THE JOURNAL OF
Archibald C. McKinley

THE JOURNAL OF
Archibald C. McKinley

EDITED BY

Robert L. Humphries

INTRODUCTION BY

Russell Duncan

The University of Georgia Press

ATHENS AND LONDON

© 1991 by the University of Georgia Press
Athens, Georgia 30602
All rights reserved

Designed by Kathi L. Dailey
Set in Caledonia by Tseng Information Systems
Printed and bound by Thomson-Shore
The paper in this book meets the guidelines for
permanence and durability of the Committee on
Production Guidelines for Book Longevity of the
Council on Library Resources.

Printed in the United States of America

95 94 93 92 91 C 5 4 3 2 1

Library of Congress Cataloging-in-Publication Data

The Journal of Archibald C. McKinley / edited by
Robert L. Humphries ; introduction by Russell Duncan.
        p.   cm.
    Includes bibliographical references and index.
    ISBN 0-8203-1187-1 (alk. paper)
    1. Sapelo Island (Ga.)—History.
2. Reconstruction—Georgia—Sapelo Island.
3. McKinley, Archibald C. (Archibald Carlisle)—
Diaries.   4. Sapelo Island (Ga.)—Biography.
I. Humphries, Robert   L., 1930-
    F292.M15J68   1991
    975.8'737—dc20   90-39090
                                               CIP

British Library Cataloging in Publication Data available

Contents

Editor's Preface

Archibald C. McKinley's family were Jacobean Scots who, in record, first appear in Invernesshire, Scotland, and later in County Monahan, Ireland (the so-called Scotch-Irish). McKinley's great-great-grandfather John left his home in Ballibay in 1744 and came to Philadelphia. While at sea, McKinley's great-grandfather William was born. The family first settled in the Virginia Valley, later moving to the Abbeville District of South Carolina. William married Mary Beatty of County Down, Ireland. He served as a soldier in the American Revolution and became a rich farmer and the tax collector of Abbeville. Their son, the first Archibald Carlisle McKinley, was born in Abbeville District in 1779.

Archibald Carlisle married Elizabeth Cummins from Mecklenburg County, North Carolina, in 1803. They moved from Abbeville to Lexington, Georgia, where Archibald died in 1861. Archibald and Elizabeth had four sons and three daughters; four of whom, or their offspring, feature in the journal: William, father of our Archibald Carlisle; Sarah Serena who married Francis Louis Upton (Uncle Frank); Charles Goodloe, father of cousins Carlyle and James J. McKinley; and Lavinia Eliza who married Francis James Robinson (Uncle Robinson).

William McKinley, father of the author, was born in Abbeville District on November 30, 1809, and moved to Lexington, Georgia with the family. He married twice, first to Precious Patience Barrow of Baldwin County, Georgia. She and her brother David Crenshaw had been orphaned before their majority. William and Precious were married in 1836 by the Rev. Francis R. Goulding (later the noted author of *The Young Marooners, Sapelo,* and other popular juveniles). Five children resulted from this union, including the journal author, Archibald Carlisle. All were born in Lexington, Georgia. Shortly after the birth of her fifth child in 1847, Precious Patience died.

About 1850 William married Lucy Anne Andrews Sims,

widow of Professor Edward Dromgoole Sims of Chapel Hill, North Carolina. Lucy Anne was the daughter of Professor E. A. Andrews, whose school in Connecticut Precious Patience had attended. It was through Precious's correspondence with Lucy Anne that William McKinley became acquainted with his future wife. She had had one daughter, Grace, who eventually married John D. Pope and moved to St. Louis; she appears only once early in the journal. The union of William and Lucy Anne produced four additional children.

Of the nine McKinley children of this generation only three—Catherine, Mary, and Guy Cummins—had offspring who survived to adulthood. In the journal only Catherine's daughter, Kate McKinley Taylor, and Mary's sons, William McKinley and Thomas R. R. Cobb, appear. The latter was named after his paternal uncle, Thomas Reade Rootes Cobb, who was prominent in the legal affairs of the state before the war and was killed leading Cobb's Legion during the Civil War.[1]

This then is the family background of our author Archibald Carlisle McKinley. That he felt strongly about family is evidenced throughout by his remembrances of births and deaths and comments on other family occasions. His feelings about his Scottish heritage are evidenced by his penning in one of the back pages of the journal, on May 8, 1870, the short verse:

> Of a' Highland Clans
> McNabs The most ferocious
> Excepting the McKinleys & the McIntoshes.
> —taken from Alastir McAlister's *Jacobite Rhymes.*

The coupling of the McKinley and the McIntosh families in the rhyme is almost prescient since Archibald married a McIntosh descendant, Sarah Spalding. Because the Spaldings and their descendants figure so prominently in the journal, some description of their family history—and a fascinating one it is—is in order.

The original Thomas Spalding had been laird of Ashintilly and other baronies in Scotland and also a Jacobite. In 1743 he lost his various estates to the courts, most probably because of his support of attempts to restore the Stuarts to the throne of Scotland. Spalding died as a member of a Scotch regiment in the service of the Dutch republic. He left several small children in Scotland, only one of which—James—grew to manhood. James became estranged from his mother and stepfather, joined an English trading house, and soon established his own successful trading business in Georgia and Florida. His home was established on Oglethorpe's old site at Frederica on St. Simons Island. He married Marjorie McIntosh, daughter of John Mohr McIntosh, the leader of the Highlanders who had settled Darien.

The Spaldings had one son, Thomas, who trained for the law but never practiced. Thomas married Sarah Leake, only daughter of Richard Leake, a prominent planter and trader. Thomas and Sarah had sixteen children, four of whom were still-born; five others did not live to their majority. Of the seven who survived we shall see five of their descendants appear in the journal, most prominently the Wyllys, the Kenans, and the children of Randolph, the only ones to carry forward the Spalding name.

In 1802 Thomas Spalding began to acquire land on Sapelo Island after selling his inheritance on St. Simons Island and in 1843 purchased the northern portion of the island as a wedding gift for his son, Randolph. He had previously given 1,500 acres of the middle of the island to his daughter Catherine upon her wedding to M. J. Kenan. Thus the Spaldings then controlled all of Sapelo except 650 acres at Raccoon Bluff owned by Anson Kimberly. Spalding's other married children—Jane Martin Leake Brailsford, Hester Margery Cooke, Elizabeth Sarah Wylly, and Charles Harris—had all received tracts on the mainland where Spalding also had extensive holdings.[2]

McKinley's uncle David C. Barrow and six of his nine children also appear in the journal. Barrow served in the Georgia state legislature and participated in the Secession Convention of 1861. His children whom we will see include David, Jr., who later became chancellor of the University of Georgia; Pope, who became a distinguished jurist and U.S. senator from Georgia; Benjamin and Henry, who both died early in manhood; Clara, who remained unmarried and managed her father's home after the death of her mother; and, most important to us, Ella, who married Bourke Spalding.[3]

William McKinley in 1850 moved his family from Lexington to his first wife's home, Beulah, in Milledgeville. He later acquired property across the Oconee River from Milledgeville and

Spalding Family

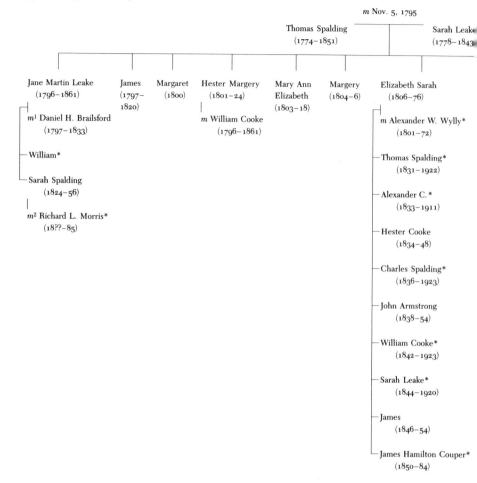

m Nov. 5, 1795

Thomas Spalding
(1774–1851)

Sarah Leake
(1778–1843)

Jane Martin Leake
(1796–1861)

*m*¹ Daniel H. Brailsford
(1797–1833)

— William*

— Sarah Spalding
(1824–56)

*m*² Richard L. Morris*
(18??–85)

James
(1797–1820)

Margaret
(1800)

Hester Margery
(1801–24)

m William Cooke
(1796–1861)

Mary Ann
Elizabeth
(1803–18)

Margery
(1804–6)

Elizabeth Sarah
(1806–76)

m Alexander W. Wylly*
(1801–72)

— Thomas Spalding*
(1831–1922)

— Alexander C.*
(1833–1911)

— Hester Cooke
(1834–48)

— Charles Spalding*
(1836–1923)

— John Armstrong
(1838–54)

— William Cooke*
(1842–1923)

— Sarah Leake*
(1844–1920)

— James
(1846–54)

— James Hamilton Couper*
(1850–84)

Note: Four children of Thomas and Sarah Leake Spalding were stillborn and unnamed (1799, 1813, 1817, 1818).

An asterisk (*) indicates that the individual appears in the journal or elsewhere in this edition.

Sources: The Spalding/Wylly family papers, collection of Charles Willingham, Marietta, Ga.; and Elizabeth Wylly Aug, Darien, Ga. McKinley family papers, collection of Ann McKinley King, Milledgeville, Ga., and Mary Cobb Trimble, Dalton, Ga. Some birth and death dates are unavailable.

Charles Harris*	Catherine*	Thomas	Emily Screven	Randolph*
(1808–87)	(1810–?)	(1813–19)	(1817–24)	(1822–62)

Charles Harris* (1808–87)
- m¹ Eliza Houstoun
- m² Evelyn Kell (1820–98)

Catherine* (1810–?)
- m Michael J. Kenan
  - Spalding Kenan* (1836–1907)
    - m Evelyn Elizabeth Livingston* (1838–94)
      - Michael J.
      - Louis Livingston* (1863–1926)
      - Randolph Spalding (1865–1910)
      - Spalding, Jr.* (1869–1918)
      - Evey (1871–1947)
      - Elizabeth
      - Catherine (1876–1954)
      - Aurie Hall (1879–1954)

Thomas (1813–19)

Emily Screven (1817–24)

Randolph* (1822–62)
- m Mary Dorothy Bass* (1823–98)
  - Sarah Elizabeth* (1844–1916)
    - m Archibald Carlisle McKinley*
      - William* (b & d Nov. 28, 1867)
  - Thomas* (1847–85)
    - m Sarah Barrow McKinley*
  - Thomas Bourke* (1851–84)
    - m Ella Patience Barrow*
      - Randolph* (1879–1954)
      - Clara Lucy* (b 1881?)

McKinley Family

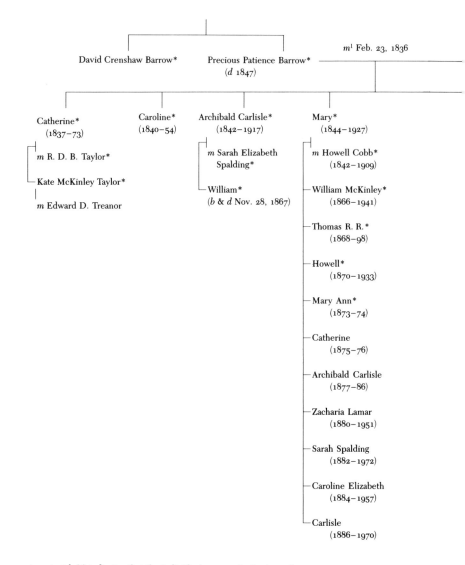

An asterisk (*) indicates that the individual appears in the journal or elsewhere in this edition.

Sources: The Spalding/Wylly family papers, collection of Charles Willingham, Marietta, Ga.; and Elizabeth Wylly Aug, Darien, Ga. McKinley family papers, collection of Ann McKinley King, Milledgeville, Ga., and Mary Cobb Trimble, Dalton, Ga. Some birth and death dates are unavailable.

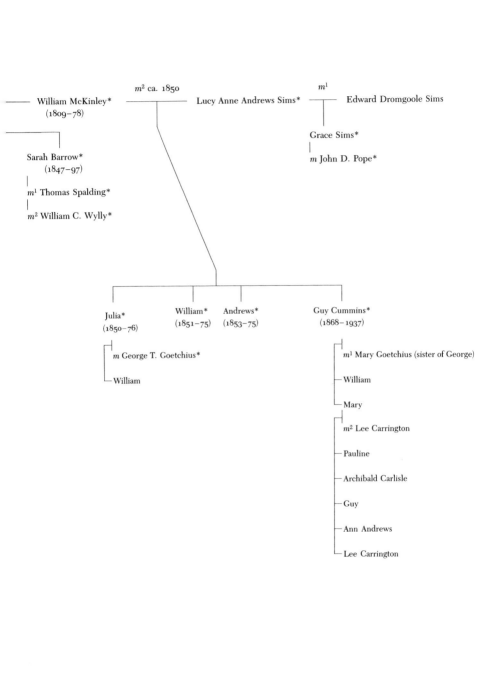

William McKinley*
(1809–78)

m² ca. 1850

Lucy Anne Andrews Sims*

m¹

Edward Dromgoole Sims

Grace Sims*

m John D. Pope*

Sarah Barrow*
(1847–97)

m¹ Thomas Spalding*

m² William C. Wylly*

Julia*
(1850–76)

William*
(1851–75)

Andrews*
(1853–75)

Guy Cummins*
(1868–1937)

m George T. Goetchius*

William

m¹ Mary Goetchius (sister of George)

William

Mary

m² Lee Carrington

Pauline

Archibald Carlisle

Guy

Ann Andrews

Lee Carrington

built a large brick home, which still stands.[4] Here the McKinley children spent their formative years. He farmed and practiced law. His farming efforts have been described as more experimental than productive.[5] McKinley was interested in archaeology and published accounts of the Indian mounds on Sapelo Island and at Kolomoki, Georgia.[6]

Archibald McKinley was eight years old when the family moved and grew up in the then state capital. He was graduated from the Georgia Military Institute in Marietta just as the Civil War began. He went through the war as first lieutenant of Company H, 57th Georgia Infantry. On his return from the war he began to farm his place called Walnut Level and on November 19, 1866, married Sarah Elizabeth Spalding.

For reasons unknown, in June 1869 McKinley began to keep a daily journal that continued until 1877 with sporadic entries afterwards. Also in 1869, at the urging of Sarah's brothers Thomas and Thomas Bourke Spalding, the McKinleys determined to move to Sapelo Island to live. Thomas and Bourke were then living at the Kenan place on Sapelo but spending much time in Milledgeville and Athens. Thus in early 1870 the McKinleys and the Spalding boys and their mother moved to the coast, first staying at "the Ridge" while housing was prepared on Sapelo. On the island they first stayed in the old Spalding barn while beginning to build a house. Before this house was finished and toward the end of 1870, John N. A. Griswold offered to lease his 7,000 acres of Sapelo and his house at High Point to McKinley for $500 per year. All then moved to High Point.

McKinley had moved to Sapelo with no clear idea of what he was to do, except help the Spalding boys. Tom intended to restore his grandfather's agricultural empire, and Bourke had the idea of raising cattle, allowing them to range freely over the island. At first each went his way: Tom contracting with the freedmen to raise cotton and sugar cane and operating his cotton gin and sugar mill; Bourke purchasing cattle and placing them on the island; McKinley contracting with the freedmen to plant cotton and cane on the Griswold lands and also acting as Dr. Sterling Kenan's agent on the island. Most of the journal entries dealing with crops are those of McKinley's efforts on the Griswold land.

At this same time the Altamaha timber trade was beginning

to grow greatly. The export trade in timber had begun in 1854[7] with construction of a mill on Doboy Island, where oceangoing vessels could load directly. Previously most of the trade had been domestic from mills in Darien. The Civil War had brought this to a halt with the destruction of the mills by the Union army. However, by 1870, seven mills were engaged primarily in squaring Altamaha logs from the interior of Georgia and loading them into vessels from many foreign countries. Lumber was produced only incidentally, usually for local consumption.

From 1870 to late 1872 McKinley and Tom Spalding continued their agricultural pursuits and Bourke tended his cattle. Of course, each helped the other as needed, and they jointly owned their boats. In December 1872, however, the possibilities of selling beef to the vessels engaged in the timber trade became attractive. A partnership was formed on December 11, 1872 between the Spalding boys and McKinley to go into the beef business.[8] Most of the journal from this point on concerns this business. Indeed, it appears they gave up agricultural activities entirely, with hardly a reference to crops afterwards, except for garden plots. In 1873 we find the cotton gin building being converted to other purposes.

Many entries in the journal describe activities such as deer hunting, shooting of doves, partridges, gannets, fishing, and so forth. These were not merely sporting activities. Such game was the primary source of protein for the McKinleys' larder and was necessary for their sustenance on the island, which was at times difficult (see November 6, 1875).

In January 1872 the McKinleys purchased 100 acres on Barn Creek, including the old overseer's house, from Tom Spalding and made this their home. They lived there until early 1877, when, at his father's request, McKinley returned to Milledgeville to live and help his father with both the law practice and the farming. McKinley had ceased regular entries in his journal, and we know little of his life afterwards. His father died the next year and McKinley replaced him as an elder of the Presbyterian church. He signed warrants as county judge in 1880.[9]

In December 1880 the McKinleys returned to their Sapelo Island home to live out their lives. The journal contains only two entries after 1877. One, in 1884, describes the death of a friend;

the other dated August 31, 1886, is a gripping account of the Charleston earthquake as felt on Sapelo Island.

It is strange that McKinley did not record in his journal the deaths of Bourke and Tom Spalding. Bourke was killed on Sapelo in 1884 by an accidental discharge of his gun. His brother Thomas was found the next year in the railroad yards of Macon, Georgia, also dead of a gunshot wound. Thomas's death is thought to have been a robbery and murder.

Sarah Spalding McKinley died on Sapelo Island in 1916 and was buried in the Spalding family plot in St. Andrews Cemetery in Darien. Strangely her headstone is no longer there. Virginia Steele Wood has kindly provided me with the inscription from this stone from her studies of McIntosh County in the 1960s. For the record, it read:

> Sarah Elizabeth McKinley
> Daughter of Randolph and Mary D. Spalding
> Wife of A. C. McKinley
> 6 September 1844

Archibald, unable to care for himself after Sarah's death, was brought to his father's home in Milledgeville by his brother Guy and there died in 1917. He was buried in Memory Hill Cemetery in Milledgeville in the McKinley family plot where he had labored to reinter his sisters. His simple stone reads:

> CSA
> A. C. McKinley
> Co. H 57th Ga.

THE JOURNAL OF Archibald C. McKinley came to light in 1969 when Sapelo and Helen Treanor of Athens (daughters of McKinley's niece Kate) were finally able to open a stuck drawer in a piece of furniture that their family had moved from Sapelo in the early 1900s. The journal had apparently been in the drawer since McKinley's death in 1917 or before the Treanors had acquired the piece from the McKinley place on Sapelo. McKinley's inscription on the inside front cover of the journal gave explicit directions for its disposition and prompted the Treanors to send the journal to the present owner, Ann McKinley King, after photocopying by Susan Tate of the University of Georgia Libraries.

His inscription reads as follows:

Archibald C. McKinley

Milledgeville

1869   Georgia

Feb. 14*th* 1876. Having completed (nearly) 230 pages of my journal and life being very uncertain I request that the following disposition be made of it in case of my death. 1*st* To my wife, 2*d* To my brother, Guy, 3*d* If either my brother or Sisters have a son named for me then it goes to him. *Destroyable at the option* of either of the two first mentioned parties. Archibald Carlisle McKinley.

Earthquake of August & September 1886—p. 249.

McKinley had purchased the commercial journal book in 1869 from a Milledgeville druggist whose label is still on the inside cover. He placed his name and address there at that time. He wrote the disposition note in 1876 but continued the journal for nineteen more pages into 1877. The original disposition note referred to his two brothers, but he later scratched out two words to reflect that only one brother, Guy, survived. Guy did have a son, Archibald Carlisle, whose daughter was given the journal, thus fulfilling McKinley's wishes.

The pages of the journal measure 7½ by 12 inches. McKinley's format was to list the year on each page in the top left margin, followed by the month and date. Ditto marks were used under the month for each entry until the next month. Sundays were almost always identified, and occasionally other days. He wrote in ink. His habit was to complete a daily entry on one page; only rarely did an entry carry over to the next page. He numbered each page, but the original pagination has not been retained in this edition.

I have attempted to keep this version as literal as possible. However, to bring the journal to print, I have made a few changes to the text for both clarity and to simplify the printing process. McKinley was inconsistent in his punctuation, using commas, periods, and dashes irregularly. Punctuation has been altered for readability though oddities remain. McKinley's orthography varied greatly. He used superscript in the manner of the day, but with some misgivings I have lowered all superscript letters or symbols. No abbreviations have been expanded; all should be self-evident to the reader. McKinley underlined for emphasis; herein these entries are italicized as are all newspapers. His spelling was generally good by any standard but there were misspellings, e.g., *champaign* for *champagne*. If the meaning is clear, misspellings have been retained; only a few words have been corrected. McKinley's use of monetary units varied; I have converted all instances to modern usage. In several places where words were repeated for no apparent reason, the repetition has been eliminated. Obvious slips of the pen have been silently corrected, e.g., *Howel* to *Howell* and *Willy* to *Wylly*. Editorial comments or interpretations are bracketed and italicized. Editorial interpolations are bracketed and in roman type.

For the names of vessels McKinley variously used underlining, quotation marks, both, or nothing. In the present edition all vessels are italicized. McKinley was quite specific and correct in his identification of vessel type: schooner, bark or barque, ship (a full square-rigged vessel), and so forth.

On one of the last pages of the journal McKinley delineated a "phonographic alphabet," a system of stenographic-like symbols using only consonants. In several entries McKinley used this alphabet apparently for secrets. I have been successful in deciphering only one of these coded words. All are bracketed as being the phonographic alphabet (*[phonographic alphabet]*). Similarly, brackets have been used to signify an illegible word or phrase (*[illegible]*) and a bracketed question mark ([?]) where the handwriting was uncertain and my transcription is a reasonable conjecture. The original journal is faded and the page edges eroded, making some final words on recto pages and end-of-page sentences indecipherable; such instances are represented by bracketed comments, e.g., *[page bottom eroded]*. I have not altered any of McKinley's capitalization, which is idiosyncratic. Apostrophes have been silently added throughout the journal.

Laid into the journal as inclusions were several papers. Only one—a letter from McKinley to his father dated December 27, 1876—is reproduced in this edition. The other papers include an authorization from Kate McKinley Taylor and David C. Barrow (executor) for McKinley to go to Early County, Georgia, and supervise the plantations of R. D. B. Taylor, deceased, dated August 3, 1865; a note, penned by McKinley, asking to be relieved as guardian of his niece, Kate, undated (most likely written in 1880, as McKinley had returned to Sapelo); a letter to McKinley from J. R. Bonner, dated July 22, 1898, dealing with their efforts to reconstruct the roster of Company H, 57th Georgia Infantry (Bonner was the company commander), apparently for veteran benefit purposes. There follow several iterations of the company roster with notes as to the fate, during the war, of the individuals. Next were two warrants for arrest signed by McKinley as judge of the County Court of Baldwin County in 1880; a receipt for his 1874 subscription to the Milledgeville *Union and Recorder;* a blank check on the Central Rail Road Bank, Savannah, Georgia; and, finally, a newspaper clipping, unidentified, in which the author meditates on the pain of saying goodbye.

In the notes I have attempted to identify the principal personages completely. I have not searched out those people of only casual appearance. Other notes are included to inform the reader of events, places, and people where McKinley's entries are not clear or need expansion.

I believe the greatest value of the McKinley journal is to the student of the period, whatever his speciality. It is not, I think, especially attractive to casual readers unless they have an interest in the family, Sapelo Island, or the Georgia coastal area. It is for this reason that I have attempted to make as few changes as possible, not to draw conclusions, and to make as much information available as possible for others to use. For the reader's benefit, an introduction has been prepared by Dr. Russell Duncan, a student of coastal Georgia in the Reconstruction period. I have also provided genealogical charts to clarify family relationships and an epilogue to bring the reader up to date on the history of Sapelo from the close of the journal to the present.

WHILE RESEARCHING the history of Sapelo Island, I was presented with a copy of Archibald C. McKinley's journal by the late Helen Treanor of Athens, Georgia. Her stories of "Uncle Arch" and "Aunt Sally," together with the contents of the journal, led to the preparation of this volume. This volume is dedicated to the memory of Helen, a practitioner of the noblest art, teaching.

Ann McKinley King of Milledgeville, grandniece of Archibald

C. McKinley, daughter of Archibald C. McKinley II, and owner of the journal, has been more than gracious in giving access to family Bibles, papers, and genealogical data, as well as in granting permission to publish the journal.

Elizabeth Wylly Aug of Darien, a descendant of Thomas Spalding Wylly, was most kind in furnishing many original Spalding and Wylly manuscripts and papers, many never before seen by researchers. In the same way, Mr. and Mrs. Charles Willingham of Marietta, he a Wylly descendant, gave free access to Spalding and Wylly family papers, including the family Bible of Elizabeth Spalding Wylly, the daughter of Thomas Spalding, and unpublished manuscripts of Charles Spalding Wylly.

Margaret Miller of Athens and Mary Cobb Trimble of Dalton, family members, also provided much of the needed genealogical information.

The staff of the Georgia Department of Archives and History provided many answers to questions and sympathy with others. One cannot believe the quality of this department of state government.

Bill Jones and Rachel Kelly of the Sea Island Company allowed access to the Howard Coffin files dealing with Sapelo Island. Lorene Gassert, librarian of the University of Georgia Marine Institute on Sapelo, provided McKinley letters and much encouragement.

William G. Haynes, Jr., of Darien and Lewis Bellardo of the Georgia Historical Society made critical comments and were helpful in many ways.

Virginia Steele Wood, of the Library of Congress, was a gracious source of information on coastal Georgia shipping as well as the inscription from Sarah McKinley's missing tombstone. Ginnie was a constant inspiration with her interest, knowledge, and publications on the Georgia coast.

The National Maritime Museum, Greenwich, England, provided shipping information dealing with the timber trade from Darien/Doboy.

Martha Turner, of Georgia College, Milledgeville, who is researching the French period on Sapelo, has provided much information as well as inspiration.

The interest and financial assistance of Annemarie S. Reynolds, widow of R. J. Reynolds, Jr., the last private owner of Sapelo Island, in making this publication possible is greatly appreciated. She is also to be thanked for making possible, at a personal sacrifice, the ownership of this gem of the Golden Isles, Sapelo, by the State of Georgia and its availability to the people of the state.

D. C. Scott of the University of Georgia first introduced me to Miss Treanor and has worked with the manuscript in many ways. He furthermore has been helpful to me for more than forty years in ways he will never know. Finally, I could never have finished the manuscript without the able assistance and encouragement of my wife, Susie, who proofed, made corrections, and put up with an irascible and erstwhile editor.

NOTES

1. All McKinley family history is derived from the family papers in the collection of Ann McKinley King, Milledgeville, Ga.

2. Spalding family papers in possession of Charles Willingham, Marietta, Ga. and Elizabeth Wylly Aug, Darien, Ga. Other information from E. M. Coulter, *Thomas Spalding of Sapelo* (Baton Rouge: Louisiana State University Press, 1940).

3. T. W. Reed, *David Crenshaw Barrow* (Athens, Ga.: 1935).

4. This gothic style house is described and pictured in John Linley's *Architecture of Middle Georgia: The Oconee Area* (Athens: University of Georgia Press, 1972), 94–95.

5. McKinley family papers. Collection of Ann McKinley King, Milledgeville, Ga.

6. William McKinley, *Mounds in Georgia* in *Annual Report of the Board of Regents of the Smithsonian Institution for 1872* (Washington, 1873), 422–28.

7. C. S. Wylly, "History of McIntosh County." Wylly family papers. Collection of Mr. and Mrs. Charles Willingham, Marietta, Ga.

8. See *Journal*, December 10, 1872, and May 22, 1873.

9. McKinley family papers. Collection of Ann McKinley King, Milledgeville, Ga.

Introduction

In antebellum Georgia everybody knew who controlled land and labor. Rich planters everywhere ran politics, economics, and society. This was especially true along the South Atlantic coastline where the wealthiest planters owned entire islands and hundreds of slaves. In Liberty and McIntosh counties, located between Savannah and Brunswick in the middle of the state's coast, Jacob Waldburg worked 255 slaves on his St. Catherines Island and Thomas Spalding worked nearly 300 slaves on neighboring Sapelo. Just to the south on Butler's Island, Pierce Butler's slaves produced millions of pounds of marketable rice—one million pounds in 1845 alone. But the war came and people were uprooted or uprooted themselves from land and laborlords. The fighting reached early into coastal Georgia as Yankee warships tightened their control of shipping and smuggling lanes and slowly choked the southern maritime economy. Whites fled the major barrier islands of Sapelo, St. Catherines, Jekyll, St. Simons, Cumberland, and Ossabaw as well as the smaller islands of Blackbeard, Colonel's, and Butler's. They took what slaves and other belongings they considered too essential, too costly, or too dear to leave behind for Yankee pilfering and made their way to mainland wagon stations or steamboat anchorages, then to railroad stations in Savannah or Brunswick where iron horses took them and their property to the safety of central Georgia. There slaveowners could safeguard their black property from enticements to run for the protection of Union navies and armies.[1]

As early as December 1861 most sea island planters acknowledged the federal navy's superiority and abandoned their coastal Georgia rice and cotton plantations. Then in April 1862, with the fall of Fort Pulaski outside of Savannah, the remaining planters moved to plantations in the state's interior, thinking that when the South won the war, they would return, reclaim their lands, gather their chattel slaves, and reestablish their labor system and way of life. They would profit more than ever before from new commercial relations with the United States, England, and the rest of the world. But, of course, the South did not win either the war or independence.

Not only did the North win the war, but northern war Congresses also placed obstacles in the way of planters' claims to antebellum lands. In the 1861 and 1862 confiscation acts, Congress authorized the seizure of all abandoned lands and the confiscation of all property found on abandoned lands. Along the Georgia and South Carolina coasts, General Rufus Saxton wasted little time carrying out the will of Congress. Saxton had wide authority to "take possession of all the plantations heretofore occupied by rebels and take charge of the inhabitants remaining thereon . . . with authority to take such measures, make such rules and regulations for the cultivation of the land and for protection, employment, and government of the islands as circumstances may seem to require." Saxton concentrated his efforts mostly on the islands of South Carolina and Port Royal particularly. Not until early 1865 did he change his emphasis to Georgia.[2]

In the fall of 1864 William Tecumseh Sherman enjoyed the accolades of Lincoln and the North for his decisive strike through Georgia from Atlanta to the sea. His army brought modern total war to the civilian and military population of the South's "Empire State," and his capture of Savannah convinced many that the end of the Confederacy loomed near. But Sherman had a problem. As his army swept through Georgia, thousands of slaves rushed to freedom and the somewhat uncertain protection of Union lines. Blacks knew that Lincoln had committed the Union to the abolition of slavery, and they hurriedly freed themselves whenever the opportunity arose. For many Sherman's march through Georgia was the greatest opportunity of their lives. Even Sherman realized that each day's march deeper into southern territory freed more people and promised them America's equal embrace. But with his army living off the land behind enemy lines, Sherman fretted over this increase in responsibility. His anxiety mounted as he informed the War Department that his column was "overloaded with two-thirds negroes, five-sixths of whom are helpless, and a large proportion of them babies and small children." These contrabands of war slowed the advance, hindered all movement, and created logistical supply problems for Sherman.[3]

Sherman never particularly cared about blacks and now turned his attention away from the contrabands and did as little as possible for them. Reports that he left some behind at a river crossing to be captured and killed by Confederate Joseph Wheeler's cavalry brought a clamor from the northern public. The northern abolitionist press began to rake the general for his negligence, and this criticism soon compelled him to do more for his charges. Sending a letter to Gen. Henry W. Halleck, the army's chief of staff in Washington, Sherman promised: "I do and will do the best I can for the negroes."[4]

On January 12, 1865, Sherman met with Savannah's black leadership in search of the means to alleviate his "problem." Four days later Sherman issued Special Field Order Number 15 ordering the resettlement of all contrabands on "the islands from Charleston south, the abandoned rice fields along the rivers from thirty miles back from the sea, and the country" southward to the St. Johns River at Jacksonville, Florida. Sherman forbade all whites except military personnel from entering this reservation. Finding a man with proven success and dedication among the freedpeople, Sherman put Rufus Saxton in charge of settling the black refugees on farms of up to forty acres each, to which they would receive possessory titles.[5]

In March, Congress formalized Sherman's reservation by sanctioning his land redistribution, explicitly calling for the division of abandoned lands into forty-acre units, and establishing the Bureau of Refugees, Freedmen, and Abandoned Lands. Lincoln appointed Gen. Oliver Otis Howard to head the bureau and to act as "yankee stepfather" to hundreds of thousands of southern blacks. In recognition of his unequaled experience, Howard appointed Saxton to continue his work in South Carolina, Georgia, and Florida.

Saxton quickly confiscated Jacob Waldburg's St. Catherines, Thomas Spalding's Sapelo, and all other Georgia islands. He also appointed civilian agents to the bureau to help him in the weighty management and resettlement responsibilities. Saxton appointed a New Jersey black, Tunis Campbell, to help him resettle black families on Sapelo, St. Catherines, Ossabaw, Colonel's, and Burnside islands. By the war's end, contrabands were busily seeking and building new lives—free lives—on Georgia's coast. Initially, many refugees moved into the tabby or log cabins they knew as slave quarters in earlier days. Later, many built homes of their own on land deeded them by the bureau. By June 16, 1865, Campbell had issued land to 312 individuals or families on Sapelo and 317 on St. Catherines. By Independence Day, 140 children attended schools on those two islands. The experiment in radical land redistribution was working. Blacks, who had labored on the land as slaves, were finally paid for the equity they had built up during more than two centuries of unpaid, unfree toil.[6]

These early successes, however, did not last. As soon as the war ended, whites demanded their land back. They held legal titles to the land and would not recognize the blacks' claim of equity. They appealed to local representatives, state governors, military officials, and the president of the United States for the return of the land. Andrew Johnson agreed and did as they asked, pardoning over twenty thousand planters and ordering their land returned to them. When Rufus Saxton protested and refused to carry out those orders, Johnson replaced him with Davis Tillson.

Early on Tillson announced: "I propose to get owners, capitalists and freed people together." Landowners and capitalists welcomed this government intervention, but the freedpeople had little to gain from it. They had already worked for a year on land to which they held possessory titles issued under Saxton and Sherman's orders with Congress and Lincoln's blessings—titles that rightfully belonged to them under their understanding of equity. With advice from Campbell and others, they tried to resist.[7]

Upon inspection of the islands, Tillson found that freedmen had formed armed militia forces and refused to permit whites access to the land. On St. Catherines and Sapelo, blacks threatened white agents who tried to regain the lands for former masters. In a letter included in this volume, Ella Barrow Spalding, who had married Thomas Spalding's grandson Bourke, relates the Spaldings' efforts to reclaim their land: "They sent a representative to the Island to take possession for the owners. But, give it up? No, indeed! When ordered to leave, the negroes declared the land was theirs, and in turn ordered Mr. Bass to leave, threatening to kill him if he did not go." Mr. Bass was Allen G. Bass, who was not only Freedmen's Bureau agent for McIntosh County but also Thomas Spalding's nephew and former wartime overseer on Sapelo. It is little wonder that the freedpeople refused to listen to a member of old master's family who told them to release the land. Tillson sent in federal troops to decide the issue, but just a show of force proved sufficient to disband the black militiamen, who had no intention of fighting the army that had recently helped free them. Tillson then not only put the planters back in control of the land but also forced the freedpeople to sign contracts by which planters regained control over black labor.[8]

With renewed control of the land, some planters were eager to lease or sell parts or all of their holdings to northern entrepreneurs who came South in hope of establishing free-labor agriculture along the coast. These "new masters" used their capital and their influence with General Tillson to obtain land and labor for their enterprises. These entrepreneurs, however, did not understand why blacks did not embrace the wage labor-contract system they offered. They failed to acknowledge what the freedpeople knew—that decades of uncompensated labor and the brutality of slavery had made the land theirs in equity. Virginia ex-slave Bayley Wyat explained it in 1867: "We has a right to the land where we are located. For why? I tell you. Our wives, our children, our husbands, has been sold over and over again to purchase the lands we now locates upon; for that reason we have a divine right to the land. . . . And den didn't we clear the land, and raise de crops ob corn, ob cotton, ob tobacco, ob rice, ob sugar, ob everything?" During Reconstruction few white Americans recognized the equity blacks held in the land. That America allowed no basic redistribution of land to four million freed slaves explains much of the failure of Reconstruction and much of the tumultuous century that followed that injustice.[9]

In 1866 the Spaldings sold the northern end of Sapelo Island to Rhode Island entrepreneur John N. A. Griswold for $50,000 and leased most of the southern end for $2,500 to two northerners, S. D. Dickson and a Mr. McBride. Dickson and McBride offered freedpeople who would sign labor contracts with them a sharecrop of two-thirds of the crop at harvest time. Even with those relatively liberal terms, blacks hesitated and refused to sign because they preferred to work for themselves—and they were making it. In December 1865, W. F. Eaton, a Freedmen's Bureau agent, reported that although 122 new arrivals needed help, 130 settlers were completely self-sustaining and 100 more nearly so. Most blacks threatened to leave the island if the old owners returned. An undetermined number managed to work for themselves until late 1867, when the bureau finalized the restoration of the land to the Spaldings. Before that, when Tillson forced blacks to leave the island or sign with the new masters, most contracted with McBride and Dickson.[10]

Those who signed realized their mistake quickly. After they harvested the crops, McBride and Dickson claimed they owed the workers nothing because the farmers had "spent" all their money by buying items on credit through the plantation store owned by McBride and Dickson. Now, at harvest time, after settling accounts, the new masters claimed that all the crop belonged to them. Toby Maxwell, a freedman who in 1871 and 1872 served as elected coroner of McIntosh County, signed the contract and worked through harvest time. He explained that, as McBride and Dickson figured accounts against the bags of cotton the freedmen brought to be weighed, they claimed "they owed them nothing . . . [and] the cotton was taken." Then, in Maxwell's words, "some of the col'd men refused to put their cotton in McBride's pile. He then had them arrested and carried to Ft. Pulaski." Siding with the landlords and refusing to tolerate any management-labor disputes, General Tillson sent twelve of the most vocal protestors to Fort Pulaski to be worked at hard labor until they would return and work peaceably under contract.[11]

Tillson blamed labor organizers for the problem. After discovering that Tunis Campbell had advised the freedpeople to stand up for their rights and not to sign bureau-promoted contracts, he made the unsubstantiated claim that Campbell swindled and used the ex-slaves for his own benefit. Tillson then banished Campbell from Sapelo "forever." Campbell left and many Sapelo freedpeople went with him rather than stay without a leader. Campbell vowed to continue his work in mainland McIntosh County. He understood the relationship of land and labor to liberty: "The great cry of our people is for land. If they can be protected they will get on well enough. . . . They want to be free-holders, land-holders, and to hold office like white men." Campbell entered a rent-to-own agreement for a 1,250-acre plantation, BelleVille, located north of Darien, and began settling black families on land of their own. They formed the BelleVille Farmers Association and grew marketable crops to pay the lease.[12]

After Congress passed three 1867 Reconstruction acts, over President Johnson's vetoes, Campbell registered black voters, who in turn elected him to local office as a justice of the peace and to state office as a state senator. In those positions he promoted equal rights and helped McIntosh blacks build a powerful political machine, which lasted for forty years. Most whites resented these Reconstruction acts, which divided the South into five military districts, each under the control of federal troops, and which allowed freedmen to vote. They resented even more the vote that put Republican Rufus Bullock in the governor's chair and sent three blacks to the state senate and twenty-nine to the house. Congress had wrenched control of Reconstruction from the hands of Andrew Johnson, who seemed determined to restore not reconstruct. In Georgia the military arm of the Democratic party, the Ku Klux Klan, arose to fight this "foreign" government; in the end—four years later—after Congress declared Georgia recalcitrant and in need of two more "reconstructions," the Redeemers (white conservatives) regained complete control of Georgia politics and Reconstruction came to an end. Yet, in reality, Georgia still needed reconstructing. On Sapelo, by January 1867, the new masters determined that conditions were in too much turmoil to try another season of planting; they let the lease lapse back into the Spaldings' hands.[13]

By October 1868, only 650 of the 39,632 acres of Georgia land that the Freedmen's Bureau had once controlled and parceled to the freedmen through possessory titles remained under the control of black families. Despite the Civil War's promised revolutionary change through the abolition of slavery and the consolidation of the South into the northern market system based upon free labor, planters had regained the political power to implement old ideas with new methods. Contract labor and the sharecrop system conspired to hold blacks to the land almost as firmly as slavery had.[14]

The suffering brought on by the war lingered in the memory of most white southerners, who resented the idea of Reconstruction because its changes directly countered the ideology and way of life whites had nurtured for two centuries. Blood had been sacrificed, sons had died, property had been destroyed or freed. Three hundred young white men from McIntosh County had marched off to secure secession, and only fifty survived the war and returned. Whites also remembered well that black soldiers of the Fifty-fourth Massachusetts and Second South Carolina regiments had torched Darien, the county seat and largest town of McIntosh County. After the war, 4,024 people in McIntosh County were slaves no more; the cost of that freedom to McIntosh planters in lost property amounted to at least $2,152,250. What had taken so long to build now had disappeared, run away, broken apart, or become freed. Whites had to cope with the monetary loss as well as the change in racial relationships, and for most of them, that was a tall, hard task.[15]

   The Journal of Archibald C. McKinley details some of the aspects of life on Sapelo and in McIntosh County during the era of Reconstruction through the eyes and mind of one white, upper-class southerner. Additionally, McKinley's glimpses of life in central Georgia around the prewar capital of Milledgeville link together powerful families and politics. From June 14, 1869, to April 30, 1877, the *Journal* illuminates many of the major themes of Reconstruction: labor and land problems; upper-class white society; black struggles for autonomy, family, and equality; the southern way of life; and black-white relations. Because Reconstruction spanned the period from the Emancipation Proclamation in January 1863 to the inauguration of Hayes and the Compromise of 1877 on March 4, 1877, the *Journal* helps us to understand what life was like for one family during most of that period. The *Journal* also adds important information to the splendid, multifarious history of Sapelo Island, whose history contains all the elements in microcosm that influenced the development of Georgia. An acceptable academic history of Sapelo has yet to be written.

   Standing twenty feet above the sea at its highest elevation, Sapelo is twelve miles long and three and a half miles wide at its widest point. The summers are very hot, 75 to 120 degrees; winters are a mild 30 to 70 degrees. Marsh and tidewater rivers separate Sapelo from Blackbeard and Little Sapelo islands. A tall grass savanna dominates the island and gives home to deer, rabbits, raccoons, and opossums. Nastier creatures also abound. Gnats, sandflies, and mosquitoes by the millions, including the malaria-carrying anopheles, bite and flit. An overabundance of rattlesnakes, black racers, and alligators make walking exciting if not dangerous. Stands of live oak, pines, palmettos, and vines rise from the soil. Today as always Sapelo and the other islands are constantly changing through the erosion and rebuilding brought by waves, hurricanes, and ocean breezes.[16]

The history of human habitation on Sapelo began nearly five thousand years ago when Native Americans lived on the island. We know very little about these early inhabitants though archeological work continues to explore their culture. Then began a history of Spanish missionary activity, which also remains obscure. Jesuits under the sponsorship of Phillip II of Spain came to Sapelo with Pedro Menendez de Aviles around 1566. By 1570, an Indian uprising killed some of the missionaries and propelled the others from the island. Three years later, another group of Catholic missionaries, this time Franciscans, arrived and founded the convent of San Jose de Zapala, a name from which Sapelo derived. Researchers conclude that the Franciscans stayed until nearly 1686, when the Spanish abandoned Santa Catalina de Guale on St. Catherines Island.[17]

In 1757 the Creek Indians ceded Sapelo to England and it became a part of the colony of Georgia. By 1762 Patrick Mackay had purchased the island and established plantation agriculture there. Sapelo changed hands once more before a group of Frenchmen, seeking refuge from the democratic revolution in France, bought the island in 1789. By 1797 another Frenchman, Marquis de Montalet, fled the slave rebellion on Haiti and settled along the Savannah River; he later relocated to Sapelo. In 1799 Englishman Richard Leake and a partner bought the south end of the island; shortly before Leake's death in 1802, his son-in-law Thomas Spalding gained control of the land.[18]

Spalding settled in among the sandflies, rattlesnakes, alligators, and mosquitoes, and managed the cultivation of the rich soil to grow indigo, long-staple cotton, and sugar cane. He advocated a "gospel of grass" and wrote many articles for the agricultural journals of his day. Spalding not only raised cattle, sheep, and hogs to sell to the navy and merchant ships that worked along the coast but also sold live oak timber to the same concerns. He served two terms in the Georgia legislature and a partial term in the United States Congress. He bought and worked human beings and built a fortune selling cotton produced by slave labor. By the time of his death in 1851, Spalding and two of his chil-

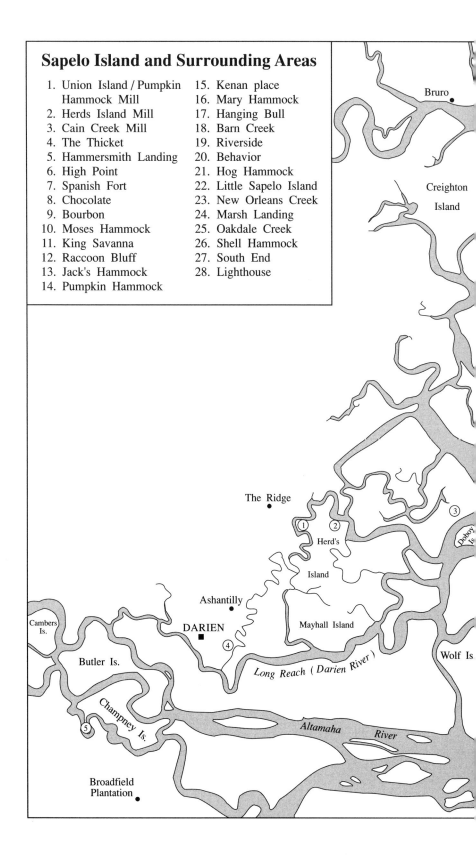

Sapelo Island and Surrounding Areas

1. Union Island / Pumpkin Hammock Mill
2. Herds Island Mill
3. Cain Creek Mill
4. The Thicket
5. Hammersmith Landing
6. High Point
7. Spanish Fort
8. Chocolate
9. Bourbon
10. Moses Hammock
11. King Savanna
12. Raccoon Bluff
13. Jack's Hammock
14. Pumpkin Hammock
15. Kenan place
16. Mary Hammock
17. Hanging Bull
18. Barn Creek
19. Riverside
20. Behavior
21. Hog Hammock
22. Little Sapelo Island
23. New Orleans Creek
24. Marsh Landing
25. Oakdale Creek
26. Shell Hammock
27. South End
28. Lighthouse

Bruro

Creighton Island

The Ridge

Herd's Island

Doboy Is.

Ashantilly

Mayhall Island

Cambers Is.

DARIEN

Butler Is.

Wolf Is.

Long Reach (Darien River)

Champney Is.

Altamaha River

Broadfield Plantation

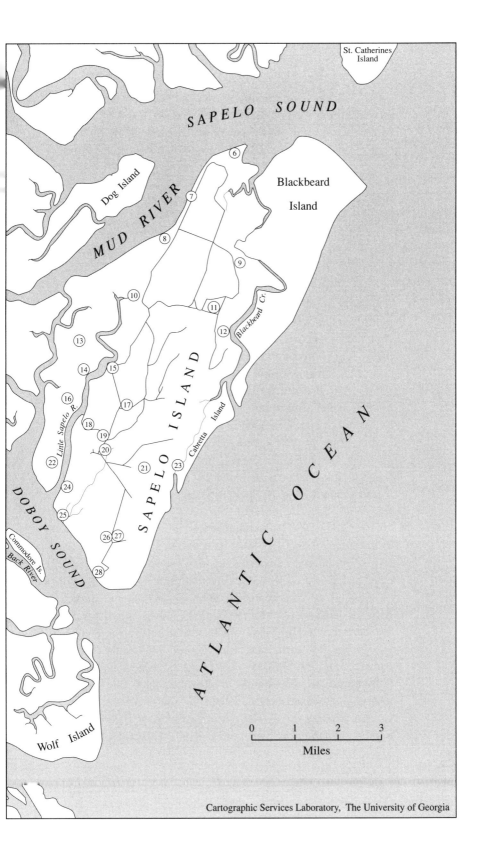

St. Catherines
Island

SAPELO SOUND

Dog Island

MUD RIVER

Blackbeard
Island

⑥

⑦

⑧

⑨

⑩

⑪

⑫ Blackbeard Cr.

⑬

⑭ ⑮

Little Sapelo R.

⑯

⑰

SAPELO ISLAND

Cabretta Island

⑱

⑲

⑳

㉒

㉑ ㉓

㉔

㉕

DOBOY SOUND

Commodore Is.

Back River

㉖ ㉗

㉘

ATLANTIC OCEAN

Wolf Island

0   1   2   3
                 Miles

dren, Catherine and Randolph, who had received parcels of land as wedding presents from their father in 1841 and 1843 respectively, owned all of Sapelo except for 650 acres along the eastern central shore. Spalding willed his property on Sapelo to his grandson Thomas II. The Spaldings continued the family business until the Civil War when Union navy raids forced them to evacuate. Randolph took most of his slaves with him, but some hid out with hopes of joining the Yankee navy.[19]

In 1964, ninety-year-old Charles Hall, a lifelong resident of Sapelo, told interviewer Fred McMurray about conditions on the island after the Civil War touched Georgia's coast. Born in 1874, the son of freed slaves, Hall grew up listening to stories of ex-slaves. He recalled that some of Spalding's slaves ran away and hid in the marshes watching and waiting for Union boats. Hall named eight slaves who made it to Yankee ships and escaped Sapelo—of those, four returned to the island after the war. He recalled that one, John Johnson, failed to dodge Spalding's bullet just before he made it aboard a Union boat. Hall's stories refute the many popular writers and some historians of Sapelo's history who refer to Spalding's kind treatment of his slaves and claim that, because of this, other planters called Sapelo "Nigger Heaven." Certainly Spalding was no Simon Legree, but those who have noted Spalding's kindness fail to understand that slavery was slavery and that blacks wanted out of it. Spalding's slaves risked life and limb to escape it—"heaven" or hell.[20]

In March 1862 Randolph died and left his share of the island to be held jointly by his wife and children. Son Tom, because of his grandfather's benevolence and now his father's, became chief proprietor even though his mother acted as trustee until he reached age twenty-one in 1868. Thomas shared the island with his mother, his brother Bourke, and his sister Sarah and her husband, Archibald C. McKinley, in return for their companionship and work. After Tom married Archibald's sister, also named Sarah, the McKinley and Spalding clans were thoroughly intertwined. In 1874 Bourke further entangled the families by marrying Archibald's cousin Ella P. Barrow of Athens.[21]

Archibald grew up the son of a prominent Baldwin County family. His father, William, was a planter-lawyer-politician who, in 1860, owned at least 66 slaves and 1,350 acres of land located just across the Oconee River from Milledgeville. By 1863, William had amassed 5,800 acres of land worth $36,550 and owned 75 slaves valued at $75,000. Representing Baldwin County in the Georgia legislature, he sat very near Archibald's maternal uncle, David C. Barrow, a representative from Oglethorpe County (near Athens), who owned 400 slaves and 2,670 acres of land in 1860 and served prominently in the Secession Convention of 1861.[22]

After Georgia seceded from the Union, Archibald served in the state militia, helped raise a company of independent volunteers (Fifty-seventh Georgia Infantry), was assigned to the army of Tennessee, and marched off to war to save the South. Because of his family's prominence and his education at the Military Institute in Marietta, McKinley wore first lieutenant's bars. He served throughout the war and saw action in Braxton Bragg's Kentucky Campaign (1862), at Vicksburg (1863), Atlanta (1864), Nashville (1864), and Bentonsville, N.C. (1865). He wore battle scars from a wound received near Vicksburg. McKinley's involvement on the losing side of the battles that severed the Confederacy in 1863, cut the transportation heart out of the South, and signaled the end was near in 1864 profoundly affected him the rest of his life.[23]

During the war members of the upper class often took with them one or more of their most trusted slaves to help ease the conditions of field duty. McKinley joined in this practice by taking his slave, Scott, to act as a camp servant. McKinley devoted the longest entry of his journal, April 17, 1870, to a eulogy of Scott. Scott endeared himself to McKinley at Baker's Creek, Mississippi, by using "the greatest care and tenderness" to nurse his master back to health from wounds that brought him near death. Scott stayed with McKinley throughout the war and did not run away to Union lines. McKinley called him "true as steel" and claimed "he was one of the few negroes who was a friend of the whites." That statement reflects the general view of southern white paternalists— that those slaves who ran away to gain freedom from bondage were deserters, traitors, and enemies, but those who remained in slavery were, in McKinley's words, "true and faithful." To other slaves, people like Scott were the deserters, traitors, and enemies. Obviously though, McKinley loved Scott and after the war rewarded him with a house and twenty acres of land.

Back from the war, Archibald married Sarah E. Spalding,

whom everyone called Sallie, and returned to farming cotton and corn. Without slaves to work the land, he hired laborers by the task or entered into sharecropping or other tenantry arrangements. These arrangements brought together freedpeople who owned no land and planters who owned no labor. McKinley also rented a portion of his land to another white agriculturalist. He received money and crops as payment for rent, and he sometimes sold his tenants mules and tools in return for crops. McKinley's journal contains sporadic records of crop harvests, selling prices for cotton, and wages paid to laborers. In 1869 McKinley's cotton fields produced a recorded 9,340 pounds of cotton. In one instance, he paid contract laborers $18.25 for picking 3,000 pounds; at that rate, total labor costs for harvest equalled less than $60. He sold his cotton for about 28 cents per pound and made approximately $2,615.20. Obviously, cotton growing was still a highly profitable enterprise for large landholders after the Civil War.[24]

His journal helps to dispel the myth that the Civil War left planters destitute. Certainly, they lost investment in their chattel slaves, and crop production was disrupted. Yet, the members of the upper class still held land as well as political and social power. McKinley was one of the Baldwin County commissioners who decided on bankruptcy cases, sold property, and ran the county's affairs. His father bought land and a house in Midway in June 1869 and four months later purchased 400 acres near Milledgeville for $2,400. The antebellum elite retained their economic, social, and political power after the war no matter how much they protested to the contrary. Because their laborers were now hired workers who could bargain, stand up to their employers, leave if conditions became intolerable, and not bow and scrape as they were required to during slavery, white southerners wailed that their fortunes, position, and lifestyle were ruined. McKinley's journal entries describe many excursions and visits, attendance at operettas and plays, buying sprees, house, land, and yacht acquisitions, investments, and hired house servants, all of which emphatically demonstrate that the landed class remained prosperous.[25]

Sometime before the cotton harvest in the summer of 1869, McKinley agreed to work on Sapelo Island with his wife's brothers, Tom and Bourke. They planned to resurrect Sapelo's fields with cotton and corn. After the crop came in, McKinley left the environs of central Georgia for the coast, but because of the unsuitable housing on the island, he rented a house at the "Ridge" just north of Darien in mainland McIntosh County. Ridgeville had been a favorite retreat among antebellum planters for escaping the extreme heat and mosquitoes of the coast and islands. Because Ridgeville's homes had escaped the Civil War fires that had burned Darien (eighty percent of whose population was black), and because of its geographical advantages, Ridgeville became the center of living for the white upper class after the war. In 1870, 192 of Ridgeville's 413 residents were white, and 72 more were mulattoes; 55 of 221 blacks and mulattoes served as domestic servants, cooks, launderers, or day laborers for the white families. McKinley fit in well with the planters, merchants, and politicians who lived at the Ridge. His neighbors included the county's richest man, Carl Epping, a timber merchant with $100,000 in real estate, planter Richard L. Morris, steamboat pilots E. M. Blount and Samuel Hubbard, timber merchant and local magistrate Joseph P. Gilson, timber merchants Charles S. Langdon, Richard Walker, and Thomas Hilton, merchant and justice of the peace Theodore Pease, attorney L. E. B. DeLorme, lawyer and politician William R. Gignilliat, and Episcopal minister Robert L. Clute.[26]

McKinley furnished the Ridge house with furniture from his Milledgeville home, including a piano, two sofas, a sideboard, and many other pieces. After renting out his Walnut Level farm for 3,300 pounds of cotton and his house for $250 a year, McKinley left with Sallie for the coast. They were accompanied by the Holmeses, who had moved to Milledgeville during the war and who now relocated to the Ridge. Dr. James Holmes became well known for his newspaper articles on early Georgia history and his glimpses of Reconstruction, *"Dr. Bullie's" Notes*.[27]

Around the time of McKinley's arrival on Sapelo, the island's population of 336 consisted of 18 mulattoes, 24 whites, and 294 blacks. Four white families controlled most of the island: Griswold on the north end, Samuel Street on the northeast corner, Michael Kenan on the central western side, and the Spaldings on the south end. Only the Spaldings had their primary residence on the island. Other whites living on Sapelo in rented dwellings included a boat pilot, a ship's carpenter, a tenant farmer, and their families. Two lighthouse operators lived in quarters supplied by the U.S. government.[28]

After McKinley and the Spaldings secured labor and planted cotton and corn, they began building homes on the island. They sawed tabby from existing structures—most likely old slave cabins —to supplement the brick and lumber they bought in Darien. They bought ten barrels of lime to use in making new tabby— a mixture of lime, sea shells, and sand. By December 5, 1870, McKinley moved his household from the Ridge to Sapelo and simultaneously sold his Milledgeville farm for $4,530; he retained his city house in Milledgeville, which he rented out. His new home had been previously occupied by John Griswold, the entrepreneur who bought the north end of Sapelo after the war. Griswold decided that the coast of Georgia did not suit him, so he rented the land he previously bought from the Spaldings to McKinley for $500 a year. He planted cotton and subleased it to black tenant farmers who paid the rent in shares equal to 6,444 pounds at harvest time.[29]

Planters did more than farm and build; they also had to maintain their political power. McKinley and the Spaldings attended agricultural conventions that brought together planters from all over Georgia. They actively attended Democratic party meetings in Darien. McIntosh County had a black voter majority that elected Republican candidates to the Georgia house and senate and generally embarrassed the white population by so doing. Overall, the county's population in 1870 had 1,196 whites and 3,288 blacks. Tunis Campbell worked actively in the county to maintain Republican strength and his own position as state senator. McKinley supported Democratic candidates such as Robert L. Morris and William R. Gignilliat. In 1860 Morris and Gignilliat had ranked ninth and seventh, respectively, as the leading slaveholders in the county with 98 and 117 slaves. In 1870 McKinley represented McIntosh County at the Democratic convention in Atlanta; in 1876 he was at the Savannah convention nominating delegates to the national convention in St. Louis.[30]

In 1870 McKinley and the Spaldings decided to diversify their interests. While expanding cotton production into new fields, including acreage on Little Sapelo Island, they now grew more food crops, rented out land to tenants, and eventually devoted most of their time to raising cattle to sell to the hundreds of ships, foreign and domestic, that docked at Darien and Doboy Island. These ships gave Darien an international atmosphere and made it Georgia's second leading port behind Savannah. Ship captains loaded their holds with lumber and cotton that arrived daily in Darien via the Oconee and Ocmulgee rivers, which reached northward through central Georgia to grab the rich cotton and timber rafts floating down to Darien. The Oconee and Ocmulgee rivers join together one hundred miles above Darien to form the Altamaha River. The convergence of these two main arteries into one greater pipeline and the cargoes the Altamaha brought to Darien gave that city enormous prominence in trade. At Darien, several large sawmills, including the one run by Joseph Hilton—captain of the local all-white cavalry company, the McIntosh Guards, to which Archibald, Tom, and Bourke belonged—cut rough logs into the finished lumber many trading captains craved.[31]

With sometimes fifty giant trading vessels at once tied up at anchor in Doboy Sound, McKinley and the Spalding brothers hoped to profit by selling fresh beef to hungry sea captains. On July 11, 1871, Bourke had built enough fences and cattle pens to bring ninety-nine cows to the island. By December 1872 McKinley and the Spaldings had built the herd large enough to begin business. Starting on December 11, they busily sold beef to vessels at Doboy Island, a main port and loading facility between Sapelo and Darien. Most of their business would be with Doboy although many ships stopped at High Point on Sapelo's northern end to buy beef. On Christmas Eve and New Year's Eve, they realized their biggest days of the year by selling 885 pounds for $80 and 993 pounds for $89.37. By the end of May 1873, from a total investment of $900, and after deducting their living expenses, McKinley and the Spaldings made $662 net profit. As an adjunct to selling beef, the partners made additional cash selling hides to tanners in Savannah, Darien, and Cambers Island, and tallow to Darien merchants.[32]

Fortified by success they expanded their business and by April 1874 had a profitable week selling fifteen "beeves." To raise money to expand, they mortgaged Sapelo and Little Sapelo islands for $5,000. They imported cattle from Savannah, Florida, and

Tennessee and paid from $12 to $60 a head. The journal attests to the success of the enterprise through its almost daily descriptions—from late October to early June—of buying and selling cattle to ships with romantic names and faraway ports: *Oriental, Roska, Jorgen Lorentzsen, Hamburg, Saturn, Huron, Gens Brandi, St. Croix*. Weekly dinner or bar visits and hunting trips with sea captains from worldwide registries helped dispel the loneliness of island life. McKinley mentions items bought from these vessels, which served as a veritable international marketplace for coastal businessmen buying exotic dogs, parrots, guns, and champagne. Soon McKinley and the Spalding brothers had serious competition when other residents entered the beef enterprise. Even though moaning over the competition, McKinley collected $1,058.36 on a single day in mid-May, bought a couple hundred cows, and spoke of the enterprise as a "prosperous business." During the winter and spring selling season of 1874, they butchered and sold 175 head; on July 15 they had 310 fattening for market. Their business had grown to the point that they bought a steamboat from Philadelphia to help them meet demand. Later, they used the steamboat to establish a triweekly passenger service from Sapelo to Darien and made nearly $25 a week. They also removed themselves from the hard job of delivering beef to ships by contracting with heretofore competing butchers who agreed to buy all their beef at ten cents, then eight cents a pound.[33]

McKinley dissolved his business partnership on February 20, 1877, and left the island on April 7. His journal fails to reveal the reasons for dissolving the firm, which seems to have been successful. McKinley tells us his father asked him to return to Milledgeville, take up law, and live with him. Tom Spalding also quit the business for reasons unknown; Bourke continued to raise and sell beef cattle. Once resettled in Milledgeville, McKinley immediately planted cotton. His last regular journal entry was April 30, 1877. When the beef business and the adventure of coastal living during Reconstruction ended, so did McKinley's journal. His last thirteen entries concern the death of a friend in 1884 and the 1886 earthquake in coastal Georgia (McKinley had returned to Sapelo by then).[34]

The journal bristles with accounts of the sporting life of the times. McKinley and the Spaldings were outdoor enthusiasts who

loved to hunt and fish, ride and sail. Sapelo and the surround-
ing seawater teemed with wildlife to be shot, hooked, netted, or
trapped. Hardly a page lacks an entry about who shot at or who
missed what; prey included sea turtles and their eggs, deer, porpoises, partridges, shrimp, crabs, rabbits, fish, clams, and rattlesnakes.

McKinley and the Spaldings made excursions to other islands
and took outings to the beaches with their wives. In April 1870,
just after moving to the coast, they helped form a social club, the
Alatamaha Boating Club. A glance at the membership roll indicates that members came from the uppermost ranks of white society, names long associated with the cotton and rice aristocracy of
the coast: Couper, Nightingale, Wylly, Spalding, Butler, Morris,
Gignilliat, Troup. Undoubtedly, the meetings of the social club
promoted fun as well as Democratic party politics.[35]

Although McKinley concentrated on the business aspects of
his life on Sapelo, on the daily routine, and on family deaths and
marriages, his journal sparkles with information about the social,
economic, and political changes of the Reconstruction era. Some
of these notations are too brief for a reader unfamiliar with Reconstruction to understand, and a full explanation of all events
and people is beyond the scope of this Introduction. Still, historians of the period and McIntosh County readers will find much
useful and familiar information to supplement their knowledge of
post-Civil War conditions along Georgia's coast.

During Reconstruction, Sapelo's freed black population tried
to live beyond the eyes of whites. Their lives consisted of impoverished autonomy to be sure, but that was better than the
impoverished slavery of prewar days. Most lived together on
land obtained from the Spaldings and the Freedmen's Bureau,
at Behavior, the Kenan place, or in the northern end community of Chocolate (see Map). Sapelo's 1870 black population of 294
counted 144 males and 150 females; 91 of those were children ten
years old or less. Nine freedpeople claimed to be at least ninety-
five years old; three of them, including Carolina Underwood and
his wife Hannah, whom McKinley mentions in the journal, had
been born in Africa. Three others were born in the Bahamas.
The 1870 census lists a total personal property value of $2,320
for the island's 312 blacks and mulattoes. That contrasts sharply

with the $31,000 in land and $13,500 in personal goods of the island's 24 whites. School was important to the freedpeople, and 52 people managed to attend school in the first half of 1870. Most of them studied arithmetic, grammar, spelling, and geography under teachers Charley Marshall and Anthony Wilson of the American Missionary Association. Sapelo blacks worked as subsistence farmers, or hired themselves as day laborers, carpenters, or domestic servants to the white landowners. Some joined the predominant labor system by signing sharecropping and tenantry agreements and farmed cotton and corn for market. They worked for new or old masters, but with one major exception, they were paid for their labor.[36]

The McKinley and Spalding cotton enterprise depended upon black labor tenantry contracts. In March 1871, blacks signed sharecropping agreements—settlement to be due at harvest time. Freedman Caesar Sams paid his rent in cash, $50 in 1872, and by so doing, gained more control over his labor than those who signed for shares. Others signed labor contracts that paid them in cash or in kind (beef or tools); this group had far more supervision from their white employers than those who signed share contracts. Labor and management did not always get along. In various entries, McKinley writes about labor disputes: "trouble with our plowhands"; "My hands, with one exception, took holiday to-day"; and "All but two of our negroes quit yesterday." These disputes indicate what freedom meant to blacks. Unlike slaves, freedpeople had the right to complain and expect redress of their working conditions or they would quit. Even on Sapelo there were other employers who needed labor and would hire it away if given the opportunity; this gave blacks some bargaining power. Additionally, blacks often took "holiday" on Saturdays, a sure expression of their freedom. By standing up for their rights, Sapelo blacks forced whites to treat them with a little respect, with a little equality. That McKinley and other whites had difficulty accepting this fact is clear in McKinley's entry: "The negroes have been annoying me very much, trying to get the money due them." That he named his stallion "Ku Klux" certainly has relevance here. And the frequency with which servants and cooks left McKinley's employ suggests his domestics were poorly treated. That McKinley fired others is an indication that they had refused to play by his rules. There is a kind of freedom in the ability to get fired that blacks did not know during slavery. The old master-slave relationship on Sapelo had been overturned and replaced by employer-employee maneuverings. The freed people were becoming free people.[37]

The journal touches other aspects of race relations during Reconstruction. Blacks sought land of their own and tried to buy it when they could. They enthusiastically celebrated the Fourth of July and the Declaration of Independence; McKinley notes that in Milledgeville "it is celebrated . . . only by negros, scallawags & carpet baggers." After the surrender of Vicksburg on July 4, 1863, coupled with Lee's defeat at Gettysburg on July 3, 1863, white southerners held to the opinion that they had nothing to celebrate on that day. Up the coast from Sapelo, in Savannah, blacks rioted in 1872 when that city decided to segregate streetcars. Shut out of the court system until 1867, blacks increasingly went through the system for redress of grievances. McKinley mentions that for the first time ever Sapelo blacks appealed to a Darien judge that they had been slandered. On another occasion, after a fight between two black men, one swore out a warrant for the other's arrest—something impossible under slavery. Certainly, some of this resort to legal avenues depended upon whether or not blacks believed the court system would be honest in its decisions. And the system was not always honest; for instance, McKinley admits he sat on the jury of a case that involved cow stealing and found the defendant guilty. Certainly a man in the cattle business should not sit as juror in a case in which he has an obvious interest. Yet, in McIntosh County, with Justice of the Peace Tunis Campbell, black ordinary Lewis Jackson and black constable Hamilton Jackson, blacks had recourse when whites pushed them too hard—at least for a while.[38]

On April 29 and 30, 1875, McKinley served on the McIntosh County grand jury that indicted Campbell on a charge of false imprisonment, an old 1872 charge that the Georgia Supreme Court had overturned in 1873. Through legal maneuvering, whites who wanted to rid the county of Campbell reactivated the case as if it had never been tried. Just to get to the courthouse to serve as a juror proved difficult as tensions worsened. In an ugly disturbance at Doboy Island, McKinley and three other whites "had to draw our pistols to quell the mob." After McKinley joined in indicting the black leader and sending him to jail, blacks exchanged gunfire with whites in the streets of Darien. There might have been a full-scale riot, but Campbell did not encourage further violence and Superior Court Judge Henry Tompkins put him on the first steamboat for Savannah. With Campbell removed, whites gained, or thought they gained, more control over their black laborers. There would be many more battles in the movement for equality.[39]

Overall, the *Journal of Archibald C. McKinley* is interesting and informative for those trying to understand life during the transition from Old South to New South. It serves as one more piece of evidence concerning the resilience of the human spirit in a world turned upside down. Blacks and whites searched for the meanings of Reconstruction—what did freedom mean, how much liberty is there, do I still have a right to the land? These questions had different answers for everyone, but the answers split generally along black-white class lines. People sought security, love, sustenance, and advancement. McKinley has helped us define the struggles and accomplishments in one localized part of Georgia. His journal helps pose questions and answers about Reconstruction Georgia.

RUSSELL DUNCAN

NOTES

1. Russell Duncan, *Freedom's Shore: Tunis Campbell and the Georgia Freedmen* (Athens: University of Georgia Press, 1986), 4–5.

2. *War of the Rebellion: A Compilation of the Official Records of the Union and Confederate Armies,* 128 vols. (Washington, D.C.: U.S. Government Printing Office, 1880–1901), 3d ser., 2:27–28, 152–53, 663–64.

3. Ibid., W. T. Sherman to H. W. Halleck, 1st ser., 47, pt. 2, 36; for the best look at Sherman's Campaign, see Joseph T. Glatthaar, *The March to the Sea and Beyond: Sherman's Troops in the Savannah and Carolina Campaigns* (New York: New York University Press, 1985).

4. Ibid.

5. Duncan, *Freedom's Shore,* 18–19. For the best discussions of the Freedmen's Bureau and Sherman's reservation, see William S. McFeely,

Yankee Stepfather: General O. O. Howard and the Freedmen (New Haven: Yale University Press, 1968); Claude Oubre, *Forty Acres and a Mule: The Freedmen's Bureau and Black Land Ownership* (Baton Rouge: Louisiana State University Press, 1978); and Paul Cimbala, "The Terms of Freedom: The Freedmen's Bureau and Reconstruction in Georgia, 1865–1870" (Ph.D. diss., Emory University, 1983), especially 231–98.

6. Duncan, *Freedom's Shore*, 22–28.

7. Tillson quote from Cimbala, "Terms of Freedom," 243; for a more sympathetic treatment of Tillson and an excellent exposition of Freedmen's Bureau activities on the Georgia islands, see Paul A. Cimbala, "The Freedmen's Bureau, the Freedmen, and Sherman's Grant in Reconstruction Georgia, 1865–1867," *Journal of Southern History*, 55 (November 1989): 597–632.

8. Cimbala, "Terms of Freedom," 271–72; see *Journal* entries for July 7, September 9 and 15, 1869 and Ella Barrow Spalding letter in Appendix.

9. The seminal work on postwar northern entrepreneurs is Lawrence N. Powell, *New Masters: Northern Planters During the Civil War And Reconstruction* (New Haven: Yale University Press, 1980). The best analysis of what Reconstruction was like for the freed slaves and why the work of "freedom" remains unfinished is Eric Foner's *Reconstruction, 1863–1877: America's Unfinished Revolution* (New York: Harper and Row, 1988); Wyat quoted in Foner, 105.

10. Duncan, *Freedom's Shore*, 33; Buddy Sullivan, *Sapelo: A History* (Darien, Ga.: Darien News, 1988), 10.

11. Duncan, *Freedom's Shore*, 33–34; Cimbala, "Terms of Freedom," 275–76; Alexander St. Clair Abrams, *Manual and Biographical Register of the State of Georgia, 1871–2* (Atlanta: Plantation Press, 1872), 114–15.

12. Duncan, *Freedom's Shore*, 35–38; Campbell quoted from *Report of the Joint Select Committee to Inquire into the Condition of Affairs in the Late Insurrectionary States*, 13 vols. (Washington, D.C.: U.S. Government Printing Office, 1872), 7:861. Campbell had been organizing labor since as early as 1853 in New York City, where he helped organize the First United Association of Colored Waiters to demand higher wages. See Philip S. Foner and Ronald L. Lewis, eds., *The Black Worker to 1869* (Philadelphia: Temple University Press, 1978), 193–94.

13. Duncan, *Freedom's Shore*, chapters 2 and 3; Cimbala, "Terms of Freedom," 292–93. For the best look at the interconnections of the Klan and the Georgia Democrats see Stanley K. Deaton, "Violent Redemption: The Democratic Party and the Ku Klux Klan in Georgia, 1868–1871" (Master's thesis, University of Georgia, 1988).

14. Cimbala, "Terms of Freedom," 292–93.
15. Luis F. Emilio, *A Brave Black Regiment: History of the Fifty-fourth Regiment of Massachusetts Volunteer Infantry* (1894; repr., New York: Arno Press, 1969), 41–44; Spencer B. King, *Darien: The Death and Rebirth of a Southern Town* (Macon, Ga.: Mercer University Press, 1981), 55–73.
16. Emory M. Thomas, "The South and the Sea: Some Thoughts on the Southern Maritime Tradition," *Georgia Historical Quarterly* 67 (Summer 1983): 162; "Sapelo Island National Estuarine Sanctuary: Sapelo Island, Georgia" (Brunswick, Ga.: Georgia Department of Natural Resources, 1977), pamphlet in vertical files, University of Georgia Library, Athens, Ga. For the best study to date on Sapelo's geological and marine history, see Mildred and John Teal, *Portrait of an Island* (Athens: University of Georgia Press, 1981).
17. The work of state archeologist Lewis Larsen and others who search for clues about early Sapelo can be found in Daniel P. Juengst, ed., *Sapelo Papers* (Carrollton, Ga.: West Georgia College Studies in the Social Sciences, 1980). Sullivan, *Sapelo*, 6–7.
18. Sullivan, *Sapelo*, 7–10; E. Merton Coulter, *Thomas Spalding of Sapelo* (Baton Rouge: Louisiana State University Press, 1940), 39.
19. Sullivan, *Sapelo*, 20; Coulter, 39–40; Malcolm Bell, Jr., *Major Butler's Legacy: Five Generations of a Slaveholding Family* (Athens: University of Georgia Press, 1986), 101. There is a need for a modern biography of Thomas Spalding. The only scholarly treatment of Spalding is the much outdated biography by Merton Coulter.
20. Interview with Charles Hall recorded in Jana Earl Hesser, "Historical, Demographic, and Biochemical Studies on Sapelo Island, Georgia" (Master's thesis, University of Pennsylvania, 1971), appendix 1. Sullivan, *Sapelo*, 22–23. For highly sympathetic treatments of Sapelo slavery under Spalding, see Coulter, *Thomas Spalding*; Betsy Fancher, *The Lost Legacy of Georgia's Golden Isles* (New York: Doubleday, 1971), 73–82; Caroline Couper Lovell, *The Golden Isles of Georgia* (Atlanta: Cherokee Publishing Co., 1970), 94–118; Burnette Vanstory, *Georgia's Land of the Golden Isles* (Athens: University of Georgia Press, 1956), 55–74.
21. *Journal*, January 3, 1871, November 4, 1874.
22. 1860 U.S. Census, Slave Schedules, Georgia, Oglethorpe County, 55–56, 81–82, Baldwin County, 18, 62–63; 1860 U.S. Census, Agricultural Schedules, Georgia, Baldwin County, 23, Oglethorpe County, 21–22; Tax Digests, Baldwin County, Ga., 1860 and 1863, Georgia Department of Archives and History, Atlanta, Ga.; Paul S. Boyer et al., eds., *The Enduring Vision: A History of the American People* (Lexington, Mass.: D.C. Heath, 1990), 1:549a.

23. *Journal,* May 10, 1870, and May 16, 1871; Anna M. G. Cook, *History of Baldwin County, Georgia* (Spartanburg, S.C.: The Reprint Co., 1978), 410–11; *Records of Baldwin County, Georgia* (Albany, Ga.: Delwyn Associates, 1975), 90.

24. *Journal,* June 16, July 3, and August 23–September 18, 1869; McKinley records cotton prices of 29½ to 27½ cents per pound (September 7 and 15, 1869). McKinley not only received "rent crops" of corn, cotton, hay, and fodder, he sold his tenants mules and equipment by taking cotton as payment. On October 18, 1869, he received his tenants' cotton at 23½ to 24 cents per pound, which he then turned around and sold for 28 cents a pound; Tax Digest, Baldwin County, Ga., 1866.

25. *Journal,* June 19, October 14, November 3, 5, 8, 20, 22–27, December 15, 16, 1869, January 5, and August 8, 1871.

26. Ibid., September 20, October 22, January 1, 18, March 31, 1870; *The Statistics of Population of the United States, 9th Census* (Washington, D.C.: U.S. Government Printing Office, 1872): 21–22, 625; 1870 U.S. Census, Population Schedule, Georgia, McIntosh County, 69–79, 117–125.

27. *Journal,* October 20, December 1, 6–13, 31, 1869; James Holmes, *"Dr. Bullie's" Notes: Reminiscences of Early Georgia and of Philadelphia and New Haven in the 1800's* (Atlanta: Cherokee Publishers, 1976).

28. 1870 U.S. Census, 117–25.

29. Monthly Report of W. F. Eaton, October 31, 1865, Bureau of Refugees, Freedmen and Abandoned Lands, Records of the Assistant Commissioner for the State of South Carolina, Record Group 105, Microcopy 869, Roll 43, p. 5; *Journal,* June 28–July 18, October 14, November 2, 3, 18, December 5, 7, 31, 1870, March 28, April 18, May 11, November 6, December 12, 1871, and January 1, 27, November 26, 1872; *Statistics of Population* 1:104.

30. *Journal,* August 16, 1870, February 8, April 25, 26, 1876, and March 3, 1877; *Statistics of Population,* 1:20, 21; in the 1868 senatorial election, Gignilliat lost to Campbell, 1256 to 539. From then on, Gignilliat worked to remove Campbell from the county, and finally succeeded through a conspiracy of trumped-up charges in 1876. A. S. Barnwell, the Democrat who replaced Campbell, is also mentioned in the *Journal.* See Duncan, *Freedom's Shore,* chapter 3.

31. *Journal,* October 27, 1870, April 12–May 13, November 29, 1871, and June 11, 1873; Duncan, *Freedom's Shore,* 2–3; Lillian F. Sinclair, "My Recollections of Darien in the Late Seventies and Eighties," 1, and Joseph Hilton, "High Water on the Bar," 3–10, Hilton Papers, Folder 8, Georgia Historical Society.

32. *Journal*, July 11, September 1, 1871, December 10–31, 1872, May 28, June 25, July 5, 1873, March 5, 6, April 22, 1874, and June 11, July 5, 1875.

33. Ibid., December 13–16, 1873, January 26, February 12, 14, March 13, 22, April 3–22, May 11, 30, June 8, 11, 15, June 19, 23, July 4–August 1, November 17, 1874, February 27, April 1, November 3, December 15, 1875, and January 25, 1876.

34. Ibid., February 6, 10, 20, April 7, 23, 25, 28, 1877; A. C. McKinley to Father, December 27, 1876, in Appendix.

35. Ibid., April 7, May 5, 16, 1870, and July 12, 1874.

36. 1870 U.S. Census, 117–25; *Journal*, June 8, 1873; American Missionary Association Manuscripts, "Letters from Georgia," Microfilm, Roll 6, nos. 23143, 23345, 23434, 23526.

37. *Journal*, July 15, August 2, 4, September 8, November 17, 18, 1869, and March 1, 7, 15, May 11, 13, 20, 27, July 8, 1871. Quotes from May 27 and July 8, 1871.

38. Ibid., July 4, 9, November 18, 1869, February 12, July 4, 1871, August 1, 1872, December 5, 1873, August 10, 1874, August 30, 31, 1875. Quotes from July 4, and November 18, 1869.

39. Ibid., April 28–May 1, 1875; for a full explanation of the indictment, conspiracy to remove Campbell, and the riot of April 30, see Duncan, *Freedom's Shore*, 103–7. That McKinley felt strongly about blacks holding political office over whites is indicated by his *Journal* inclusion of the Georgia Supreme Court decision that blacks were indeed eligible to hold office; *Journal*, June 16, 1869.

THE JOURNAL OF
Archibald C. McKinley

1869

JUNE

14 Ames circus & menagerie exhibited in Milledgeville to-day.
Sallie[1] delighted at sight of the animals. A good slow, re-
freshing rain to-day—the first in a month—crops needed
it badly.

15 Weather clear—been planting corn in my garden to-day
in ground formerly occupied by garden peas, also planted
pop corn.

16 Went to Walnut Level[2] this morning. My cotton is pretty
good, but corn is backward. We hear to-day of a Radical
Supreme Court's decision[3] that the negro is eligible to
office.

17 Weather cloudy & warm—toward evening light rain with
high winds, the latter tearing small limbs from the trees.

18 Weather cloudy & very warm. I have been assisting my
father[4] to make out interrogatories for Willie Wylly[5] & a

1. Sarah Elizabeth Spalding McKinley (1844–1916), wife of Archibald C.
McKinley.

2. McKinley's farm, adjoining the then northern boundary of Milledgeville
and the west bank of the Oconee River at Tobler Creek. On December 31,
1870, McKinley describes it as 282½ acres. Baldwin County records the
deed of sale from McKinley to "Vaugn and Wall" for $4,500 and describes it
as 283¾ acres (Deed Book "O":113–14).

3. *White vs. Clements.* Georgia Supreme Court, June 1869. Decision that
black men had the right to hold office.

4. William McKinley (1809–78), father of A. C. McKinley. Milledgeville
lawyer and farmer.

5. William Cook Wylly (1842–1923), a first cousin of Sallie McKinley.

man named Carr, in the case of J. W. Anderson's Sons &
Co. against Mrs. Spalding[6] for price of two mules.

19 Weather clear and very warm. J. C. Whitaker's (Bankrupt)
property sold to-day. Waitzfelder & Co.[7] bought a 2000 acre
plantation for $2026. My Father bought his Midway[8] house
& lot for $413. Jim McKinley[9] left here to-day for Savannah.

20 Weather very warm & clear. Mercury 90° in shade. Attended Presbyterian Church. Sermon by Rev. C. W. Lane.[10]

21 Weather clear & warmer still—94° in shade. Received a
barrel of rice from Dillon & Stetson. Met Wm. S. Stetson
from Savannah, we were Lieutenants in the same company
& served through the war together.

22 Weather clear & exceedingly warm—mercury 95° in the
shade. Prospects of rain now (9 P.M.). My Father is in Eatonton attending an arbitration. I went to Walnut Level this
morning. Some of my cotton three feet high, but as yet no
blossoms.

23 We had a glorious rain last night. Weather not so warm.
Father returned from Eatonton. Mrs. Spalding buying up
blackberries for wine.

24 We had a light rain last night—to-day the weather is clear
& pretty warm. My garden cotton showed the first blossom
this morning. Uncle David Barrow[11] arrived this afternoon.
Charity, our cook, left us on the 22d, and Sallie Ball took her
place the same day.

25 Weather clear & warm. Seven cotton blossoms in my garden
to-day. A fight between Jerome Tuttle and a man named
Bonner from Augusta, about a gambling debt. Tuttle put in
the calaboose. My two bull puppies, Argus & Tabarman-

---

6. Mary Dorothy Bass Spalding (1823–98), McKinley's mother-in-law.

7. A Milledgeville mercantile and manufacturing concern.

8. Midway was a small community 2.5 miles south of Milledgeville. Site of
Oglethorpe College before the Civil War.

9. James J. McKinley, of Savannah, a first cousin of McKinley.

10. Charles W. Lane was pastor of the Milledgeville Presbyterian Church
from 1869 to 1872.

11. David Crenshaw Barrow, McKinley's maternal uncle.

tona (called Tonna, for short),[12] bit a negro woman who was foolish enough to come in the yard unprotected.

26 Weather very warm. Had a good rain at Walnut Level, although there was only a sprinkle in town, enough cloud however for a flash of lightning to strike the town hall—no damage done. Uncle David left today for Athens.

27 Weather clear & warm. Attended [Milledgeville] Presbyterian Church.

28 Weather warm & clear—mercury 91°. Went to Walnut Level this morning. I have some pretty cotton, from half leg to waist high & pretty grassy. Found blossoms for the first time in my field cotton to-day. Good deal of excitement in Milledgeville over a velocipede rink[13] just established.

29 Weather clear—thermometer 94°. Sister Kate Taylor[14] has been spending a few days in town with us. Capt. John A. Cobb[15] & family passed through Milledgeville last night enroute to Athens.

30 Weather warm & clear—thermometer 94°. Went to Walnut Level this morning before breakfast. I have hired two extra plows, at $2 per day, each. Plowing with sweeps,[16] four furrows to the row. Blossoms thick. Afterwards went with Father to see the Whitaker house[17] in Midway, which he has bought.

JULY

1 Weather clear during the day—thermometer 95°. After supper we had a light rain with a great deal of thunder &

12. This name is evidently an attempt to latinize the biblical site Mount Tabor.

13. A bicycle rink.

14. Catherine McKinley Taylor (1837–73), a full sister of McKinley.

15. Captain John A. Cobb, son of General Howell Cobb; settled after the war in Americus as a planter and served in various elected offices. They evidently were en route to his family's home in Athens.

16. A type of plow blade that only disturbed the top inch of the soil, used to weed cotton.

17. The home of bankrupt J. C. Whitaker, which had just been sold.

lightning, one flash of which struck one of the lightning rods on my Father's house, with out doing any damage however.

2 Weather clear until afternoon, when we had a light sprinkle —thermometer 93°. Went to Walnut Level—have discharged my extra plows—counted twenty cotton blossoms without moving out of my tracks.

3 Weather clear—thermometer 94°. Tom Spalding[18] and myself drove out to Walnut Level. Cotton is looking very promising—knee to half thigh high—tallest waist high. A day or two now will finish the third plowing. Am now running three or four sweep furrows to the row.

4 Weather clear—thermometer 96°. Today is the sixth anniversary of our surrender to the Yankee army at Vicksburg.[19] It is now celebrated in this section only by negros, scallawags & carpet baggers.[20]

5 Weather warm & clear, with light showers in the afternoon. Sallie & myself spent the day at Dr. Spalding Kenan's,[21] five miles from town, and on our return this afternoon, we were caught in the rain above mentioned. Since seeing other people's cotton, I am better satisfied with my own.

6 Weather cool, damp & misty. Been engaged most of the day with interrogatories in the case of J. W. Anderson's Sons & Co. vs. Mrs. Spalding. This day twenty-two years ago at 5 o'clock P.M. my mother[22] died, at Lexington, Oglethorpe County, Georgia.

7 Weather same as yesterday—mosquitos very bad. Took Sallie to ride before breakfast, out past Jake Gunn's on the

18. Thomas Spalding (1847–85), Sallie McKinley's brother. He later marries McKinley's full sister Sarah. See January 3, 1871.

19. Vicksburg, Mississippi. A decisive Union victory under Gen. Ulysses S. Grant. The city was surrendered July 4, 1863, after a lengthy campaign and a siege of six weeks.

20. Scalawags were the native white southerners who joined the Republican party and embraced Reconstruction efforts. Similarly, carpetbaggers were white northerners who came to the South to exploit the situation.

21. Dr. Spalding Kenan (1836–1907), a first cousin of Sallie McKinley, a physician, and, after his mother's death, the owner of the Kenan property on Sapelo.

22. Precious Patience Barrow McKinley.

Walker's ferry road.[23] Mrs. Spalding received a telegram this morning, announcing the dangerous illness of her brother, Dr. Bass.[24] She & Bourke[25] left this afternoon for Savannah.

8 Weather clear & warm. Went to Walnut Level this morning with Father's wagon for wood but broke down about half way back & had to send my little wagon for the wood. Some of my cotton is breast high, but generally from knee to waist high. Finishing its *third* plowing.[26]

9 Clear & warm. Fifteen years ago last night at one o'clock my sister Caroline[27] died of cholera, aged fourteen & a half years. The radical negroes[28] in this section have had a large 4th July celebration to-day with visiting colored fire companies[29] from Macon. The procession numbered probably 500 men and youths. All peaceable so far, but they have a dance tonight.

10 Clear & warm. Uncle David arrived last night on his return home—this morning he, sisters Kate & Sallie & little Kate[30] left for Athens. Tom Spalding and I went as far as Camak[31] with them. A company of Yankee Soldiers arrived this afternoon, to prevent Alexander, lessee of the Penitentiary, from

23. Jacob Gunn, Jr., lived eight miles from Milledgeville. Knight, *Georgia's Landmarks*, 1:276.

24. Dr. Sterling Bass (d. 1869), Sallie McKinley's maternal uncle. A Savannah physician.

25. Thomas Bourke Spalding (1851–84), Sallie McKinley's younger brother. He later marries Ella Barrow, daughter of David C. Barrow and first cousin of McKinley. See November 4, 1874.

26. Cotton was usually plowed for weeds only twice using sweeps, the plant then being high enough to shade out the weeds.

27. Caroline McKinley (1840–54), full sister of McKinley.

28. Blacks affiliated with the Radical Republicans, a coalition within the Republican party that worked to promote the civil and economic rights of freedpeople after the Civil War.

29. Blacks formed fraternal organizations, often as volunteer fire companies, in the South after the war.

30. Sarah Barrow McKinley (1847–97), full sister of McKinley, and Kate Taylor, niece of McKinley. McKinley later served briefly as little Kate's guardian. Kate later married E. D. Treanor of Athens.

31. A small town in Warren County, Georgia, and junction of the Macon branch with the main line of the Georgia Railroad. Named for James A. Camak, first president of the Georgia Railroad Company.

making distinction in treatment of white & black convicts. They camp in the old Court House Square.[32]

11 Sunday—clear & very warm—thermometer 97°. Called out of church this evening to get a telegram announcing the death of Dr. Sterling Bass, from dysentery. He was an uncle of my wife.

12 Weather hot. This afternoon a light shower of rain. Served interrogatories on Judge Harris[33] in case of Anderson's & Co. vs. Mrs. Spalding.

13 Clear & warm. Went to Walnut Level this morning. Cotton fine—bolls nearly as large as a guinea egg.

14 Very warm—thermometer 97°. About six and a half o'clock P.M. we had the most violent wind & rain storm I ever saw. About ⅙ of the trees in town were prostrated by it. My yard suffered severely that way.

15 Weather clear & much pleasanter after the storm of yesterday. I, this morning, discharged my servant boy Owen for impudence & have in his place another one named Bulloch.

16 Very warm & clear—toward evening pleasant breezes. I forgot to say at the time that Mrs. Livingston[34] of Columbus, Ga. arrived here on Tuesday the 13th inst.

17 Clear & warm. Went to Walnut Level this morning. Crops fine—cotton from knee to chin high and some of it beginning to lock across the row. I lost my boy Bulloch, spoken of before. He was bound by a prior contract to Capt. Jack Jones, who to-day claimed him, which leaves me without a servant boy. I yesterday sent my mare Kate to my Father's pasture to have a colt.

32. On July 13, 1869, the *Southern Recorder* (Milledgeville) reported that part of Company C, 18th Infantry had arrived the previous Saturday to inspect the penitentiary and to investigate alleged whippings of convicts employed in the construction of the Brunswick Railroad. Old Court House Square was apparently a corner of the old state capitol grounds, now Georgia Military College.

33. Judge Iverson L. Harris, Milledgeville. Attorney for J. W. Anderson's Sons Co. and later justice of the Georgia Supreme Court.

34. Elizabeth Bass Livingston (1816–88), Sallie McKinley's maternal aunt and wife of Lewis Livingston of Columbus, Ga. Their daughter, Evelyn Elizabeth, married Dr. Spalding Kenan.

18 Sunday. Warm & clear. I have been suffering considerably from rheumatism to-day.

19 Monday—warm, with good breeze—light showers of rain this morning. Good rains passed around us. Having no servant boy yet, I am having to do my own work.

20 Warm & dry, except some sprinkles. Commencement at Oglethorpe College[35] tonight. Mrs. Spalding & Bourke return from Savannah tonight.

21 Clear & pleasant. Went with the boys to Tom shoals[36] in the Oconee river to-day. Cotton crop very fine. Anniversary of the first battle of Manassas.[37] Sallie wants me to record the fact of her having rheumatism.

22 Cloudy, with light showers—good rain I hear at Walnut Level. We started a shrimp net to-day, preparatory to a trip to Sapelo Island. This is the fifth anniversary of a very severe battle I was in near Atlanta in 1864, in which Jas. Foshee of our company & Maj. Genl. Wm. H. T. Walker our division commander were killed.[38]

23 Warm & somewhat cloudy—no rain. Hired a servant boy named Jackson, to-day at five dollars a month. Methodist District Meeting commenced here to-day.

24 Weather clear during the day—light, slow rain in town after dark. Found we were knitting our shrimp net with the wrong stitch—quit it and started another one.

25 Sunday—Cloudy & raining all the forenoon, so much that we could not go to church.

26 Weather clear. To-day I had my garden walks (which had become filled with crab grass) cleaned out. Mrs. Spalding & Tom went out to Dr. Kenan's to-day, the latter on business for me [*phonographic alphabet*].

35. Then located at Midway, Oglethorpe College moved to Atlanta in 1870.

36. A shoal in the Oconee River near the mouth of Tobler Creek and McKinley's Walnut Level farm; associated with Tom's path, an early trading route.

37. In July 1861, the first major battle of the Civil War and a strategic victory for the South.

38. The battle of Atlanta was fought July 22, 1864.

27 Clear in the morning. A wagon & horses ran away down town this morning, smashing up two buggies & doing other damage. A light shower later in the day.

28 Wednesday. Walked out to Walnut Level early this morning. I have some cotton there which is as fine as any I ever saw—from 25 to 91 squares, blossoms & bolls to the stalk. Showers in afternoon—one heavy rain.

29 The Methodists are getting up a revival here—preaching twice a day since Monday.

30 Cloudy & damp, now & then a shower. It rained the first dog day, and it really seems as if it will rain every one.

31 Still cloudy & damp, with some rain. Julia, Willie[39] & Tom Spalding left for commencement at Athens this morning. Bought a load of wood to-day.

AUGUST

1 Sunday—Cloudy & damp. Miss Mary White joined the Presbyterian Church this morning. Rev. Charles W. Lane, Pastor.

2 Clearer & warmer. This is little Tom Cobb's[40] birth day. Discharged Martha, washerwoman. Methodists still carrying on their revival.

3 Clear & warmer. Mrs. Spalding called out to Dr. Kenan's. The latter's fourth son has just been born to-day. To-night we received by express from John K. Nightingale[41] of Brunswick two large soft shell turtles.

4 Wednesday. No rain & pretty hot. I have been suffering for some days past with a very sore toe—under the nail—am afraid it will be serious. Just after dark this evening, 7½ o'clock, my mare Kate gave birth to her first colt—a very fine one.

39. Julia (ca. 1850–76) and William (1851–75) McKinley, half sister and half brother of McKinley.

40. Thomas R. R. Cobb (1868–98), nephew of McKinley named for his uncle who was prominent in state politics before the war. He later became an attorney in Atlanta.

41. Member of a prominent coastal Georgia planter family.

5 Clear, hot & dry. I walked out to my Father's to see my mare's colt—a pretty little bay (at present), mare colt, we call her Fanny. The servants all sleep off the lot now, because they have a ridiculous story that there are ghosts on it.

6 Very warm. A fine shower this afternoon. Father went out to look at a tract of 400 acres of land, belonging to Oliver P. Bonner, which he wishes to sell.

7 Cloudy & damp. Partial eclipse of the Sun this afternoon, obscured by clouds. First open cotton reported at Walnut Level to-day. "Laid by" the last of the crop there yesterday.

8 Sunday. A cloudless sky with weather so *cold* that winter clothes have been almost universally worn during the day. Went to see Kate's colt. Mrs. Spalding returned from Dr. Kenan's. [They] call his baby "Spalding." Service in Episcopal Church, by Rev. H. K. Reed of Macon, there being no resident minister here.

9 Clear & cold. My Father left for Atlanta this morning, to attend the Supreme Court.[42] Commenced hauling wood from Walnut Level with one of my mules. Cotton opening fast. Rust[43] is appearing in it. Commenced pulling upland fodder. Discharged our negro cook, Sallie Ball.

10 Clear & dry. Our first cook, Charity, returned to our service this morning, at $10 per month for cooking and washing. Mrs. Miller Grieve[44] died this evening of Bright's disease.

11 Went to Walnut Level this morning—still hauling wood from there.

12 Thursday. Weather clear & warm. Mrs. Grieve was buried this morning at 9 o'clock.

13 Weather still clear & getting very warm. The warm weather is making cotton open very fast.

14 Dry & warm. Finished pulling upland fodder. Father returned from Supreme Court at Atlanta.

42. The *Georgia Reports* for this session do not indicate that William McKinley attended as an attorney of record. He was possibly there as an observer.

43. Cotton "rust" is a necrosis of its leaves caused by a potassium deficiency.

44. Sarah Caroline Grantland, wife of Miller Grieve, editor and publisher of the *Southern Recorder* (Milledgeville).

15 Sunday. Very warm & dry. Attended Presbyterian Church.
In afternoon called on Mrs. Chas. K. Hall, my wife's cousin.
16 Hot. Went to Father's to get irons for a two-horse wagon.
After dark, a fine, slow rain is falling in town.
17 Weather very hot. Nothing of interest transpiring.
18 Wednesday. Very hot. My brother Andrews[45] spending
the night with us. Mrs. Spalding pretty sick. Tom Spalding
returned from Athens this afternoon.
19 Weather very hot & dry. This morning before breakfast I
took Sallie out to Walnut Level. The first field of upland
cotton she ever went through. In some places, six open bolls
to the stalk.
20 Very hot. I forgot to mention that on the 17th Bourke went
out to Dr. Kenan's, to stay until he returns from Macon.
Bought a pair of pump sole boots this morning. We hear this
morning of a bad shooting affray which occurred in Hancock
County just over Town Creek (the County line), in which
a young white man named Posey was shot in the hip, &
his little brother three years old shot through the thigh by
three negro men. In the affray one of the latter (Father of
the other two) was killed outright, having the top of his head
blown off.[46]
21 The hottest day of the season, so far—thermometer down
town reported as being at 102° in the shade. Bourke returned from Dr. Kenan's.
22 Sunday—Very hot. Went to Presbyterian Church. A very
light sprinkle of rain this afternoon.
23 Dry & hot. Got my two horse wagon from the shop this
morning, just finished. Commenced picking cotton at
Walnut Level to-day. The Superior Court for this County

45. Andrews McKinley (1853–75), half brother of McKinley. Sometimes
referred to as Arnie.
46. The *Southern Recorder* of August 24, 1869, reports that a Mr. Posey
of Hancock County killed an unnamed black man whose children had
allegedly bothered Posey's fruit and been impudent to his wife. Posey
thrashed one of the children and the child's father came to settle the score.
Each fired his gun; Posey and a child were wounded. The black man
died soon after being shot. Later, the coroner's jury returned a verdict of
justifiable homicide.

commenced its session this morning. 399 lbs. cotton picked
to-day.

24 Dry & warm. My bulldog, Argus, liked to have killed my
little terrier, Victor, to-night. 558 lbs. cotton to-day.

25 Dry & hot. A good deal of interest manifested by the community in the trial, now going on in court, of John T.
Arnold for killing Newton J. Pugh on 14th August 1868.[47]

26 Dry & hot. John T. Arnold was this afternoon convicted of
voluntary manslaughter for the killing of Pugh in 1868. Our
case of Jno. W. Anderson's Sons & Co. vs. Mary Spalding
was commenced this evening & was progressing when Court
adjourned. 534 lbs. cotton picked yesterday, and 436 lbs.
picked to-day.

27 Dry & hot. The case in Court against Mrs. Spalding, mentioned on the 26th, came to trial this morning and resulted
in a verdict in her favor, relieving her of the whole debt.
William McKinley, Attorney for her—Judge I. L. Harris
against her. I was sworn as a witness. 363 lbs. cotton picked
to-day. Commenced pulling low ground fodder.

28 Dry & hot. The continued drought is ruining the crops.
Received a load of hay from Walnut Level this morning.
Superior Court still in session. 180 lbs. cotton picked.

29 Sunday. Dry & hot. Service at the Episcopal Church by
Rev. Mr. Leacock,[48] who staid at our house while here.

30 Dry & hot up to this time (8 o'cl. P.M.), but with a little prospect of rain to-night. Had my mare Kate & her colt Fanny
brought back to town this morning & rode her once more.
Mr. Leacock left for Macon this afternoon. 224 lbs. cotton
picked. Our cook, Charity, has been sick two days. A fine
rain after 9 o'cl. P.M.

31 Cloudy, with damp North East wind. The rain of last night
made cotton too wet to pick. Dr. Kenan dined with us.

47. On August 14, 1868, a quarrel arose between Newton J. Pugh and
John T. Arnold at the distillery of Obadiah Arnold, sheriff of Baldwin
County and father of John Arnold. Pugh was shot twice and died in a short
time. John T. Arnold was found guilty of voluntary manslaughter.

48. The minister of the Milledgeville Episcopal Church. Also spelled
"Laycock" in the journal (edited to Leacock).

SEPTEMBER

1 Weather clear & cool. Julia and Willie McKinley returned from Athens this afternoon. 805 lbs. cotton picked to-day.

2 Weather clear & cool, N.E. wind still blowing. To-day is my dead Mother's birth-day. She would be fifty two years old, if alive. Dr. S. G. White, P. Thweat & myself, as commissioners to-day, set apart the widow's twelve month support to Mrs. Orme, in this case it was $2500. 1032 lbs. cotton weighed in to-night.

3 Weather clear and cool, built our first winter fire. Rode out to Walnut Level this evening. The crops are ruined—the top crop of cotton bolls is a total failure. The August drought has entirely destroyed that portion of the crop. My corn crop is cut off fully one-half. 1165 lbs. cotton picked to-day.

4 Weather moderating. The telegraph reports ice in Vermont on the 1st inst. & snow in New York on the same day. Commenced hauling cotton to John Edwards' to be ginned. Mrs. Livingston is staying with us; she is returning to Columbus.

5 Sunday. Weather cloudy & warm. Attended the Presbyterian Church—preaching by Rev. Chas. W. Lane. The negroes seem to be drilling at night on the flat down on the river, as we hear their drum beats frequently.

6 Warm & cloudy during the day—clear at night. To-day is Sallie's birth day—she is twenty five years old. Bought 18 yards of bagging and 55 yards of rope, to pack three bales of cotton with. Bought a thermometer.

7 Dry & warm—mercury 88°. I sold three bales Walnut Level cotton this afternoon at 29½ cents a pound. They weighed 500 lbs., 507 lbs. & 527 lbs. Mrs. Spalding is sick this evening. This morning she, Mrs. Livingston, Sallie, Bourke & Charlie[49] went in a carriage to James Dickson's over the river, where the two first named were born.

8 Weather cool & pleasant. Mrs. Spalding Kenan came [to] town to-day, to stay a few days. I went to Walnut Level this

---

49. Charles L. Bass, a first cousin of Sallie McKinley and son of Allen G. Bass. Also spelled "Charly" in the journal (edited to Charlie).

afternoon. 1344 lbs. of cotton picked to-day. I neglected to state in the proper place that my servant boy Jackson quit me on the 4th inst., and was replaced by one named George Bonner on Sunday, 5th inst.

9   Thursday. Weather cool & pleasant. I was up in the Court of Ordinary as a witness in the case of Grantland's estate against Orme's estate. My sister Julia came in to-day to spend a few days with us. Just before going to bed, much to our surprise, the omnibus drove up to our door with Mr. A. G. Bass,[50] Mrs. Dr. Bass[51] and five children in it. All on a visit to us. About 1050 lbs. cotton picked to-day.

10 Cool, dry & pleasant—thermometer this morning 59°. Paid our cook, Charity, ten dollars this morning. Mr. Bass and I went to Walnut Level this evening. About 1250 lbs. cotton picked.

11 Paid my cotton pickers, $18.25 for a little over 3000 lbs.

12 Sunday. Went to Presbyterian Church.

13 Tom Spalding & I start to Athens this morning, on a visit, where we arrived all safe about 4 o'clock P.M., after a pleasant trip.

14 Cloudy with occasional showers during the morning. This morning Sister Kate, Tom & myself walked down to Mrs. Genl. Howell Cobb's,[52] to see the family. In afternoon Capt. J. A. Cobb & Cousin Lucy[53] arrived on the cars. Crops have not suffered so much for rain in this section as they have with us.

15 Tom & I started for home this morning, where we arrived all safely at 4 o'clock this afternoon. Bourke Spalding has

50. Allen G. Bass, Sallie McKinley's maternal uncle. A Spalding overseer and the Freedmen's Bureau agent for McIntosh County.

51. Mrs. Sterling Bass.

52. Mary Ann Lamar Cobb, widow of Gen. Howell Cobb and mother of Howell and John A. Cobb. Howell Cobb (1815–68) had been governor of Georgia from 1851 to 1853, member of the U.S. House of Representatives from 1842 to 1849 and from 1854 to 1855, Speaker of the House in 1849, secretary of the Treasury from 1857 to 1860, and major general in the Confederate army. His family is prominent in the *Journal* because of Howell Cobb, Jr.'s marriage to McKinley's sister Mary and frequent visits among the families.

53. Lucy Pope Barrow Cobb.

been weighing my cotton in my absence. He also sold three bales for me at 27½ cents per lb. Mrs. Dr. Bass & family left for Eufaula this evening. Mr. Allen Bass & Mrs. Livingston & Charlie Bass left Monday.

16 Thursday—Warm & dry. Tom Spalding's birth day—twenty two years old. He & Bourke Spalding left for Sapelo Island this afternoon, via Savannah. I am to follow on the 20th inst. Tom's dog, Bly, is missing to-night.

17 The price of cotton having fallen so much, I stored two bales weighing 463 & 485 lbs., to wait for a rise in price. My brother William came this evening, to take care of my lot until I return from Sapelo. Tom's dog Bly came home to-night almost starved. One load of rent corn received from Walnut Level to-day. I bought me a gun to-day—a Winchester Rifle, shooting sixteen times.

18 Dry & warm. Another load of rent corn from Walnut Level. This being Saturday, the town has been crowded with negroes.

19 Sunday. Service at the Episcopal Church to-day by Rev. Mr. Leacock.

20 I left Milledgeville at 4 o'clock on my way to Sapelo.

21 Arrived at Savannah at 5¼ o'clock A.M., after a very pleasant ride all night on the Central R. Rd. Met Tom & Bourke in Savannah & left with them on the Steamboat *Nick King* at 10 o'clock for Sapelo. Went outside where the sea was rather rough, making a good many passengers sea sick. Arrived at the North end of Sapelo Island about 4 o'clock, where we left the boat & went to Mrs. M. J. Kenan's[54] place.

22 Went fishing. I only caught five—the whole party 73.

23 Went fishing again. I caught eleven—the whole party caught forty-six. Tom caught a bass fully three feet long. It took all of an hour to get him in. After getting him home they put him in a fish car.

24 Raining. This morning on waking we found the car containing the Bass had broken loose. We have just recovered it.

25 Tom & I rode down to his Plantation landing this morning. This afternoon we all went fishing, but owing to very high winds and too short an anchor rope we had no luck.

54. Catherine Spalding Kenan (1810–?), Sallie McKinley's paternal aunt.

26 Sunday—Some rain, and rather a dull day.
27 Went fishing this morning—I caught twenty one fish. Later in the day Tom & I rode out to look at a 400 acre place on the Island, which he wants to sell me. This afternoon we all went over to Pumpkin Hammock, just opposite, & the boys shot one Gannet,[55] one White Crane and one blue Heron.
28 Went fishing this morning to Moses' Hammock—had pretty fair luck, but lost one rudder hook & split a hole in the bottom of our boat. Sailed back, I very well scared.
29 Wednesday. We all went out to the Beach. Surf very rough with N.E. wind. Afterwards went to the South End to see Baba[56] & to see the live oak grove there which is truly grand.
30 The wind still N.E. That together with the fact that we can not fix a rudder to our boat, makes us have a lazy day.

OCTOBER

1 Wind still N. East, with stormy, bad weather—too bad to fish or do anything else with either pleasure or success.
2 Wind N.E.—cloudy, with some rain. Tom & I rode down to look at the Oakdale place. It has a beautiful view of Doboy Sound, but is too low to build on. On our way back a heavy shower of rain caught us, and we got a thorough drenching.
3 Sunday. Weather clearing. Nothing to do but read & sleep.
4 Wind West, with beautiful weather. Went fishing & altogether we caught one hundred & two fish. Went to the North end of the Island to-night to take the Steamboat *Lizzie Baker* on my return home, but on reaching the wharf, found the boat had not left Savannah.
5 Wind gone back N. East, but the weather still clear. Went to Moses' Hammock fishing, but owing to bad winds we had poor luck.

55. The bird now known as the Wood stork, *Mycteria americana*. This bird has not nested on Little Sapelo Island in over fifty years.
56. Nickname for Betsey Beagle, a former slave of Thomas Spalding, who had been nursemaid to two generations of Spalding children. See E. M. Coulter, *Thomas Spalding of Sapelo* (University: Louisiana State University Press, 1940), 84.

6 This morning we all went over to Raccoon Bluff on the ocean side of the Island but owing to bad weather, had poor success fishing. Having had to paddle our canoe against wind & tide and to walk a good deal, we got back home after dark well tired. On our return we found Mr. A. C. Wylly,[57] and I found a letter from Sallie, written a week ago.

7 We have had rather a dull day. Wind N.E., with some rain. Bourke went hunting & jumped twelve deer,[58] and killed three of them.

8 We all left Sapelo Island at 8.48 o'clock this morning in a sail boat for Darien. We had a fine breeze for our purposes, sailing across Doboy Sound in just twelve minutes. We all waited in Darien for the *Nick King*, the boat bound for Savannah, which came along at 11 o'clock P.M.

9 Taking the boat at 11 o'clock last night, I arrived in Savannah about 10.30 o'clock this morning—just 2½ hours after my train on the Central Rail Road left, which compels me to stay in Savannah until Monday morning before I can leave for home.

10 Sunday. Attended church at the Independent Presbyterian Church on Bull Street this morning, with Wm. S. Stetson. Dined with Capt. Chas. Wylly[59] on Jones Street—called on the McIntoshes in the afternoon, and went to the same church at night.

57. Alexander Campbell Wylly (1833–1911), a first cousin of Sallie McKinley. Referred to as Campbell.

58. Jump hunting. In this method the hunter moves through the cover attempting to flush deer and to get a shot. At this time on Sapelo it was usually done on horseback. Deer and other game were important food sources for the residents of Sapelo at this time. See also the Ella Barrow Spalding letter in this volume.

59. Charles Spalding Wylly (1836–1923), a first cousin of Sallie McKinley. Author of *The Seed That Was Sown in the Colony of Georgia and the Harvest and the Aftermath, 1740–1870* (1910); *The Story of Sapelo* (1914); and *Annals and Memoirs of Glynn County* (1920). Subsequent writers on the history of the Georgia coast have depended heavily on Wylly for source material, much of which proves to be unreliable. In the manuscript of *The Story of Sapelo* (the published version was abridged), Wylly states: "In the picturing of the early French owners [of Sapelo] and others, I have not felt myself bound to an absolute verity, capable of proof, and have thought that there is a touch of art infinitely more valuable and instructive than the mere dead bones of a biography." (Collection of Helen Treanor.)

11   Left Savannah at 8 o'clock this morning, on the Central Rail Rd. After a tedious day's ride, arrived at home 9 o'clock at night—found Sallie expecting me.

12   Tired out by yesterday's long ride. Rode out to Walnut Level this afternoon. I find the cotton crop has all opened & been gathered in already.

13   Wednesday. Rode out to Father's this afternoon.

14   Went with my Father to look at a 400 acre tract of land on Fishing Creek, six miles from town, which he purchased from Oliver Bonner, for six dollars an acre. It can be made a very fine place.

15   Weather fine, with westerly winds, and very much cooler than on Sapelo Island.

16   Weather rather cool in the mornings and warm at midday. Willie McK. went fox hunting—caught none.

17   Sunday. This morning as my brothers Andrews & Guy[60] and John Moore were coming to church in a buggy, a bolt broke and the horse ran away through the river bridge, upsetting the buggy, hurting Guy badly and bruising Andrews severely. Went to Presbyterian Church.

18   Have been busy hauling in rent hay & fodder, and making a final settlement with my tenants. Sold them a pair of mules for $468, payment made in cotton at 24¢ per lb., which took 1950 lbs. They paid me a balance due me, $104.13, also in cotton 434 lbs. at the same price. I bought the remainder of their cotton (237 lbs.) at 23½¢ = $55.69—paid by a check on "So. Insurance and Trust Company."

19   Very pretty weather. No news.

20   Wednesday. I partially rented my Walnut Level place this afternoon to Clayton Vaughn for 3300 lbs. lint cotton.

21   Letters this morning from Tom & Bourke Spalding. I go to Savannah this afternoon to meet Tom Spalding on business.

22   After an all night ride on the Central Rail Road I arrived in Savannah about 6 o'clock A.M. Met Tom at the Pulaski House, where it was arranged that I should live on the "Ridge" near Darien next year. Saw Tom off for Sapelo on the Steamer *Lizzie Baker* at 9 o'clock A.M. Afterwards called on the McIntoshes, Wyllys and William S. Stetson.

60. Guy Cummins McKinley (1868–1937), half brother of McKinley.

23 Left Savannah for Milledgeville at 8 o'clock this morning—got home 9 o'clock to-night. When I left Savannah it was very cloudy and raining hard. When I arrived home found it clear and it had scarcely rained at all.

24 Sunday. Attended the Presbyterian Church where I heard an excellent sermon by Mr. Wm. Flinn, the former pastor, now residing in New Orleans.

25 Cousin Lucy Cobb, her family & Miss Mayou[?] Cobb passed through Milledgeville this afternoon en route to Macon. We met them at the depot. Wrote to Register Murray for an order to sell property of Thomas Humphries and Thomas S. Bagley, both Bankrupts.

26 A cold wet day. I am suffering with a cold and sore throat.

27 Wednesday. The weather cleared up last night and to-day is beautifully clear. Paid W. & J. Caraker $24 in full for all wagon work. My mare Kate has been out of harness so long that driving her is like breaking a young horse.

28 Paid my last quarter's dues to the Episcopal Church. First heavy, killing frost this morning.

29 Weather clouding up and turning warm.

30 Warm and pleasant this morning, but during the day a North wind sprung up, and this evening it is getting very cold.

31 Sunday. The coldest October day I ever saw. Went to the Episcopal Church this morning and afternoon & heard Rev. Mr. Leacock preach—in the evening went to hear Mr. Flinn of New Orleans preach at the Presbyterian Church.

NOVEMBER

1 Have been "trying" a horse drover's horses a good part of the day. I forgot to say that Mother[61] left home for Atlanta on Thursday last.

2 The principle event of to-day is the marriage of Rev. Wm. Flinn, formerly Presbyterian Minister at this place (Milledgeville) but now of New Orleans, to Miss Mary Orme

---

61. Lucy Anne Andrews Sims McKinley (?–1882), stepmother of McKinley.

of Milledgeville. Married at two o'clock in the afternoon
by Rev. Charles W. Lane and left for New Orleans at four
o'clock same evening.

3 Wednesday. Been driving & trying horses yesterday & to-
day, wanting to buy one, but have not done so yet. I have
also been rebreaking my mare Kate to harness. She had for-
gotten all about it almost. This afternoon at 4 o'clock Sister
Kate, little Katie Taylor and Sister Sarah arrived here from
Athens. All looking pretty and well.

4 Weather warm again. Rode out to my Father's this morning
to see my Sisters & staid nearly all day. Our cook, Charity,
took sick this morning with breakfast half done & Sallie had
to finish it.

5 Warm, cloudy & some rain. Bob Hammond has just hauled
me five loads of wood. Paid G. W. Haas & Co. this morning
$50.00 on my bill with them.

6 Weather clear & pretty. No news.

7 Sunday. Went to the Presbyterian Church.

8 Father went to Savannah this afternoon to attend the United
States Circuit Court. I bought another mare this evening
from a horse drover named Thomas Jefferson of Kentucky.

9 It began to rain this morning & has rained nearly all day.
We burnt out all our chimneys.

10 Wednesday. Weather clear. Sisters Kate & Sallie have been
spending the day with us. I forgot to say that Sallie Wylly[62]
& her little niece Mattie [Wylly] arrived Monday night
(8th inst.).

11 Weather clear. My Father left this afternoon to attend a
Bankrupt Court in Macon.

12 Sallie Wylly and her niece moved to our house this afternoon. My Father returned home to-night. I tried my new
mare this afternoon.

13 Rain again this morning. On the 11th inst. George Hollins-
head killed a negro. My Sister, Mrs. Mary Cobb,[63] arrived
this afternoon with her two fine boys, William McKinley
Cobb and Thomas R. R. Cobb. They came from Athens and
are at present stopping at my Father's.

62. Sarah Leake Wylly (1844–1920), a first cousin of Sallie McKinley.
63. Mary McKinley (1844–1927), full sister of McKinley.

14 Sunday. Weather cloudy and cold. Attended the Presbyterian Church.

15 Sallie Wylly left for Savannah this afternoon. The cars going towards Macon to-day were crowded & jammed with people going to the State fair which opens to-morrow at Macon. In the crowd I met Uncle David C. Barrow, his daughters Clara & Ella & his son Ben. Tom Spalding arrived to-night from Sapelo Island.

16 My boy George quit me this morning. He was taken sick on Saturday & took offense at my hiring a man while he was sick. Sister Sallie left for Macon this afternoon. Tom Spalding also. The cars crowded.

17 Wednesday. Cars going toward Macon still packed with people. Yesterday was warm & cloudy & last night we had a severe storm, from South West, which raged nearly all night. To-day clears off cold. I hired Pompey, one of our former slaves, this morning, by the month at seven dollars a month.

18 A Thanksgiving day appointed by Grant & Bullock.[64] Most of the stores in Milledgeville are closed, to allow their clerks and owners to attend the Fair now going on in Macon.

19 My brother Willie & I went over to Macon this morning to see the Fair. It rained most of the day & I was in most of it. I saw some magnificent riding at the tournament—also saw a great many articles & stock on exhibition. Met my Sisters, cousins, Miss Mary Hamilton of Athens, Tom Spalding, and a great many other friends & acquaintances—got back home to-night at twelve o'clock, wet, tired, sick & sleepy. I lost Willie in the crowd which was estimated to consist of about thirty-five thousand persons. To-day is the third anniversary of my wedding.

20 Willie got home from Macon all safe this morning. I lost him yesterday. Have been busy to-day selling Bankrupt property. I sold Tom Bagley's land (158½ acres) for $883.92 to E. Waitzfelder & Co. of New York. I have been sick all day,

64. President Ulysses S. Grant and Georgia governor Rufus Bullock, proclaimers of Thanksgiving Day. The holiday was first proclaimed by Abraham Lincoln in 1863 and subsequently each year by presidents and governors until the 1930s when legislated as a national holiday.

caused by yesterday's exposure. My mare Kate was taken with a severe attack of distemper on the 18th inst.

21 Sunday. There being no service at the Episcopal Church to-day, although it was the regular day, I attended the Presbyterian Church. Very cold.

22 Cold & clear. To-night is the fourth anniversary of the night on which I addressed my wife. Dr. Kenan & family & Mrs. M. J. Kenan dined with us to-day.

23 Uncle David & Ben Barrow called on us to-day. They are on their way to Athens from Macon & got left by the cars this morning. Raining heavily since twelve o'clock.

24 Wednesday. Owing to an accident on the Macon & Augusta R. Rd. yesterday, there was no train eastward this morn-ing, so that Uncle David & Ben were detained another day. Sallie & I dined at my Father's, where besides my relatives, I met Major & Mrs. Lamar Cobb and Genl. Wm. M. Browne, a cousin of the Marquis of Sligo in En-gland. This evening I went to Templeton's Operetta now performing here.

25 Ben Barrow staid with me last night. He and Uncle David got off this morning. This evening Sallie & I went to the Operetta, where we met cousins Clara & Nellie Barrow[65] & Miss Mary Ann Cobb,[66] all of whom last night arrived & are staying at my Father's.

26 I attended the Operetta again to-night. There was not a white woman there during the performance. One of my mares & colt still very sick with distemper.

27 Sallie & I have been spending the day out at my Father's. I do not go to the Operetta to-night, but furnished my servant Pompey with a half dollar to go.

28 Sunday. Attended Baptist Church, sermon by Col. Butler of Madison. To-day two years ago our first & only child was born & died.[67]

65. Clara and Nellie (Ella) Barrow. McKinley's first cousins.

66. Mary Ann Lamar Cobb, daughter of General Howell Cobb.

67. Archibald and Sallie had one son, William, who was born and died on November 28, 1867. The only references to this child are in the *Journal* and the McKinley family Bible. The child was buried between the Ridge and Darien, most likely in the Spalding family cemetery at Ashintilly. See *Journal*, May 31, 1870.

29 Tom Spalding and my brother Andrews left to-day for Sapelo Island. Weather unusually warm. Mrs. Spalding has been to Mrs. DuBignon's,[68] returned yesterday. I have been driving my new mare Fannie & am very much pleased with her. We change the colt's name from Fannie to Sallie.

30 This is my Father's sixtieth birth-day & thank God he is well enough to enjoy it, with all but one of his children around him. To-day is also the fifth anniversary of the bloody battle of Franklin in Tennessee, which I missed by being detached to guard a salt mine. My Father & Miss Mary Ann Cobb left for Macon this afternoon.

DECEMBER

1 Cousins Clara & Ella Barrow left for home (Athens) this morning. I have rented my house to-day to Samuel Whitaker for $250 per annum. Sister Mary Cobb & her children, Willie & Tom are with us now—also my Sister Sarah.

2 Thursday. My Father returned from Macon to-night.

3 Weather cold & raw. Mother returned from Atlanta this afternoon. Bishop Beckwith of the Episcopal Church preaches in Milledgeville this evening. Sister Kate has been spending the day with us.

4 A municipal election in Milledgeville to-day—at this writing (8 o'cl. P.M.) result not known. Sister Kate again spent the day with us.

5 Sunday. Raining all morning. Service at the Episcopal Church by Rev. Mr. Leacock.

6 Clear, cold weather. Boxed & shipped my piano to-day, [to] Darien. A collision between white and black people very imminent, growing out of a personal difficulty between a white & a black man. My Father went to Eatonton to-night.

7 Shipped to Darien to-day 1 sideboard, 1 secretary, 1 box marble & 2 whatnots. McCombs old hotel was fired last night by an incendiary, but was discovered in time to extin-

68. Anna V. Grantland Dubignon. Her husband, Charles, was a grandson of Poulain Dubignon, one of the French who purchased Sapelo Island in 1789.

guish the fire before it injured anything. Very bad feeling prevails between whites & blacks, and we are expecting every night for the town to be fired by the negroes. My brother-in-law Capt. Howell Cobb[69] arrived last night from Macon and is staying with us.

8 Wednesday. Shipped to Darien to-day 2 mahogony chairs, 2 sofas, 1 centre table, 1 bedstead, 1 bureau, 1 washstand, 1 towel stand, 1 table. Father returned from Eatonton yesterday. Bad feeling still prevails between whites & negroes, but as yet no violence.

9 Better feeling to-day between whites & negroes & danger considered to be over. Still shipping furniture to Darien. Howell Cobb & sister Mary left us this afternoon—the former for Americus—the latter for Father's.

10 Very busy shipping furniture.

11 Finished shipping furniture to Darien. Sent my horses to my Father's & moved out ourselves. Sold the furniture that I did not care to ship.

12 Sunday. A day of rest. Did not go to Church. Howell Cobb returned last night.

13 Sallie & I went to town to pick up the few things left about the house. Sam Whitaker commenced moving into my house to-day. Sent my cow & calf to Father's. Mrs. Spalding is staying for the present at Mrs. Mike Kenan's. Charity, our former cook, is taking care of my house until Whitaker finishes moving in. I paid her ten dollars to-day.

14 Finished moving out of my house in Milledgeville to-day, and Mr. Whitaker took possession. Brought my two bull dogs out to my Father's.

15 Wednesday. Bourke Spalding arrived in Milledgeville, from Sapelo, last night. Tom F. Newell marries Miss Colquitt of Baker County to-night. Raining this morning—clear this evening. Sam Whitaker paid me to-day $56.75 for furniture &c. bought. I paid Bischof's bill ($35) this evening.

16 Father paid me $250 this morning on his debt to me. I paid L. W. Hunt & Co.'s bill ($27.45), J. M. Clark's ($36.53) &

---

69. Howell Cobb (1842–1909), son of General Howell Cobb, and an Athens attorney. Later a judge and a professor of law at the University of Georgia. He is on his way to his brother's, John A. Cobb, in Americus, Ga.

also Mrs. Spalding's at Clark's ($79.87), and $75.00 on my own bill at G. W. Haas & Co. Wrote to Bill Stetson to get a package of money out of the Savannah Express office & forward to Tom Spalding.

17 Paid Pompey seven dollars, wages for the past month. My sister Julia left for New York this afternoon. My Father accompanies her as far as Savannah.

18 It rained most of last night, followed in the latter part of the night by a terrific wind. To-day very cold with high wind.

19 Sunday. Drove my new mare Fannie to town this morning. Attended the Presbyterian Church.

20 It was so cold this morning that I preferred to walk in to town. Mrs. Spalding came out yesterday, to spend part of her time with us at Father's. Cotton selling in Milledgeville to-day at from 22½ to 22⅞ cents.

21 All excitement to-day, looking at John Robinson's Circus & Menagerie come into town. One of his best showmen is a Milledgeville boy named Jerome Tuttle. Altogether however it was rather a poor show. Cloudy and warm.

22 Wednesday. I was woke up about three o'clock this morning by loud thunder & found one of the hardest wind & rain storms going on out doors that I ever saw. It did no damage however out here, except to blow down some new fence just built. My Father returned from Savannah to-night. He met Uncle David Barrow at Gordon & brought him home with him.

23 Uncle David left this morning after sitting up till three o'clock last night. Bourke Spalding & Willie McKinley left Milledgeville for Darien, overland to-day at 1 o'clock. They travel in a one horse wagon & on a saddle horse—are well armed & take my two bull dogs & colt with them.

24 Weather hazy & cold. Bourke & Willie have a good day for travelling & ought to get in the vicinity of Dublin by night, with good luck. Walked to town & back to-day.

25 Christmas, & a dark rainy one at that—bad for travelling. Presents have been exchanged during the morning. I got an exquisite box of razor, brush, comb &c. presented by Mrs. Spalding.

26 Sunday. Raining nearly all day—too much to go to Church without danger of getting wet.

27 Some rain. Had an interview with A. H. Kenan[70] in reference to a claim of one Joseph against Mrs. Spalding.

28 Weather cleared up to-day. It is the first sun shine that
Bourke & Willie McK. have had since they left here. Town
crowded with negroes.

29 Wednesday. This morning while in Milledgeville I received
a telegram for Mrs. Spalding about her business in Savannah. As I had intended going to Savannah tomorrow anyway,
I will start one day sooner and see what I can do towards
collecting money for her in Savannah.

30 I left Milledgeville yesterday afternoon at four o'clock and
after a ride of nearly all night reached Savannah at five & a
half o'clock this morning. I have not succeeded in making
any definite arrangement for Mrs. Spalding's benefit & as
I have to go out to Darien tomorrow morning, I have telegraphed my Father to come down and finish what I have
begun. My sister, Mrs. Mary Cobb, is twenty-five years old
to-day.

31 The last day of the year. I left Savannah about nine o'clock
this morning on the Steamer *Lizzie Baker* for Darien, where
I arrived about five o'clock this afternoon. The boat was
crowded with Yankees travelling south for their health. I
was glad to see before I landed Bourke & Willie McK. drive
down to the wharf—they got through all safe, making the
trip from Milledgeville to Darien overland in exactly eight
days reaching here to-day at one o'clock. Dr. Holmes[71] &
family also moved from Milledgeville to Darien with me.

70. Augustus H. Kenan, brother of Michael J. Kenan. State legislator and
delegate to Secession Convention of 1861, where he voted no.

71. Dr. James Holmes (1804–83), physician of Darien and Milledgeville.
Author of "Dr. Bullie's" Notes in the *Darien Timber Gazette*. See *"Dr.
Bullie's" Notes*, ed. Delma E. Presley, (Atlanta: Cherokee Publishing
Co., 1976).

1870

JANUARY

1 The first day of the year. I rode out to the Ridge last night in my own wagon & slept in *our* own house. I met Tom & Bourke Spalding here—also my brother William McKinley. Paid this afternoon over $128 freight on my furniture. Hired a negro named Tom Bell, at the rate of $15 a month, to take care of my property on the Ridge until I move my family down.

2 Sunday. We all rested to-day. Nothing transpired.

3 Bought 250 lbs. fodder to-day for my horses during my absence. Tom, Bourke & myself bought a skiff to-day from Carl Epping for $100 payable in thirty days. It was formerly called the *May*, but by common consent we christened her the *Sallie*. We left Darien at 4 o'clock P.M., I to take Steamer at Doboy for Savannah, the others for Sapelo, but after getting to Doboy I concluded to go on with them to Sapelo, where we arrived about 9 o'clock, & where I met my brother Andrews & Charlie Bass.

4 All the boys have gone deer hunting, leaving me alone to keep house. Very cold. I forgot to record that it snowed in Darien yesterday—the first time in many years.

5 Wednesday. The boys killed no deer yesterday, and some of them have gone out to-day again, to try their luck— but with no better success. Tom, Andrews McK. & myself spent the day at the barn, where I for the first time saw a McCarthy gin.[1]

---

1. A roller gin, as opposed to a saw gin, specifically designed for ginning long staple (sea island) cotton.

6   Bourke & Willie McK., in despair, quit driving for deer
    & this morning rode out jump hunting. Bourke killed one
    and Willie two & got well smeared[2] for killing his first deer.
    Afterward we all, except Tom, pull[ed] around in our new
    skiff, the *Sallie*, to the Lighthouse and beach, saw the pilots
    seining & got from them some very fine bass, so that our
    store room is now well supplied with venison and fish.

7   This afternoon Tom, Bourke, Charlie Bass, Willie & Arnie
    McK. & myself with two trunks started for Doboy, in the
    Sallie. The sound was as smooth as glass & we crossed it with
    three oars in 15 minutes. Waited at Doboy till 11 o'clock at
    night—then took steamer *Nick King* for Savannah.

8   Willie, Arnie & myself arrived in Savannah to-day at 12.20
    o'clock, after making an outside trip, which is unusual
    coming northward. We missed our train on the C. R. Road
    & found our Father had left Savannah just before we got
    there. We took the night train for Gordon.

9   Sunday. Arrived at Gordon about daybreak—left Arnie and
    the trunks there & Willie & myself walked to Milledgeville,
    where we arrived a little after 1 o'clock. Father returned
    from Savannah last night, where he had been to collect
    Mrs. Spalding's money from Capt. Gué.

10 Since I got to my Father's yesterday, I have been completely
    broken down by my walk from Gordon. I left on the cars at
    4 o'clock P.M. for Macon to attend Bankrupt Court tomorrow
    in case of Thomas S. Bagley. Arnie got home on the cars
    from Gordon to-night.

11 Reached Macon at 6.40 o'clock P.M. yesterday. Attended my
    Bankrupt Court, bought me a pair of boots & returned to
    my Father's to-night.

12 Wednesday. Quite a panic, I hear, was created in Milledge-
    ville yesterday—caused by Mrs. S[palding] paying up her
    accounts at the stores. While in Macon yesterday, I sub-
    scribed for one year to the semi weekly *Macon Telegraph*.

13 This is my sister Caroline's birth-day—or would be if she
    were living. She would be to-day thirty years old. I sub-
    scribed to-day for the *Milledgeville Federal Union*. Walked
    in to town this morning & rode out in the carriage.

2. The practice of smearing the deer's blood over the hunter on the
occasion of his first kill.

14 I have been busy most of the morning getting trunks ready to ship to Darien. Got them all off—to Central R. Rd., to go by the *Nick King.*

15 Willie McKinley left this morning for Athens, to enter the University High School at that place. Soon after he left the wind commenced to blow almost a gale from S. West & the rain to pour in torrents, but by three o'clock it stopped and Mrs. Spalding, Sallie & myself started for Savannah, on our way to Darien.

16 Sunday. We reached Savannah about 5½ o'clock this morning & drove to Mrs. McIntosh's (89 Jones Street). They were so crowded that I left Sallie there & I went to the Pulaski House. Sallie & I attended the Independent Presbyterian Church.

17 Spent most of the day buying stoves, groceries and crockery & everything for housekeeping.

18 Sallie & I left Savannah this morning at 10 o'cl., on the steamer *Nick King*, for Darien. The boat was crowded with Yankees, among them Mrs. Harriet Beecher Stowe with her husband & two daughters. All of them going to Florida to spend the winter. We arrived at Darien about 7 o'clock P.M. & drove to our new home on the Ridge.

19 Wednesday. Have spent the day getting things to rights & making ourselves as comfortable as possible. Owing to sickness Mrs. Spalding staid in Savannah.

20 We are getting fixed somewhat comfortably in our new home. We have not seen the sun since our arrival. I forgot to say that I paid Tom yesterday my third of our skiff.

21 Rode into Darien to receive some freight shipped from Savannah on the steamer *Water Lily*, but had to wait nearly an hour for its arrival. She left Savannah yesterday morning at 8 o'cl. & arrived here to-day at 1 o'clock P.M.

22 Tom & Bourke Spalding left for Savannah last night on the *Nick King.* Willie Wylly drove out from Darien & paid us a visit yesterday. He is living at present on Cambers Island, up the Altamaha. I have been suffering the most intense pain all day, caused by neuralgia.

23 Sunday. I have been in bed nearly all day, being very sick from yesterday's sickness & medicine.

24 I have been feeling sick all day & have done little or nothing.
25 Mrs. Spalding & Mr. Allen Bass arrived last night at twelve o'clock, from Savannah. Mr. Richard A. Bird, the former Judge of the Court of Ordinary of this County died to-day.
26 Wednesday. After a very hard rain on Monday night, the weather has cleared up & is now beautiful.
27 Tom & Bourke arrived from Savannah this afternoon, bringing with them four good mares. They rode through on horseback.
28 Bourke, Charlie & Mr. Bass went down to Sapelo this morning. Tom & I drove one of his new mares into town to-day— she balked badly.
29 The party which went to Sapelo, returned this morning. They got caught in a fog & laid in Doboy Sound nearly all night. Col. [Charles] Spalding came last night & left this morning. Went in last night expecting to meet my Father, but he did not come.
30 Sunday. Had visits from Sallie[3], Campbell, Willie & Hammie[4] Wylly. The two latter & Tom left this afternoon, Willie & Tom for Cambers Island.
31 Mr. Bass left for Savannah this evening. Sallie & Campbell left for home the same time.

FEBRUARY

1 Rode into Darien to-day. No news.
2 Wednesday. Nothing of interest transpiring.
3 Bourke & myself, with two negro boat hands carried our boat, the *Sallie*, from the Ridge to Darien. Bourke & Charlie Bass went up to Cambers Island. I came back to the Ridge.
4 We carried all our horses, but one, into Darien this morning & put them aboard a flat, preparatory to taking them to

3. Sarah Leake Wylly.
4. Hamilton Couper Wylly (1850–84), a first cousin of Sallie McKinley. Referred to variously in the journal (edited to Hammie).

Sapelo, but after we had loaded the flat the weather got so rough that we had to unload & postpone the trip. We paid Epping for our boat to-day.

5 Weather very cold & cloudy and everybody trying to keep warm. I have been a little sick to-day.

6 Sunday. Attended Episcopal Church. Services by Rev. Mr. Clute, in the old Trezevant dwelling.

7 Still waiting on the weather to moderate, so as to get our horses to Sapelo.

8 Very cold & windy. Mr. Allen Bass returned from Savannah to-night.

9 Wednesday. We have at last got our flat loaded & off for Sapelo. On reaching Doboy we ventured to cross the sound at 10 o'cl. at night, although it was flood tide, but owing to a N.W. wind which sprung up while we were in the sound, we landed fully two miles below the mouth of our creek,[5] & had a very hard & tedious time beating up to it against the wind.

10 Ebb tide met us about three o'cl. last night, just below Little Sapelo & we had to wait there until 9 o'clock this morning for the flood. We then cut loose & beat up the river against the wind, arriving here (Kenan's place)[6] about three o'clock this afternoon, after a most exhausting trip the whole way.

11 I went out this morning with Tom & Bourke deer (jump) hunting. Tom killed one. Mr. Campbell Wylly left here this morning.

12 Tom started with the flat to Darien last night, but on account of rough weather he had to leave it at Little Sapelo & return, himself, here. He left in the small boat this morning for the Ridge. Bourke killed a fine buck this morning.

13 Sunday. Bourke & I rode out to the beach this morning & from thence to the South End.

14 I have spent most of the morning at the barn. Tom returned this afternoon bringing letters & papers. I hear that the steamer *Two Boys* drifted out of Sapelo Sound a few nights

5. Refers to the mouth of Little Sapelo River, also known as the Duplin River.

6. The Sapelo property of Mrs. M. J. Kenan, also known as Duplin. See Map.

ago, in a high wind, and capsized outside. All the passengers not heard from.[7]

15 Rain, rain—nothing else doing. Little Lizzie Cobb, youngest child of the late Genl. Howell Cobb, died in Athens on the 3d inst.

16 Wednesday. We all went deer hunting to-day. The party killed three small ones. I got two shots at a long distance, but killed nothing.

17 Tom, Bourke & I went dove hunting. We killed eighteen doves, nine partridges[8] & two rabbits. Wind N.E. with a little rain.

18 This morning Bourke & I started at 5.20 o'clock for the Ridge & reached there at 9 o'clock. It rained nearly all the way from Kenan's place to the Sound.

19 Very cold with high wind from West.

20 Sunday. Went to Church, and for the first time kept up with the service through the Prayer book.

21 Took boat at 3 o'clock this afternoon & reached Sapelo a little after 5 o'clock. Had a remarkably pleasant & smooth trip, crossing the Sound in ten minutes. Sallie came down with me. Very cold.

22 Weather continues very cold. Tom is to-day finishing the ginning of last years cotton crop.

23 Wednesday. On waking this morning I was very much surprised to find it raining. Rained nearly all day.

24 This morning, the weather having cleared up, we took Sallie in a two-horse wagon to the barn, and she & I walked around & looked at our new place while Tom paid off his hands.

25 We all, Mr. Bass excepted, left Sapelo at 9.40 o'clock this morning for the Ridge, which we reached a little before two o'clock.

7. This steamboat bound from Darien to Savannah had a boiler explosion in Sapelo Sound on February 8, 1870. A gale blowing, her anchor line parted and she was swept out to sea. Eight of the crew swam ashore but the captain, eleven of the crew, and three passengers were never found.

8. The Bob White Quail. From the *Journal* it seems that these birds were common on Sapelo when the island was farmed. Today they are almost nonexistent on the island.

26 Weather delightful—the first Spring day of the season. The Catholics have been holding a fair most of the week, in Darien, to raise money to build a Church.

27 Sunday. Went to Church, but the house being rather too small for the congregation, I came back home. Left for Sapelo at 11 o'clock to-night.

28 Arrived at Sapelo at 2 o'clock this morning. After breakfast, rode down to the plantation. Sick to-day.

MARCH

1 Left Sapelo this morning at 5 o'clock for the Ridge, to meet sister Kate & Nellie Barrow on to-night's steamer, but they did not come.

2 Wednesday. Left the Ridge this afternoon for Sapelo— taking Sallie with me. Doboy Sound pretty rough, but crossed safely.

3 Been deer hunting most all day—got a shot at only one deer & missed him. Bourke killed a large buck.

4 Left Sapelo this morning about 5 o'clock for the Ridge, to meet sister Kate & Nellie, but again they did not come. Sallie returned with me—also a young Mr. Ravenel, who went down with us last Sunday night.

5 I have been a little sick for a day or two past. A friend of Mr. Bass, a Yankee named Gregory, arrived to-day. [*Marginal note:* Mrs. Hazard began to cook.]

6 Sunday. Weather very warm. Campbell & Sallie Wylly and their cousin, Miss Rebecca Couper, took dinner with us to-day. The latter lady is very pretty. Tom brought up a flat of Mr. Nightingale's last night, from Sapelo—the same which carried our horses down, a month ago.

7 Weather exceedingly warm for this season. Raining nearly all day—part of the time very hard. We had to-day the first thunderstorm of the season.

8 Sister Kate, Nellie Barrow and little Katie Taylor & nurse arrived to-night about 8 o'clock on the *Nick King*. Tom and I met them in Darien.

9 Wednesday. Weather fine & dry. We have been amusing
   our visitors by taking them down on the plank walk. Bourke
   & Charlie returned from Sapelo this evening.
10 Weather dry. We took Katie and Nellie in our boat to Herd's
   Island on a pleasure trip.
11 Our visitor, Mr. Gregory, came up to-day from Sapelo
   and left to-night on the *Nick King*. We did not see him.
   Mr. Campbell Wylly, Sallie & Willie Wylly and John Nightingale called to-day. The two first spend the night with us.
   Commenced raining after dark.
12 Raining nearly all day. Campbell & Sallie Wylly left for
   home this afternoon. A pretty severe wind & rain storm
   from S.W. at 8½ o'clock P.M.
13 Sunday. Did not go to Church to-day.
14 Hired a negro boy named David, about sixteen years old,
   this morning—am to pay him $5.00 per month.
15 Raining nearly all day—cleared off towards night and at
   mid-night a stiff, cold west wind sprang up. Mrs. Spalding,
   Lou & May Holmes[9] left for Sapelo to-night at 9½ o'clock.
16 Wednesday. Clear & cold. Rode into Darien this morning—
   then hauled a load of wood.
17 Mrs. Spalding, Sallie, Sister Kate, Nellie, little Katie
   & nurse, with Tom, Bourke, Charley & myself started
   for Sapelo at 11.15 o'clock to-night and arrived there at
   2 o'clock A.M.
18 We took the ladies out deer hunting to-day. Most of [them]
   went in the wagon. Tom killed one [deer].
19 The fifth anniversary of my last battle (Bentonsville N.C.,
   fought March 19th 1865). The party went to the South End
   & Sapelo light house to-day—some by wagon & some by
   boat. Campbell & Sallie Wylly arrived yesterday afternoon.
20 Sunday. The party spent most of the day on Sapelo Beach.
   The up-country members of the party delighted with
   the Beach.
21 Some of the ladies went sailing. Katie, Sallie and myself
   walked down to the plantation. The first crabs of the season
   to-day.

9. Mary Louise and May Kell Holmes, daughters of Dr. James Holmes.

22 Willie Wylly & Willie Nightingale arrived this evening from Cambers Island.

23 Wednesday. Went hunting—Willie Wylly and Bourke each killed a deer—Bourke's very large.

24 All the party started for Blackbeard Island this morning, but Blackbeard Creek was so rough that they had to return without crossing—carried our boat over there on a wagon.

25 Wind N.E.—rain nearly all day.

26 More rain, and our party of ladies compelled to keep within doors.

27 Sunday. Nothing transpiring.

28 Campbell & Sallie Wylly left for home this morning. Bourke & Charlie went to Darien for the mail & to give our servants on the Ridge something to eat.

29 The party, except Mrs. Spalding, Sallie & myself went to Blackbeard Beach. I have been confined to my bed most of the day with headache.

30 Wednesday. Raining most of the day—thunderclouds. Tom's cook, Rose Boson, quit him last night, and Sallie has done most of the cooking to-day.

31 Mrs. Spalding's birth day—forty seven years old. Clear weather—wind West. Corn is up, with two leaves.

APRIL

1 Left Sapelo this morning just before day, bringing Mrs. Spalding, Lou & May Holmes back to the Ridge. My mare Fannie being about to have a colt, I had to walk into Darien with the mail. Got back to Sapelo at 5 o'clock this afternoon. Sister Sarah's birth-day—23 years old.

2 The rest of our party left Sapelo this evening & reached the Ridge at 10½ o'clock to-night.

3 Attended the Episcopal Church this morning.

4 Monday. Beautiful weather.

5 Bourke has at last finished him a sail. He left the Ridge this afternoon at 2 o'clock, went to Sapelo & returned to-night at 10 o'clock.

6   Wednesday. Walked into Darien early this morning for
    the mail. My old army friend, William S. Stetson, arrived
    to-day, from Savannah. He will spend a few days with me.

7   Bourke, Charlie Bass, Stetson & myself went by boat from
    the Ridge to Cambers Island to organize a boat club, which
    we did, calling it the A-*lat*-a-ma-ha boat club. The follow-
    ing members organized—P. M. Nightingale, president—
    J. M. Couper, vice pres't.—A. C. Wylly, sec. & treas.—
    Robt. Couper, C. Bass, A. C. McKinley, J. K. Nightingale,
    W. Nightingale, T. Spalding, T. B. Spalding, W. S. Stetson,
    W. D. Waples, W. C. Wylly & H. C. Wylly—members.

8   Left for Milledgeville this evening at 6½ o'clock. Stetson
    left shortly after for Florida. Willie Wylly came as far as
    Savannah with me.

9   Reached Savannah at 4 o'clock this morning, took the car on
    the Central Rail Road at 8 o'clock A.M. & reached Milledge-
    ville at 9½ o'cl. P.M. Raining some to-day.

10 Sunday. Attended Presbyterian Church in Milledgeville.
    Rev. C. W. Lane preached. Church crowded.

11 Rode into Milledgeville with Father. Old friends seem glad
    to see me.

12 My Father left for Savannah this afternoon, to attend U.S.
    Circuit Court. I started to Macon, but turned back at
    the depot.

13 Wednesday. Rode into town—nothing occurring.

14 Miss Smith, a friend of Mother's, has been spending the day
    with us to-day.

15 Attended the funeral of Mrs. Wm. H. Scott at the Episco-
    pal Church this morning. She died, I think, in Marietta &
    was brought here for interment. Father returned to-night
    unexpectedly from Savannah.

16 Weather fair & pleasant. The farmers in this section of the
    State are all very busy planting cotton.

17 Sunday. Cousin Clara Barrow, Sister Sarah & I attended the
    Easter services at the Episcopal Church in Milledgeville—
    services by Rev. Mr. Philson. Weather windy & very cold.
    During the afternoon I received news of the very sudden
    death of my former faithful slave, SCOTT. He died about one

o'clock to-day apparently in perfect health. After eating very largely during the morning, he smoked his pipe & laid down on his bed to take a nap—in a few minutes he had a spasm & died in a few minutes more, without speaking. Poor fellow, he was one of the few negroes who was a friend of the whites. He followed me into the army, as a camp servant, in October 1861 & remained with me, true as steel, until May 1865, or the end of the War. He followed me through "Bragg's Kentucky Campaign" in 1862, was with me at the battle of Baker's Creek (Champion Hill), the siege & surrender of Vicksburg—crying when he heard it reported that I had been killed at the above named battle, but finding that I was only wounded he nursed me with the greatest care & tenderness until I recovered. When Vicksburg fell he followed me in spite of Yankee threats & promises of freedom & good situations, back into the Confederate lines, remaining with me through the Georgia campaign of 1864, and through Genl. Hood's advance on & disastrous retreat from Nashville in the same year. And lastly through the North Carolina campaign of 1865—being true and faithful to me and the Cause I fought for, until the day of his death. He was about forty-five years old when he died, and was an old family servant, his father (Peter) having been a slave of my Mother's father. I am proud to record the fact that he was liked & befriended by all his *true Southern* white acquaintances, and his death lamented by all of them. After the war, in consideration of his good conduct and attachment to me, my Father gave him a house & twenty acres of land for his (Scott's) life, and he was cultivating the land industriously.

18 My Father & I left Milledgeville this afternoon for Savannah—he to attend U.S. Circuit Court, & I on my way to Darien. Thermometer stood at 40° this morning, but owing to clouds & wind during the night, there was very little frost.

19 Arrived at Savannah about 6 o'clock this morning & left at 10 A.M. on the steamer *Nick King*, arriving at the Ridge about 9 P.M. I brought Mrs. Spalding a little negro servant girl named Eliza.

20 Mrs. Spalding, Sister Kate & little Kate left for Savannah
on the 11th inst. Mrs. S. to attend Jimmie McIntosh's wedding on the 13th. Nellie Barrow & Tom Spalding left for
Milledgeville on the 18th inst. Bourke's mare, Susie, gave
birth on the 7th inst. to a mule colt. Bourke & Charlie sailed
to Sapelo this afternoon.

21 Thursday. Bourke & Charlie returned to-night, [Bourke]
having killed two deer. Campbell Wylly is here.

22 Mrs. Spalding returned from Savannah this evening.

23 Bourke started for Brunswick this morning.

24 Sunday. Attended Church twice to-day—Rev. Mr. Clute
officiating. Rather warm, thermometer showing 91°, but
owing to pleasant sea breeze, the heat was not oppressive.

25 Thermometer 90°, with land breeze. All the family who are
at home, except myself, are spending the evening at Col.
Barclay's.

26 A cold N.E. wind blowing, bringing with [it] clouds &
making very unpleasant day of it. Bourke returned from
Brunswick this evening.

27 Wednesday. My bay mare, Fannie, gave birth to a very fine
mare mule colt before day this morning.

28 Bourke, Charlie & myself left this afternoon, between 1 & 2
o'clock for Sapelo. We sailed most of the way. After waiting
for the Sound to become calmer, we crossed just before dark
& found it rather rough.

29 Went fishing & caught five fish & several crabs—the others
caught more.

30 Went hunting & did not see a deer nor get a mouthfull to
eat until nearly dark. Rain this morning.

MAY

1 Sunday. Took a walk from the Kenan house to my place and
Tom's, to look at our garden & the crop. Cotton and corn
are up, with a very fair stand.

2 Went hunting this morning, on foot, and killed my first deer
at the Patch of Pines at Belle drive—a medium sized buck.

Bourke bloodied me. Returned to Ridge this evening. Sound very rough.

3 Rest day with me. I neglected to state that Tom was elected a vestryman of this Episcopal Church on the 30th ult.

4 Wednesday. Our White cook, Mrs. Hazard, & her daughter quit us last night in high dudgeon, the secret of which was that they didn't have enough to keep them from idleness & so got to stealing the food sent to be cooked.

5 We walked into Darien this morning & then went to Cambers island to attend a meeting of our boat club. Seven new members joined the club, viz.—Miss Fannie Butler,[10] Mr. Thos. Forman, R. L. Morris, B. Troup, R. Troup, W. R. Gignilliat & H. Bryan. During the day there was a race between Miss Butler's skiff the *Miss Fannie* with two pairs of sculls & Mr. J. M. Couper's canoe the *Lela* with one pair of sculls–the latter coming out ahead & winning a basket of champaign on the race. Got a new cook named Rose—not much of a one.

6 A Norwegian bark, loaded with R.R. iron for Brunswick went aground on the South breaker at Doboy inlet on the 3rd inst. Will be a total wreck I hear. I neglected to state that on the 7th of last month William Nightingale gave me a puppy, aged then about one month. He is a cross of a "Dandy Dinmont" (see Guy Manering)[11] father upon a Skye terrier mother—both parents imported dogs. I call my puppy "Pat Cleburne," after my old general.

7 Big trouble in Darien over the Office of Inspector General of Timber. Chas. H. Hopkins, a noted radical, some days ago got Col. Barclay, the incumbent, displaced & got the office himself—to-day I hear the tables have been turned on Hopkins & Barclay is back in his office. Bourke, Charlie & Jas. Dunwoody went to Sapelo to-day. Rain yesterday & a little this morning.

10. Frances Kemble Butler (1838–1910), daughter of Pierce (Mease) and Frances Anne Kemble Butler. She later married the Rev. James Wentworth Leigh in 1871 and was the author of *Ten Years on A Georgian Plantation* (1883).

11. Dandie Dinmont was a character in *Guy Mannering* (1815), a novel by Sir Walter Scott.

8 Sunday. Attended Episcopal Church. Raised my boy David's wages to-day from five to six dollars.
9 Weather a little cool. I am having a very dull time staying on the Ridge with the women folks.
10 It is eight years to-day since I helped to organize our company for the Confederate Army (before that time I had served six months in the State troops raised by Gov. J. E. Brown).[12] Our new cook, Rose, left us this morning, and another one named Ella set in this evening. The boys returned from the Island to-day. They killed one deer, but wounded several.
11 Wednesday. Mrs. Aiken[13] gave birth to a daughter last night. She names [her] Varina for Mrs. Jas. E. Holmes.[14]
12 Mrs. Spalding, Sallie & Bourke were all taken suddenly ill last night with something resembling Cholera Morbus. Still very sick, all of them.
13 The sick are better to-day. I drove my mare Fannie nearly as far as Darien to-day—the first time since she had her colt—leaving the colt at home. Tom Spalding returned from Milledgeville this afternoon.
14 Tom, Bourke & myself went alligator hunting this morning. I killed one & Tom two—the last mentioned two we could not get, as they sunk in deep water.
15 Sunday. Heard a very intolerant sermon by Mr. Clute, the Episcopal Minister here, on confirmation.
16 This is the seventh anniversary of my first battle, Baker's Creek, near Vicksburg, Mississippi, where I was wounded in the shoulder. Our boat club met in Darien to-day & after receiving two new members, T. & G. Gignilliat, we adjourned to Mr. Morris' place, Ceylon, where we had a good dinner & plenty of champagne.
17 The hottest day so far—thermometer 94° in the shade.
18 Wednesday. We left the Ridge this morning at 2½ o'clock for Sapelo. The cotton crop on the Island is suffering for rain. Corn knee to waist high and looking very fine.

12. Joseph Emerson Brown, governor of Georgia for four terms, 1857 to 1865.

13. Mrs. Isaac M. Aiken, of Herd's Island.

14. Varina Bryan Holmes (1839–69), first wife of James E. Holmes (son of Dr. Holmes).

19 Spent most of the time in the cotton field with Tom and Mr. Bass.

20 Left Sapelo at 5.45 this morning for the Ridge. Very warm.

21 Warm and very dry.

22 Sunday. Warm and dry.

23 Still dry. Sallie & I drove our mare Fannie into Darien to-day and staid there a few hours.

24 I drove into Darien this afternoon to meet Uncle David Barrow, who came on the Steamer *Nick King* about 8 o'clock this evening.

25 Uncle David, Bourke, Charlie and myself came down to Sapelo this morning, sailing all the way from the head of Long Reach.

26 Thursday. Uncle David, Mr. Bass, Tom & myself rode all over the Island to-day showing it to the former—trying to make the former buy a portion of the Island. In all we must have ridden nearly thirty-five miles.

27 My twenty-eighth birth-day. Bourke & Charlie returned from the Ridge this morning, whither they went yesterday. Uncle David left this morning at 10 o'clock—going to Darien & on to Brunswick, Decatur &c.

28 We all went down to the plantation, where we intend building, & tried our hand sawing tabby. We sawed twenty blocks & blistered our hands. Tom & I started at 11½ o'clock tonight for the Ridge.

29 Sunday. Sallie & Hamilton Wylly took dinner with us.

30 Tom & I rode into Darien. Notified the Ordinary's clerk to make F. L. Gué, administrator of estate of R. Spalding, deceased,[15] make an annual return. I forgot to mention that one of Tom's mares gave birth on the 16th inst. to a male horse colt.

31 Sallie & I rode down to the cemetery where our baby is buried, this afternoon. Bourke & Charlie came up from the Island.

---

15. Randolph Spalding (1822–62), Sallie McKinley's father. A colonel in the Confederate army, he died of fever in Savannah while on duty.

JUNE

1   Wednesday. Birth-day letters from Milledgeville received.

2   Bourke, Charlie & myself came down to the Island this morning—sailed all the way. I took a lesson at sailing. This afternoon we all went hunting & Tom killed one deer.

3   We have moved down to-day from the Kenan House to a small two room house near Tom's barn. So far it is much pleasanter.

4   Tom, Bourke, Charlie, Mr. Bass & myself commenced enclosing about five acres of one of the savannahs on the Island to-day, for a pasture. I see by the paper that Col. *Augustus H. Kenan*, of Milledgeville, died last Thursday, of dysentery.

5   Sunday. Little Katie Taylor's sixth birth-day.

6   Still at work on our pasture. A little rain fell to-day.

7   Still working on our pasture. I found squares on the cotton yesterday. Corn is tasseling.

8   Wednesday. I came up to the Ridge this morning with two boat hands. We have taken our boat, the *Sallie*, out of the water on the 6th to paint her. Rode into Darien this afternoon.

9   Been answering letters this morning. A little rain on the Ridge. Mrs. Spalding taken sick. More rain. Started for the Island at 6½ o'cl. Brisk breeze blowing when I reached the Sound. Waited on it about an hour & then crossed— pretty rough.

10   Commenced painting our boat green yesterday. Finished our pasture this afternoon.

11   Repairing and painting our boat still.

12   Sunday. Walked out to the beach this morning, all of us, & on our way back got caught by a rain. Rain the balance of the day, with high wind from S.E. to-day and yesterday.

13   Sister Kate's thirty-third birth day. Cloudy & cool. Rain, with heavy thunder & lightning.

14   Giving the finishing touches to our boat. Rain, with heavy thunder & lightning.

15   Wednesday. Rain, with heavy thunder & lightning.

16 We launched our boat to-day. She looks very pretty. At 4 o'clock we started for the Ridge & arrived all safely. Rain, rain, rain.

17 My horse being sick, Tom & I walked to Darien to get some lumber—also went to Herds Island. Tom hears to-day of his cotton crop of last year being damaged—a swindle no doubt. More rain.

18 Walked into Darien with Tom, where we made arrangements with H. Huntington to get our lumber on 60 days' time. More rain.

19 Sunday. Sallie & I attended the Presbyterian Church, services by Mr. Quarterman. Heavy rains. My mare Fannie has been sick to-night. Hired a negro boy named Charles last night, for $5 per month.

20 Heavy rains. Tom left for Charleston this evening, to look after his cotton.

21 More rain. Hired a house maid named Bellah to-day for $4 per month. Jno. Frazer, a Scotch boy aged 17 & in Tom's employ, shot a negro man to-day on Sapelo, with 12 buckshot; he is not dead yet. Bourke & Charlie left for the Island. Negroes excited.

22 Wednesday. Jno. Frazer was arrested last night & taken to jail in Darien. No rain to-day.

23 Dry weather at last. Bourke & I went to Mayhall Mill to-day to get lumber to build with—sailed most of the way.

24 Our new maid Bellah left us this morning. Mrs. Charles Wylly & little daughter, Mattie, arrived this afternoon, from Savannah.

25 Dry & pretty weather.

26 Sunday. Wm. & Campbell Wylly & John McQueen McIntosh dined with us to-day. Bourke, Charlie & myself came down to Sapelo to-night.

27 Went fishing in Little Sapelo river[16]—caught a mess.

28 Had two hands sawing tabby this morning, sawed sixty-eight blocks, 2 ft. × 15 in. × 9 inches. Tom Spalding returned from Charleston yesterday. Bourke & Charlie left for the Ridge. Stopped sawing tabby as one of my two men quit.

16. Also known as the Duplin River; see Map.

Killed an alligator about seven feet long in the creek just in front of our door.

29 Wednesday. Can get no hands to saw tabby.

30 All the boys have gone to Altamha, on the Altamaha, to attend a meeting of our boat club.

JULY

1 Friday. We (Mr. Bass & myself) eat our first watermelon, from the patch of the former, to-day.

2 The boys returned to the Island this afternoon, bringing with them three pairs of new sculls.

3 Sunday. Charlie & I started for the Ridge this morning at 3 o'cl. Attended Presbyterian Church.

4 Sallie & myself left the Ridge at daylight—got to Sapelo for breakfast. Tom & Bourke went to Mayhall Mill for lumber.

5 Sawing tabby nearly all day. The hands brought down 8 or 10 thousand feet of lumber this morning.

6 Wednesday. My Mother died this day twenty three years ago, aged 29 years, 10 months & 4 days. Tom & Bourke returned this morning. We moved up to the barn this afternoon.

7 Went fishing with Sallie. Rains all around us, but we get none.

8 Tom & Bourke left for the Ridge early this morning. Mr. Bass a little sick.

9 Tom & Charlie Bass came down from the Ridge this morning. Sister Caroline died to-day sixteen years ago. My mare, Fannie, again sick.

10 Sunday. Very dry—wind North East.

11 Tom, Charlie & Sallie left the Island for the Ridge this morning at 1 o'clock.

12 Weather very warm & dry. Schooner *Welcome Return*, Capt. Crane, arrived about five o'cl. this afternoon, bringing for us 10 bbls. lime, 2000 brick, nails, groceries &c.

13 Wednesday. Weather intensely hot—a good heavy rain about two o'clock.

14 Sallie, Bourke & Charlie arrived about three o'clock this after noon. Very good rain.

15 The Steamer *O. F. Potter* arrived this morning at 5½ o'cl., with Tom on board. She landed at the lower hammock on our creek & brought my wagons, mare Fannie & colt, shingles, furniture &c. &c. Bourke, Charlie & myself went on the *Potter* on her return as far as Pumpkin Hammock, towing our boat behind. We went to the Ridge.

16 After suffering from a very severe sick head-ache all yesterday afternoon & evening, I, with the others, left the Ridge about 12 o'clock last night, bringing with us Mrs. Spalding & May Holmes. Arrived at Sapelo just after daybreak. All living in Tom's barn.

17 Sunday. Sallie & I drove down to the South End this morning, with our mare, Fannie, & spring wagon.

18 Piling our lumber & levelling our house inside. Palouie [?] (man in charge of her) has just brought my Morgan colt, "Little Sallie," (that was foaled Aug. 4th 1869) to the door fully harnessed.

19 Dry & hot. Work on house progressing slowly.

20 Bourke, Charlie, myself & my servant Charles caught seventy two fish this morning.

21 Thursday. Anniversary of 1st battle of Manassas. Charlie Bass' 17th birth-day. I am suffering very much from a swollen finger.

22 Six years since I was in a very severe battle near Atlanta, Ga. (see July 22d 1869). Steamer *Lizzie Baker* stopped running to Darien this afternoon. She stops now at Doboy & sends the mail to Darien by small boat.

23 Some insect stung me about a week ago on the middle finger (1st joint) of the left hand—since which time it has been steadily rising & inflaming.

24 Sunday. Sallie, Tom, May Holmes, Charlie & myself left for the Ridge to-night. My hand is getting so painful that I must see a doctor.

25 Although I have been under the influence of morphia all day, yet I have been suffering very much & have been delirious a little, from my hand.

26 This morning Dr. Holmes lanced my finger—making an incision about 1 inch long diagonally across the inside of my finger—cutting to the bone. The pain was the most intense I ever suffered in my life. The doctor thinks the swelling is caused by a spider bite. About 10 o'cl. at night we started for the Island—leaving May Holmes & bringing with us Miss Lou Holmes.

27 Wednesday. Still laid up with my hand.

28 The brick mason commenced his preparations to work on our house to-day. Bourke & Charlie left for Brunswick yesterday.

29 Dog days began last Tuesday. Warm & dry.

30 Dry & warm. Still disabled with my hand. Long letter from Father.

31 Sunday. Spent island Sunday, i.e. did nothing. Bourke & Charlie returned this morning.

AUGUST

1 Some prospect of rain. Light, slow rain from about 12½ o'cl. to about 3½ o'clock.

2 Still disabled with my hand. First open cotton (short staple) found last Saturday. Dry & warm.

3 Wednesday. Tom finished plowing. Rode out to Big Marsh to see Dixon cotton.

4 Kate's colt—little Sallie we call her—is one year old this evening. Very good shower with heavy thunder at 12 o'cl. We started a mullet & a shrimp net about a week ago.

5 Miss Lou Holmes, Bourke, Charlie & myself started for the Ridge at 7 o'cl. A.M. Dry.

6 We left the Ridge about 9 o'cl. A.M., leaving Miss Lou Holmes & bringing with us Lula Clute, the Episcopal Minister's daughter.

7 Sunday. Spent an Island Sunday—i.e. doing nothing.

8 Very warm. Cotton beginning to open a good deal.

9 Tom, Bourke & myself went deer hunting to-day but did not kill one. Some rain.

10 Wednesday. Work on our house progressing very slowly. Letters from Father & Sister Sarah. My room on the Ridge was struck by lightning about 11 o'cl. yesterday morning. I don't know yet what damage was done. Left Sapelo about midnight for the Ridge. Sallie, Tom, Charlie & myself.

11 Arrived at the Ridge a little after daylight. The lightning struck my room on the N.W. corner on the 9th inst. Part of it passed down a tree nearby. The other part tore off the weather boarding & ceiling on that corner—injured a writing desk, bored a hole through a sheet of zink, smashed a china foot tub & passed down a pillar to the ground.

12 Nothing of importance occurring.

13 Took boat at Darien & went to Butler's Island, on my way to Atlanta to attend an Agricultural convention. Went with John Nightingale to Carteret in Glynn County, where we staid all night.

14 Sunday. Drove into Brunswick & stopped at Mr. Nightingale's house. Attended the Episcopal Church, and in the afternoon Wm. Nightingale & I drove around Brunswick. It is a pretty town, but very much scattered through the woods.

15 Mr. Nightingale & myself took the cars on the Macon & Brunswick R. Rd. at 4.45 o'clock this morning. Arrived in Macon about 6.30 o'cl. this evening & left for Atlanta at 9 P.M.

16 Arrived at Atlanta about daylight this morning. Hotels too crowded to get in—so went to Judge Pope's. Attended Agricultural Convention at 10 o'cl. this A.M. Got a telegram asking me to represent (in connection with W. R. Gignilliat) McIntosh Co. in the Democratic Convention tomorrow.

17 Wednesday. Attended both conventions to-day. Have met Uncle David Barrow, Uncle Robinson [17] & Pope Barrow. [18] Staid at St. James Hotel to-night.

18 Found my brother William in Atlanta, with amaurosis of one eye. He is under medical treatment. Pope Barrow & myself

17. Francis James Robinson, McKinley's paternal uncle.

18. Pope Barrow, first cousin of McKinley. Barrow later became a U.S. senator and distinguished jurist.

left on the Ga. R. Rd. at 7 o'cl. A.M. I reached Milledgeville about 6 P.M.

19 Find my Father knocked up with a boil on his ankle. Beautiful crop at Walnut Level.

20 Rode into Milledgeville with Father and called on Mrs. Mike Kenan's family.

21 Sunday. Attended the Milledgeville Presbyterian Church, Rev. Chas. W. Lane, Pastor.

22 Have been suffering for two days past with severe cold & cough.

23 Baldwin County Superior Court met to-day. I called on Mrs. Spalding Kenan at her Mother-in-law's.

24 Wednesday. I left Milledgeville this afternoon at 4½ o'clock, for Savannah.

25 Arrived at Savannah this morning about day-light & stopped at the Screven House. Dined at Mrs. McIntosh's. Bought gun caps & dog collars.

26 Left Savannah at 9 o'clock this morning, on Steamer *Lizzie Baker*. Went outside & came in at Doboy bar at 2½ o'clock. Bourke & Charlie met me at Doboy Island with our boat. Got to Sapelo about 5 o'cl. Found all well.

27 Rode out to Big Marsh to see Tom's Dixon cotton—about 4 feet high & 40 to 70 bolls.

28 Sunday. Lula Clute left yesterday with Charlie, who returned to-day. Wind N.E. for 2 days.

29 The brick layer, who has been working on our house, has absented himself, so that no work on the house is going on to-day.

30 Tom & I left at 5.45 this A.M. for Darien to see a lawyer & get the former appointed Administrator on his father's estate—did not see a lawyer & had to write one.

31 Brick-layer resumed work this morning. Tom & I returned from Darien about daylight.

SEPTEMBER

1 Thursday. A sailboat belonging to a negro named Glascow (a former slave of Tom's) arrived here on a trading expedition yesterday, though it is against Tom's orders.

2 My Mother's birth-day. Work on house progressing slowly.
3 Tom, Bourke & I went deer hunting at the North end of the Island. I wounded one deer, which Bourke afterwards killed. Tom missed one. [*Marginal note:* Evened off with Bourke May 15, 1872.]
4 Sunday. Warm & dry. Nothing occurring.
5 Work on house getting on faster with two masons.
6 Sallie's twenty-sixth birth-day. Wind very strong from N.E., threatening a gale. A small rattle snake killed in front of our new house.
7 Wednesday. Very strong N.W. wind, with clouds. Commenced the first chimney to our new house.
8 Wind still N.E. & stronger, with occasional showers. Hard rain to-night—wind blowing almost a gale.
9 Rain nearly all morning—all work suspended.
10 Rain. No work doing. Wind N.E.
11 Sunday. Wind N.E. with rain. The negro preacher from Savannah preaches at Hanging Bull.
12 Wind N.E. & strong, increasing at night fall to a storm. Some work going on on the house. Heaviest rain tonight I ever heard fall.
13 Too wet to work much.
14 Wednesday. Bourke went to Darien to get iron for building chimneys. Cessation of rain.
15 Wind N.W. Weather clearing up and cool. Bourke returned this morning, having spent most of the night at Doboy. Tom sick with fever.
16 Tom's 23d birth-day. He is still sick & left for the Ridge today, accompanied by Sallie, Mrs. Spalding & all the rest but Mr. Bass & myself. Mrs. S. & Sallie have been on the Island since the 4th & 16th of July.
17 Raining again, with wind N.W., but changing. Our house has the rafters on, some boxing, all the chimneys started & one nearly finished. I neglected to state that we have a new steam boat touching at Darien & running to Savannah & Charleston. She made her first trip day before yesterday & is called the *Eliza Hancox*. Charlie returned from the Ridge this morning & he & I started for the Ridge this evening, reaching there about 9½ o'cl.

18 Sunday. Attended the Episcopal Church. Heard last night of the severe illness of my Father.

19 Bourke & I reached the Island about 9 o'cl. this morning. The negroes have been stealing our lumber. My wagon shaft broken this morning.

20 Being out of all meat to eat, Bourke & I took two negroes & went hunting. We hunted nearly all day without even jumping a deer.

21 Wednesday. Bourke & I went hunting again to-day & late in the afternoon Bourke killed a large buck near Chocolate. Weather stormy. Boat returned from Darien with corn, oats & meat.

22 Cloudy, with high N.W. wind. Wind went back N.E. & blew a gale to-night.

23 Wind still N.E. & very strong. Finished sheeting over house. The brick layer has not worked since the 16th inst.

24 All the negroes at work on our house have stopped work to go deer hunting.

25 Sunday. Bourke & I started for the Ridge about 1 o'cl. Brisk N.E. breeze & we sailed nearly all the way.

26 We did not go down to-day because Tom wanted to see about his taxes. Bourke returned from Cambers Island where he went yesterday, bringing 4 doz. rice birds.

27 Tom went to Darien & arranged his taxes. Wind N.E.

28 Wednesday. We intended going to Sapelo to-day, but it being a wet day we were prevented from going.

29 We started for Sapelo to-day—arriving there just before dark. Carpenters shingling our house.

30 The bricklayer has absented himself for two weeks so that all our brick work is suspended. Some rain.

OCTOBER

1 Carpenters have shingled the house, excepting the holes left for the chimneys to be built through.

2 Sunday. We all rode out to the beach this morning & down it nearly to the light house. Some rain.

3   The weather has at last cleared up & it is much cooler. It
     is the first pleasant weather we have had since 5th ultimo.
     Carpenters all gone to Darien & all house work suspended.
4   Weather clear & pretty—decidedly cooler. Wind N.W.
     Bourke & I, with Tom's servant Bermuda went fishing—
     caught over half a bushel of fish. I caught 56.
5   Wednesday. The carpenters commenced laying the floor in
     our new house. Weather beautiful.
6   Wind gone back N.E. Cloudy & cool. Since Monday Tom
     has been measuring his land, preparatory to receiving
     his rents.
7   We all went partridge hunting—Tom & Bourke killed
     eighteen between them. Weather cloudy & windy.
8   Mr. Campbell Wylly arrived this morning. We all went up
     to an old Spanish fort [19] on the N. End, for a granite post.
     We dug it up, but did not bring it home. Bourke killed one
     deer. Weather too rough to go to the Ridge. Wind N.E.
9   Sunday. High N.E. wind with a good deal of rain. Very
     high tides.
10   Wind moderated somewhat—still cloudy. About 4 o'cl. P.M.
     we all started for the Ridge. Before we had gone a mile the
     rain commenced & continued with little intermission until
     we reached the Ridge.
11   This afternoon we went over to Pumpkin Hammock Mill [20]
     to look at some lumber which we want to buy. As heavy rain
     last night & to day as I ever saw.
12   Wednesday. Tom, Bourke & Charlie left for Sapelo this
     morning, I staying on the Ridge.
13   Spent the day at Pumpkin Hammock Mills helping Bourke
     to have a raft of lumber built. A plank fell on my head &
     shoulder nearly knocking me down. We got 4589 feet of

19. An Indian shell ring on the north end of Sapelo Island, constructed
about 1800 B.C. See *Sapelo Papers: Researches in the History and Pre-
history of Sapelo Island, Georgia*, ed. Daniel P. Juengst (West Georgia
College Studies in the Social Sciences: Carrollton, Ga., 1980).

20. The sawmill owned by the Hilton & Foster Company located on the
north end of Union Island near the Ridge and opposite the present Blue
and Hall Landing, not the Pumpkin Hammock just across the Duplin River
from Sapelo Island. (See Map.) This mill burned the night of June 2, 1875
(see journal entry).

lumber in all. My dog Argus died last [night] from the effects of poison. Supposed to have been given by some free nigger.

14 Weather clear & cold. Letter from Griswold last night offering to rent me the North End. Bourke & myself came to the Island this afternoon.

15 Weather clear. Our raft of lumber, from Pumpkin Hammock, arrived last night. We have been lathing in our new house nearly all day.

16 Sunday. Raining at daylight—afterwards cleared up & we had a pretty day.

17 Finish lathing one room—sawed some palings and slept in the new house to-night for the first time. Tom hauling corn & had a chill. Our bricklayer started work again last Saturday, but took a chill and had to stop.

18 Weather damp. Rain nearly all day yesterday. The bricklayer starts work again this morning. Bourke hauling corn.

19 Wednesday. Still hauling corn, but finished this evening. Went fishing & caught some fine fish at the landing. Wind N.E. & somewhat cloudy.

20 Wind S.E. to S.W. in the morning with excessively heavy rain. Afternoon wind N.W. & blowing off cold. Been lathing the second room in the new house.

21 Bourke killed a deer & a very large rattle snake this morning. I caught some fine sheephead & school bass at the landing. Went hunting this afternoon but killed nothing but mosquitos.

22 Came up to White Shells on our way to the Ridge. I caught a very large Whiperee[21] & Bourke a channel bass three feet long. Weather clear, wind N.W.

23 Sunday. A Memorial Meeting for Genl. Lee (who died on 12th inst.) in Darien yesterday.

24 Turned off our cook, Ella, this morning, who raised a big row about wages when she thought Bourke & I had left for Sapelo. When she found we had not, she left in a hurry. It was with the greatest difficulty I restrained B. from whipping her.

21. A stingray.

25 I hired a new cook this morning at $5.00 per month. Her name is Mollie—a former slave of Mr. Norman Gignilliat, & a genuine negro. Bourke left for Sapelo yesterday, I staying on the Ridge. Cloudy & wind high from N.E.

26 Wednesday. Long letter from Father this morning. The boys came up from Sapelo this evening. Weather clear, wind N.E.

27 We have about adopted the plan of small cropping on Sapelo next year, renting out some land & raising cattle. Weather clear, wind N.E. Have been engaged part of the day copying a list of persons to be invited to my Sister Sarah's Wedding.

28 Mrs. Spalding & Tom left for Savannah this morning at 10 o'clock, on the Steamer *Eliza Hancox*. Sallie, Bourke & I left for Sapelo at 3½ o'cl. this afternoon, leaving Charlie in charge of the Ridge house. Weather clear, wind East.

29 Sallie has been busy all day, setting our plants in our new front yard. I have been lathing. Weather clear & very warm indeed—too much so to wear a coat. Wind West. Campbell Wylly staying with us while he has his corn, at the Kenan place, shelled.

30 Sunday. Bourke planted his first orange seed to-day. Sallie & I rode down to the South end to see her old nurse, Baba.

31 Took Sallie to ride before breakfast—went as far as Hog Hammock. Carpenters finished the roof entirely to-day & we have torn away the front scaffolding. The chimneys were finished last Thursday (27th). I have been building a fence, fixing a front walk &c. &c. Sea breezes, weather clear.

NOVEMBER

1 Busy tearing down the scaffolding from around the house & cleaning up generally. Bourke & I have also [been] sawing palings. Weather for the past three days clear & very warm. Wind E.

2 Wednesday. Hired a negro girl named Sarah Hillery at $2 for the 1st month—$3 afterwards. Got a letter from Griswold renting me the North End next year for $500 & his

house balance of this year. Bourke killed a deer. Rain, wind
N.E.

3 Sallie, Bourke & I rode up to the extreme North end of
Sapelo, to look at the house which Mr. Griswold offers
to rent me. Very much pleased with it. The view is really
magnificent—overlooking Sapelo Sound. While there, the
Steamer *Eliza Hancox* passed with Mrs. Spalding & Tom
aboard, returning from Savannah. Weather cleared up, but
still warm. Wind N.W.

4 We left Sapelo at 10½ o'cl. this morning, and after a delightful sail, reached the mainland about 2 o'cl. Weather clear,
but wind N.E.

5 I walked into Darien to attend an informal and private meeting of the Democratic party. We decided to nominate no
candidate for the legislature, but to support R. L. Morris,
independent candidate.

6 Sunday. Attended Presbyterian Church—services by
Rev. Mr. Quarterman. Some rain. After 9 o'cl. P.M. high
West wind.

7 Walked into Darien where Tom was appointed by a negro
Judge,[22] "Administrator de bonis non"[23] on his father's
estate, in place of F. L. Gué, deceased, former administrator. Weather cold but cloudy—wind West to N.E.

8 Tom, Bourke & I sailed down to Sapelo. Finished laying the
floor of our new house. Cloudy & warm.

9 Wednesday. Cloudy & very warm. Carpenters putting in
door facings. Went fishing. Had oysters for dinner for the
first time this season.

10 Bourke went to Darien last night. Tom started his gin this
morning. Weather cloudy & cold. Wind N.

11 Weather wintry—wind North & blustering. Our boat could
not return last night on account of it. Wm. Nightingale
arrived about dinner time.

12 Tom, Willie Nightingale & I went deer hunting—jumped
several, but only Tom killed a large buck. Willie N. left this
evening. Weather clear & warmer, wind West.

22. Tunis G. Campbell, Sr. See Introduction.

23. An administrator who oversees the unsettled estate of a deceased
person (i.e., the estate of Randolph Spalding).

13 Sunday. Mr. Campbell Wylly came last night. This morning he, Tom & I went to Doboy for a wagon pole of ours which had been left there last Thursday. Weather delightful. Wind S.E.

14 I have been lathing my room most of the day. Have got two doors hung & one window put in in the Southern end of the house. I neglected to record that on the 2d inst. my sister, Mary Cobb, gave birth to her third son, who Howell, his father, wishes to call for myself, but his mother calls him Howell for his father. Cloudy—some rain. It afterwards rained nearly all night.

15 After last night's rain it blew off very cold. Our first real winter day. Bourke returned from Savannah and got off the boat at the North End. Tom & I have been putting in windows at the South end of our house.

16 Wednesday. Very cold & high wind from N.W. Bourke was very sick last night, but is better this morning. Busy fixing windows.

17 We had our first white frost this morning—a very heavy one. Had a 'possum for supper.

18 Frost again. We all came up to the Ridge this morning. Letters announcing an offer of $25 per acre for my Walnut Level place in Baldwin County.

19 This is the fourth anniversary of my marriage with Miss Sarah E. Spalding. Owing to my absence at the time I failed to record that on the 9th inst. we hired another cook, Lucinda, at $5 for 1st month & $6 afterwards.

20 Sunday. Attended Presbyterian Church. Afterwards walked down to Ashantilly & Black Island.

21 Bought half a cord of wood from Arthur Bailey. Warmer, with some rain—wind S.E.

22 At five o'cl. this morning high West wind & turning cold as it clears off.

23 Wednesday. Bourke came up from Sapelo, where they killed, on the 20th, a porpoise weighing 482 lbs. Mrs. Spalding & Charlie Bass are staying in town to attend some Charades & tableaux. Wind West.

24 Wind N. East & clouding up & cold. Rain commenced falling at night. The charade & tableaux exhibition, under

Mrs. Spalding's management, takes place to-night in
Darien. All have gone in except Sallie & myself.

25 High Westerly winds to-day & clearing up cold. Bourke &
myself, with two boat hands, came to Sapelo, sailing except
across the Sound—pretty rough water at the mouth of Little
Sapelo river.

26 Tom, Bourke & myself rode over most of the land line between the former's & Kenan's land. Bourke killed a fine
buck. The former and Mr. Bass left for the Ridge this afternoon—the first time the latter has been off the Island since
Feb. 21st.

27 Sunday. Bourke & I drove my two mares to & down the
beach—having a delightful trot on it.

28 We hauled our two secretaries from Kenan's place down to
our new house. Mr. Bass & Tom returned from the Ridge.
A negro boy accidently shot & killed on Little Sapelo. Three
years ago to-night my only child was born & died.

29 We have been burning some of the savannas to-day for
cattle, but the grass is too green to burn well. After I had
gone to bed to-night, I received a note from Sallie saying
that her Mother was dangerously ill on the Ridge. We were
afloat in 15 minutes & made the trip in 2½ hours.

30 Wednesday. Mrs. Spalding better to-day. This is my
Father's sixty-first birth-day. Pouring rain all day.

DECEMBER

1 Some rain with very high N.W. wind. Jno. McQ. McIntosh
arrived from Savannah. Campbell Wylly spent the night
with us. 10 o'cl. P.M. clear as whistle.

2 We left the Ridge about 10 o'cl. A.M. Sailed most of the
way—very pleasant trip. Wind N.W. Mrs. Spalding
better this morning. We have put in one window & swung
one door.

3 Weather clear—wind N.W. Swung one door and put in one
window.

4 Sunday. Tom & I, with two boat hands, came up to the
Ridge, where we met Col. & Mrs. Spalding, Wm. Wylly &
John Nightingale & Jno. McQ. McIntosh.

5   Commenced moving the family from the Ridge to Sapelo.
    I came down with Bourke in a large boat, which is moving
    our goods. Tom came in our skiff.

6   While coming up Little Sapelo river last night we were over-
    taken by Wm. Wylly, Jno. Nightingale & J. M. Couper, all
    coming to hunt deer. We reached the Island about 1 o'cl.
    this morning and all went hunting to-day. We jumped plenty
    of deer & thirteen shots were fired & not a deer killed.

7   Wednesday. I forgot to record in the proper place that on
    the 3d I got a letter from my Father stating that he had
    sold my Walnut Level place to Clayton Vaughn for $4500
    & 1 acre of woodland for $30. We all went hunting again
    to-day, but killed nothing.

8   Mr. Bass & myself started between 12 & 1 o'cl. this morning
    for the Ridge to bring a load of furniture, & returned with a
    heavy load at 4 o'cl. P.M. Mr. Couper & Bourke each killed
    a deer.

9   We all went hunting again to-day, but did not even jump a
    deer. Our company left for home about 4 o'cl. this afternoon.
    Wind N.E.

10 Tom, Bourke & myself carried a load of furniture to the
    North end. Cold, high wind from N.E. with a great deal of
    rain, nearly all which we have been in—a stormy night.

11 Sunday. Wind gone S.E. & clearing up.

12 At 3½ o'cl. A.M. Bourke & I started for the Ridge in our skiff
    & Tom in a large boat. Brought back the last of our furni-
    ture & all of us moved down to the Island. Bishop Beckwith
    preached on the Ridge yesterday & confirmed a large class.

13 We moved up to Griswold's house at High Pt. to-day. Tom
    & Charlie going back to Riverside, Bourke & I staying at the
    Point, where I keep my mare, Kate. Wind West.

14 Wednesday. Tom has to go to Darien to attend the Superior
    Court as a petit juror. Bourke drove down to Riverside, re-
    turning to-night at 10 o'cl. Five sail boats have passed in
    front to-day. Sapelo Sound rather rough on flood tide. Wind
    N.W. & cold.

15 Another load of furniture &c. from Riverside. Steamers
    Eliza Hancox & *San Antonio* passed to-day. Wind N.W.,
    but warmer & clouding up.

16 Wind N., stormy & great rain. *Lizzie Baker* passed going
South & *Eliza Hancox* going North.

17 Steamer *Nick King* delayed & went North this morning.
Wind N.W., cold & cloudy but dry.

18 Sunday. Tom returned from attending court. We all spent
the day at High Point. Another load of goods from Riverside.
Letter from Father containing $150 of my rents. Mr. Bass &
I returned to Riverside & spent the night there.

19 Returned to High Pt. this morning. Tom killed a deer. At
9 o'cl. to-night Mrs. Spalding, Sallie, Bourke, Charlie,
myself & Eliza (Mrs. S's servant) took the Steamer *Lizzie
Baker* for Savannah. Wind S.W. & high—some rain. Rough
getting on the Steamer.

20 Reached Savannah about 7 o'cl. A.M. Sallie & I stopping at
Pulaski House—the others at Mrs. McIntosh's. A three
days' election commences throughout the State for Con-
gressmen and some of the States offices.

21 Wednesday. Left Savannah about 8 o'cl. A.M. & reached
Milledgeville 9½ o'cl. P.M. Sallie, Charlie & I go to my
Father's. Mrs. Spalding and Bourke to Mrs. M. J. Kenan's.

22 Spent the day at my Father's, where I find Sister Mary Cobb
& children and Ben Barrow in addition to the usual family.

23 Walked into Milledgeville. Weather clear and very cold.
Thermometer this afternoon 36°. Took dinner at Mrs. M. J.
Kenan's.

24 Walked into Milledgeville this morning, where I met
Dr. Spalding Kenan. Very cold. Wind N.W.

25 Sunday. Christmas. Intensely cold. Thermometer in Milledgeville to-day 6° above zero. Wind North West to North.

26 I caught a very bad cold indeed by exposing myself too
much to the intense cold of Saturday. Weather moderating,
wind West with some sleet & some snow.

27 This morning at 11 o'clock Cousin Ella Barrow & Miss Mary
Ann Cobb arrived from Macon. Wind North.

28 Wednesday. Mrs. Jno. D. Pope (Grace Sims),[24] three children and my brother William arrived at 9 o'clock P.M. from
Atlanta. The latter is suffering greatly with his eyes, having

24. Grace Sims Pope, stepsister of McKinley.

lost the use of one entirely and the other being impaired greatly.

29 Cousin Clara Barrow arrived by the 2 o'clock train from Augusta. Walked into Milledgeville this morning & spent most of the day there. Swapped overcoats with Bourke.

30 This is my Sister Mary McK. Cobb's twenty-sixth birth-day. With a house full of company, we are having a jolly time.

31 My brother-in-law, Capt. Howell Cobb, arrived on the 2.30 train from Athens. Guests are arriving to the wedding rather rapidly. To-day, Clayton Vaughn & John Wall, the men who purchased my Walnut Level farm of one hundred and eighty two and a half acres, paid the first installment of the purchase money, viz.—$2500. Another installment of $1000 is due on the first day of March 1871, and the other and last installment of $1000 is due December 25th 1871. Thomas Spalding, the bride-groom elect, arrived in Milledgeville on the 9.30 P.M. train.

1871

JANUARY

1   Sunday. New Years day. Attended the Milledgeville Presbyterian Church and heard a very excellent statistical (of this church) sermon by Mr. Lane.

2   Weather beautiful & delightful. All the family very busy preparing for the approaching wedding.

3   Tuesday. This evening at about 9 o'clock my youngest full sister (Sarah Barrow McKinley) & my Mother's youngest child married Thomas Spalding of Sapelo Island, my wife's eldest brother. They were married by Rev. Chas. W. Lane, pastor of the Milledgeville Presbyterian Church, though by request he married them by the Episcopal Marriage Service. The wedding was the pleasantest social gathering I ever attended in my life. I went to bed at half past four A.M.

4   This afternoon Uncle David Barrow, Ben Barrow, Cliff Kenan, Judge J. D. Pope, Mrs. Spalding, Tom & my sister (his wife), Sallie, my brother William, Bourke, Charlie Bass, Cousins Clara & Nellie Barrow, Miss Mary Ann Cobb & myself left Milledgeville on the 4.30 train, the first four for Macon, the twelfth, thirteenth, & fourteenth for Augusta & the balance of us for Savannah, arriving at the latter place, after a tedious ride, at 5.30 the next morning.

5   After sleeping from 6 to 9.15 A.M. I started out in the city & was busy until a hour after dark purchasing family supplies &c., buying over $500 worth & paying my bill at Dillon & Stetson's of $62.00. Went to the theatre where I saw Laura

Keene act in the comedy of Tony Lumpkin[1] or "She Stoops to Conquer."

6 Mrs. Spalding, Sallie, Bourke, Charlie, Willie McK. & myself left Savannah at 9 A.M. on St. *Lizzie Baker*, & arrived at Sapelo at 3.20 o'cl. P.M., bringing with us quite a large supply of groceries. Had a nice pleasant trip outside—just enough swell to be pleasant. Wind S.W. to S.E.

7 Willie McKinley, Bourke & Charlie drove down to Riverside. I have been busy unpacking, stowing & putting to rights our groceries.

8 Sunday. Walked out with Sallie to Dumese field.[2] Weather clear & delightful.

9 Clear & cold. Drove down to Riverside & spent the day. The boys went deer hunting, but killed nothing. Tom's man Jack Underwood quit to-day.

10 Paid off my cook to the 9th inst. ($11.00) & my housemaid to the 2d inst ($3.25 + Dec. 13th $1.75). Tom & his wife (my sister) arrived this evening on the Str. *Nick King*, from Savannah.

11 Wednesday. To-night about 6½ o'cl. Bourke & I left for Riverside—reached there at 8½ o'clock. Weather very pleasant.

12 Spent the day at Riverside. Wind gone N. East.

13 Tom came down this morning & on his way back killed a young buck. I have just had a wheel of my little wagon repaired & this afternoon Bourke & I hitched Tom's and my mares (Sallie & Kate) to it & had a very pleasant drive up to High Point. Wind N.W. & cloudy.

14 Went hunting & took Sallie & my sister Sallie with us in a wagon. Willie McK. killed a buck which had been badly wounded before. Wind N.E. some rain.

15 Sunday. Spent an island Sunday.

16 Charlie, Bourke & Willie McK. went to Riverside.

1. A character in Oliver Goldsmith's *She Stoops to Conquer: or, The Mistakes of a Night* (1773).

2. Dumese Fields on the north end of Sapelo Island, named after Francis Marie Loys Dumoussay de la Vauve, one of the French owners of the island in the 1790s.

17 All the boys have gone to Darien to attend a meeting of their boat club. I resign at this meeting.

18 Wednesday. Received a letter from Spalding Kenan, asking me to act as his agent on the Island. Some Ship Captains have come over to hunt with us.

19 In two days hunting the party killed two deer, but the Ship men killed none. I did not hunt. I have stopped my mare Fannie from working—she is looking so badly.

20 At 2½ o'cl. P.M. a boat arrived from Capt. Brailsford's[3] in Bryan County, bringing a Yankee friend of his, named Capt. Hussey, to take a hunt. He brought four fine hounds & just before dark he & Tom rode down to Riverside. The latter returning to-night.

21 All went hunting—Tom, Charlie, & I in the wagon. Tom, Bourke, Charlie & Capt. H. each killed a deer—Willie McK. missed one. I did not see a live deer the whole day.

22 Sunday. Capt. Hussey left for Capt. Brailsford's this morning in his little yacht.

23 We all took a sail in Mud River—except Mrs. Spalding. The boys then sailed over to Black Beard island.

24 Campbell & Sallie Wylly arrived a little after dark. We have been expecting Sister Kate on the Str. *Nick King*, but she did not come. The boat started to come outside this morning, but on leaving Warsaw Sound she met a dense fog & turned around & tried to come inside—but stuck in Romney Marsh & passed here at midnight.

25 Wednesday. I came down to Riverside this morning. Carpenters commenced ceiling my room to-day. Wind N.E. & clouding up.

26 Campbell Wylly & Bourke came down to-day.

27 I returned to High Point this morning to meet Sister Kate, but she did not come. Bourke is hauling fodder. I paid $5 for fodder. Some rain.

28 The Wyllys left this morning in a canoe with Mud river rather rough. The *Nick King* should have passed here last night, but owing to dense fogs she has not gone by yet.

3. A cousin of Sallie McKinley.

29 Sunday. The Strs. *Nick King* & *Eliza Hancox* passed together about sun rise. Weather foggy.

30 Tom & I took our wives down to Riverside & spent the day.

31 Again looked for Katie on the *Nick King*, and was again disappointed. Weather foggy.

FEBRUARY

1 Wednesday. On Monday we bought thirty one chickens, two turkeys & two ducks.

2 Nothing interesting going on.

3 Willie McKinley, Bourke & Charlie sailed in the *Sallie* from High Pt. to Marsh landing. Wind W. & water rough. I met them this evening at Riverside.

4 Bourke & I, with two boat hands, started for the Ridge at 4 o'cl. A.M., reaching there at day break. He & I walked to Darien & back. My servant David went on a visit to his father on the Main to-day. We reached Marsh landing on our return about 4 o'cl. P.M., where I got out & Bourke & his two hands sailed on to High Pt. I was so unwell that I spent the night at Riverside. My room was sufficiently finished to-day to move into.

5 Sunday. Willie, Charlie & myself drove up to High Pt. this morning with a load of corn & fodder. Wind S.E.

6 Mr. Bass & Mrs. Spalding intended going to Savannah to-night on the *Lizzie Baker,* but owing to a sudden & severe N.E. storm they could not get off. From a clear, pretty warm day, it changed in fifteen minutes to a cold N.E. storm.

7 A cold & severe N.E. storm prevailing all day.

8 Wednesday. It being calm, after the fog cleared up Tom & his wife & Sallie & myself with two boat hands went in our skiff to Bruro (Col. Chas. Spalding's place).

9 After breakfast I rode with Col. S. over to the Forest (Mrs. Wylly's place) & staid there—he returning. At 8½ o'cl. P.M. Tom arrived by water with the ladies. Weather very beautiful & mild.

10 Left the "Forest" at 1.40 P.M. for Sapelo, wind being N.E. As we progressed & the river widened, the wind got stiffer

& as we neared Sapelo Sound we stuck on a mud bank & the water getting very rough commenced to pour over our gunwales so that we had to run the boat ashore. After waiting on the flood tide we were able, by pushing over the marsh to wade to Dog island where we built a fire & disembarked at 12 o'clock at night.

11 After nodding the night through we woke at day light to find our boat high & dry a hundred yards from the water, but after very hard work we launched her & got to our landing at 8.10 o'cl. this morning—being out about eighteen & a half hours. The other side of Mud river was very rough. Those at home yesterday report seeing two whales about 40 feet long in the Sound. Mrs. Spalding says she opened a bbl. of flour yesterday & a can of kerosine to-day.

12 Sunday. Charlie Bass went to the Ridge yesterday. We hear to-day of the intention of a good many of the negroes on the Island to buy the "Street" land[4] & make a black settlement.

13 Went down to Riverside & staid all night. One of the hardest rains fell from 9 to 12 o'cl. to-night that I ever heard.

14 Cold with high W. wind. Paid our cook up to date & 95¢ over ($10). Our maid Sarah quit our service yesterday. Charlie Bass returned from Darien on the Str. *E. D. Morgan* this evening.

15 Wednesday. I staid at High Point to-day to take care of things while the other men were gone.

16 I staid at High Pt. to-day for the same reason as yesterday. Bourke started for Broadfield & Darien.

17 Staying home to-day for the same reasons as yesterday. Willie McKinley caught a fine string of small sheephead yesterday & day before. Mrs. Spalding & Mr. Bass left for Savannah to-night on Str. *Nick King*. Willie Wylly arrived on same boat.

18 Tom & Bourke shipped their cotton from Doboy on Str. *Eliza Hancox* to Charleston.

4. A parcel of 650 acres at Raccoon Bluff on the northeast tip of Sapelo, the only part of the island never owned by the Spaldings. It was owned by Samuel M. Street and others when it was purchased in 1870 by a consortium of freedmen known as the William Hillery Company.

19 Sunday. Willie Wylly left this morning. I see by the newspapers that the Prussian Army will occupy Paris to-day—
having captured it.

20 All preparing to go to Darien to-morrow, to witness a boat
race. This afternoon I carried the ladies of the house down
to Riverside. I slept to-night in my room in our new house
for the first time.

21 After an early start from Sapelo all our party reached Darien
about 10½ o'cl. A.M. A very pleasant trip. Near Doboy I
took the government boat, to lighten ours. I rejoined the
boat club, after resigning about a month ago. We had two
races between the *Sunny South*, an eight oared boat pulling to-day six oars, & our new race boat, the *Pierce Butler*
pulling four oars. The following gentlemen composed the
crew of the former, viz.—Jas. M. Couper, A. C. Wylly,
———— Floyd, G. Gignilliat, J. E. Holmes, Robt. Couper
& myself as coxswain. Those pulling the latter were—
Wm. Nightingale, Thos. Spalding, T. B. Spalding, ————
Jones & C. L. Bass coxswain. Each boat beat one race. The
first time was 2.13 the last 1.31—each race half mile. The
ceremonies closed with a sumptuous dinner & a dance at
Cogdell's hotel. There was also a race between Jas. Couper's
single scull skiff & Robt. Couper's 2 oared boat—the latter
beating.

22 Wednesday. We bought a canoe this morning, 10 months
old for $30. Our party left Darien about 12 o'cl., but before
we reached Pico a head (N.E.) wind rose & it was with great
difficulty we reached Doboy. We could not cross Doboy
Sound & had to spend the night on Doboy Island.

23 We got a tug to tow us across the Sound this morning. This
is Bourke's twentieth birth-day. We have been plowing for 4
or 5 days.

24 After staying last night at Riverside we drove up about
12 o'cl. to High Pt. Our former cook Lucinda left last Tuesday & we now have one named Rachel. Mrs. Spalding sent
out to-day per Str. *Lizzie Baker* a large supply of groceries.
Sister Kate & little daughter arrived this afternoon. A man
named Miller brought down 50 bus. corn, 11 bus. peas & 3
turkeys from Creighton Island.

25 I have been unwell all morning. The U.S. Rev. Cutter
    Nansemond[5] left her anchorage just down Sapelo Sound this
    morning, after lying there several days.
26 Sunday. The Str. *Lizzie Baker*, having lost an anchor in Mud
    river some time ago, left her Mate, a man named Decker,
    here to look for it while she went to Florida & back. A heavy
    blow from S.W., with heavy rain this afternoon.
27 Tom & Bourke left on Str. *Lizzie Baker* for Savannah at mid-
    night. The wind being N.W. and very high made boarding
    the Steamer an exceedingly rough business.
28 Wind N. & cold. Hauled a load of wood.

MARCH

1 Wednesday. Mr. Bass, Sallie & I came down to Riverside
   last night by moon light. I have been busy to-day writing
   contracts & trying to make my mare, Fannie, work in double
   harness, & succeeded.
2 I drove up to High Point & brought Sister Kate, little Katie
   & Sister Sarah down to Riverside.
3 Carried all the ladies down to the South End. The live oak
   grove there has been trimmed out & looks much better.
   Been very much worried again by my bay mare's refusal
   to work.
4 All of us except Mr. Bass returned to High Point. Spent the
   afternoon cutting & hauling wood.
5 Sunday. Bourke returned from Savannah, bringing with him
   a stallion & a magnificent black mare. He paid for the first
   $125 & for the last $300. He came by land & flatted them
   down from Bruro. A serious misunderstanding between
   Sister Sarah & myself which may cause me to leave the
   Island.
6 Hired a boy named Cato, for $5 a month. Willie McK.,
   Bourke & myself came down to Riverside. Breaking up corn
   land & preparing to plant sugar cane.

5. The *Nansemond* was a revenue vessel, now called a customs vessel.

7 Hired a house girl named Sallie, at $2 for the first month
   and $3 a month after that. Tom returned from Savh. to-day
   on Str. *Nick King.*

8 Wednesday. I staid to-day at High Point. Bourke driving
   down to Riverside.

9 Warm weather. Nothing interesting going on.

10 Maj. Lachlan McIntosh & Mr. D. C. Winans arrived on the
   Steamer *Lizzie Baker.* The latter thinks of buying a place
   on the Georgia Coast. He is very wealthy, & a native of
   Baltimore, but living now in Scotland.

11 All the gentlemen but myself went deer hunting. Only one
   deer killed & that by Willie McKinley.

12 Sunday. Heavy rain with thunder & lightning before daylight. We drove to Hanging Bull and witnessed a negro
   wedding—then drove to the South end & to the Beach.

13 Went hunting & jumped twenty one deer & killed only
   one—killed by my brother William. Our guests left to-night
   at 8½ o'cl. on Str. *Lizzie Baker.*

14 Tom, Willie & I came down to Riverside & jumped two deer
   on the road. We commenced building a fence to-day near
   the landing, to enclose a colt lot.

15 Wednesday. Hard at work on our lot fence. The negroes on
   Tom's place signed the contract to-day. Bourke struck one
   on the N. end Friday.

16 Still hard at work on our fence. A warm South wind blowing
   & gives me a very bad cold.

17 St. Patrick's day. Very heavy rain this afternoon & night,
   from S.W., with thunder & lightning.

18 Rain all morning. Came up to High Point this afternoon. My
   mare Kate started to plowing on the 15th inst.

19 Sunday. A quiet island Sunday.

20 We have made an arrangement by which Tom & his wife
   stay one week at Riverside & I & my wife one week—
   alternating.

21 In pursuance of yesterday's arrangement, Tom, his wife, Sister Kate & little Katie went down to Riverside this morning.
   Wind west.

22 Wednesday. We got, to-day, from Creighton island a boat
   load of sugar cane, which Col. Spalding gave us for seed.

23 Charlie & Willie McK. went to the plantation, leaving Sallie & I alone at High Pt. The weather is exceedingly warm for the season.

24 Mrs. Spalding returned from Savannah on the *Lizzie Baker* this afternoon. Bourke got out by the same boat, 10 bushels of oats.

25 A stiff Northeaster blowing, but still warm. The party of home people returned from Riverside.

26 Sunday. Wind S.W. A hurricane almost at 5.30 o'cl. P.M. with some rain.

27 Willie McKinley left us to return to his home at Milledgeville. He took Str. *Lizzie Baker* about 10.30 o'cl. to-night. Poor fellow, he is about to lose one of his eyes from amaurosis. Wind West.

28 I came down to Riverside this morning. Tom commenced having Griswold's cotton (which he is to gin) hauled from Chocolate to his gin. Bourke & I put the first coat of paint on the inside of our boat, the *Sallie*.

29 Wednesday. Cutting & hauling poles for our fence all morning. Worked on the fence in the afternoon. Sallie came down to-day. A little rain—wind N.E.

30 As we finished breakfast, it commenced to rain & has been a steady rain since (3 P.M.). Heavy thunder—wind S.W.

31 Mrs. Spalding's forty-eighth birth-day. Been trying to make my bay mare pull in harness. Wind S.W.

APRIL

1 Working with my mare again. Some rain. This afternoon Sallie & I came up to High Point. Wind W. This is my Sister Sarah's twenty-fourth birth-day.

2 Sunday. Two men are here, who were shipwrecked some days ago on Blackbeard island. Wind W.

3 I took the Str. *Lizzie Baker* about 9½ o'clock to-night, on my way to Savannah.

4 Reached Savannah wharf at 7½ o'cl. this morning. I stopped at the Pulaski House. My Father, whom I hoped to meet, left for Milledgeville a few days before I arrived.

5 Wednesday. I went to the theatre this evening & saw Lydia Thompson's troup of blondes act. I bought a shot gun to-day.

6 Yesterday I quit the Pulaski House & went to stay at Mrs. McIntosh's at 89 Jones Street.

7 Left Savannah this morning at 10 o'clock on Str. *Lizzie Baker*—reaching our landing about 4 o'cl. P.M. Very pleasant trip outside.

8 Charlie Bass has gone out drum fishing this morning, but did not catch anything.

9 Sunday. Mrs. Spalding went down to Riverside this afternoon. Weather very warm.

10 Sallie & I came down to Riverside this afternoon. Clouding up, with prospect of rain. Commenced cutting marsh grass for horses. Finished our horse lot fence last week.

11 An agent of Swift Brothers has been looking at the live oak on the Island to-day, but he only offers Tom 10 cents per foot, which he refuses.

12 Wednesday. Been in the field nearly all day superintending corn planting & preparation of land for cotton.

13 Been painting our skiff. A Nor'west storm this morning, with heavy rain.

14 Weather clear, after morning, with cool North West wind. Plows bedding up cotton land. Sallie & I came up to High Point this afternoon.

15 Heavy showers of rain most of the day, accompanied by heavy thunder & vivid lightning. About midnight cleared off with a terrific North West wind.

16 Sunday. Very pretty Spring weather. Mrs. Spalding returned from Riverside this afternoon. I got my first no. of *N.Y. Day Book* to-day.[6]

17 The Str. *Lizzie Baker* on her return trip to-night landed for us 25 sacks of corn, 1 bbl. flour & 579 lbs. bacon. It (the water) was so rough last Friday that she could not land them on her outward bound trip. This morning Charlie Bass caught, off the N. pt. of Blackbeard Is., a large drum fish, weighing all of sixty pounds.

6. A weekly periodical.

18 Katie & daughter, Sister Sarah & Tom & Charlie all left
for Riverside this morning. Commenced planting cotton
yesterday.

19 Wednesday. Been sick to-day.

20 Sick to-day. Rain at night, with heavy thunder.

21 Clear this morning. Launched our skiff last Tuesday night.
Str. *Lizzie Baker* landed fifty bushels corn & 1 keg of ale for
us this afternoon.

22 All of us, except Mrs. Spalding & Bourke, went fishing at
Blackbeard—poor luck.

23 Sunday. Nothing of importance occurring.

24 Went down to Riverside. Bourke & I hauled 351 lbs. fodder
from South End.

25 Bourke brought 450 lbs. fodder from S. End. Preparing
more corn land. My Father arrived this afternoon on Str.
Nick King.

26 Wednesday. Father and I rode down to Riverside, going
by the Kenan place. He is very much interested in the old
Indian mounds on the Island.

27 Took my Father over the Southern end of the Island—
started for High Pt. this afternoon & at Moses Hammock
were overtaken by a tremendous rain & again from the old
fort to the Point. Clouds greatly charged with electricity.
Giving our sugar cane its first hoeing & planting corn.

28 Spent the day at High Pt. Str. *Lizzie Baker* landed us
twenty-five sacks of corn.

29 Rode with Father to Chocolate & Bourbon. Weather hot.

30 Sunday. Walked down with Father to look at the Indian
Mounds, called the "Old Spanish Fort."

MAY

1 Tom shot a large rattle-snake near the house. Strange to
say, although near five feet long, yet he had but one rattle.
Father, Sister Kate and little Katie Taylor left on the Str.
Lizzie Baker this evening at 7 o'clock, for Savannah.

2 Mr. Thos. Bond arrived on Str. *Nick King* from Savannah on
a visit to Tom. Bourke started yesterday morning to Bruns-

wick via Cambers island, to attend a party at Mr. Forman's and a boat club meeting.

3 Wednesday. Charlie, Tom & his visitor went down to River- side. The latter brought a hound to Tom, sent by Col. Nichols of Savannah.

4 Commenced raining about 10 o'clock A.M. & has continued slowly nearly all day. After a few hours' intermission the rain recommenced at dark and continued nearly all night.

5 Charlie & Mr. Bond returned from Riverside. Bourke re- turned on Str. *Nick King* from Brunswick & Darien. Str. *Lizzie Baker* landed a lot of groceries for us.

6 My cousin, Carlyle McKinley[7] arrived on *Lizzie Baker* yesterday from Savannah. All the men except myself went deer hunting to-day. Bourke killed two. Weather clearing & turning cold. To-night we have to sit around a fire.

7 Sunday. Weather very cold for this season.

8 Weather moderating very slowly. Sallie & I came down to Riverside. Mr. Bond left on *Lizzie Baker* to-night. He was getting sick.

9 Finished plowing corn & cane immediately around the house, for the first time. Balance of the family came down to Riverside this evening.

10 Wednesday. Carl. McK., Tom, Bourke, Charlie & I went to Doboy to get a "Retriever" brought out from England for Tom by a ship Captain.

11 Replanting corn and hoeing cotton around the house. All the family excepting Sallie and myself, went off to the South end grove and to the Beach.

12 I forgot to mention yesterday that while at the South end grove, Tom killed a rattle snake with eight rattles, on the front porch of the old house. Bourke started to Valdosta to look up cattle. Some rain in afternoon.

7. Carlyle McKinley (1847–1904), a first cousin of McKinley. Born in Newnan, Ga., he for many years worked as a journalist for Charleston, S.C., newspapers. Noted for his poetry, he wrote, among others, "Sapelo." He also wrote *An Appeal to Pharaoh: The Negro Problem and its Radical Solution* (1889). McKinley's newspaper account of the Charleston earth- quake of 1886 was reprinted in *Ninth Annual Report, U. S. Geological Survey, 1887–88* (1890).

13 All our hands hoeing cotton first time in New Ground.
14 Sunday. Carl McK., Tom, Charlie & myself rode to the Beach this morning. In the afternoon Sallie, Charlie & I drove up to High Point.
15 Been greasing & washing boots to-day. Str. *Lizzie Baker* passed going North over an hour earlier than usual. She brought Mrs. Spalding's hat rack from Mr. Nightingale's in Brunswick.
16 It is eight years ago to-day since I fought in my first battle (Baker's Creek, Mississippi) & was wounded.
17 Wednesday. Came back to Riverside this afternoon. A good rain at High Pt. this morning, but scarcely any South of Bell drive.
18 Bourke returned from Valdosta this afternoon. He saw a man drowned in Long reach off the tug *E. A. Sonder*. Eight years ago to-day the siege of Vicksburg commenced.
19 I was busy yesterday boating fodder from Little Sapelo. Took Sallie over there with me. Rode up to High Pt. this afternoon expecting to get a milk cow off the boat, but was disappointed.
20 We built a pen for our stallion, "Ku Klux," this morning. I have been finishing the lathing in my room. Most of the family went to High Pt.
21 Sunday. Spent an island Sunday.
22 Commenced listing ground in Big Marsh, preparatory to planting late corn—also plowing & hoeing corn in New Ground. Crops suffering for rain.
23 Commenced planting corn in Big Marsh this morning. Still listing & hoeing corn in New Ground. Crops suffering for rain. Have not had a good rain at Riverside & below since 27th inst.
24 Wednesday. Finished listing corn ground in Big Marsh. Letter & telegram from Father saying that he had sent Tom a cow & calf & me a cow, calf & bull.
25 Carpenters commenced ceiling the third room of our house this morning.
26 I drove up to High Pt. this afternoon. Bourke carried our skiff to the same place. The Str. *Lizzie Baker* brought my sister one cow & myself a cow & a young bull—all sent by

my Father. The boat also brought me some groceries, which I will sell.

27 My twenty-ninth birth-day, and thank God I have been peculiarly blessed in reaching it in perfect health, surrounded by friends & above all in having a loving & beloved wife. Bourke, myself & Bermuda brought my cow & bull down to Riverside this morning. We had some trouble with our plowhands yesterday, but they are all straight again.

28 Sunday. Weather warm & dry. Been sick to-day.

29 I went with the two-horse wagon to Moses Hammock & got 268 lbs. fodder. Jumped a deer on the way. Mrs. Spalding & Bourke went to High Point—the latter on his way to Savannah.

30 Plowing corn & cotton in the New Ground. Our crop is suffering from the drought, & although it has been raining in sight all around us to-day, yet we have not had enough to wet one much. We had the first roasting-ears of the season for dinner to-day.

31 Wednesday. Still plowing corn & cotton in "New Ground." No rain yet. Mr. Bass finished a cow pen this morning.

JUNE

1 Working still in "New Ground." No rain yet. My cousin Jas. J. McKinley arrived at High Pt. last Tuesday. He, Carl McK. & Charlie Bass came down here to-day.

2 Jas. & Carl McK. & Charlie went back to the Point. The former leaves on Str. *Nick King* to-night. No rain yet. A great many of the negroes gone to Darien to see a negro hanged for murder.

3 A light shower this morning—cloudy all day. Bourke returned from Savannah yesterday & came down to Riverside to-day. Finished plowing "New Ground" at 4.15 o'cl. yesterday—plowing corn on South side of road to-day with sweeps. Got from Sav'h a bbl. of syrup & two boxes crackers. Bought three Pigs.

4 Sunday. Cloudy all day with a good deal of rain. Carl McK. & Charlie arrived last night at 11 o'cl. with the boat from High Pt. We have a new anchor for our skiff.

5 Plowing corn around the house, with sweeps. We have been busy nearly all day, sinking what is called a "Driven Well"— an iron pipe 2 inches in diameter with a pump attached. We commenced before breakfast & had excellent water for dinner. We sunk it about 15 feet. Some rain & very warm.

6 Sallie & I started for High Pt. this morning at 5.50 o'cl. Tom & his wife went down to Riverside this afternoon. My terrier Missy has been nearly dead with blind staggers, but is getting well, but I am afraid my terrier Pat is taking it—having been sick several days.

7 Wednesday. The wagon came up this afternoon to commence moving tomorrow. Not a steamer or sail has passed over Sapelo to-day. Col. Spalding landed here from Str. *Nick King* yesterday.

8 Carried the first wagon load of furniture &c. to Riverside this morning, so that our move has commenced.

9 Heard this morning of the death of my little cousin Wilson Cobb—he died of congestion of the brain. Miss Hettie Kell arrived on Str. *Lizzie Baker* & was met here by Col. Spalding. Carried down another load of furniture &c. to-day.

10 I have been sick all day, having had an attack of cramp colic last night, which lasted all night—a terrible attack & one which frightened me.

11 Sunday. I have been feeling very sick & bad all day.

12 Bourke started to Cambers Is. for a flat, to carry his horse to the mainland to start after cattle. I have been sick all day. High wind from S.W. all day, with heavy clouds & rain in afternoon.

13 Sister Kate Taylor's thirty-fourth birth-day. Sent off another load of furniture to Riverside. Bourke did not go to Cambers Is. until to-day.

14 Wednesday. It is two years to-day since I commenced my journal. Sent off another load of furniture &c. to Riverside. Still laid up with colic from 9th inst. I hear that they eat the first ripe watermelon of the season, to-day at Riverside.

15 Sent off another load of furniture &c. to Riverside. Bourke was to have carried his horses up to Hammersmith on the mainland last night. Yesterday at dusk a rattle-snake was killed between the house & kitchin, near the door of the latter.

16 Sent off another wagon load of furniture &c. A rain storm this afternoon from N.W. The view of the storm, across the Sound, as it approached was grand—seeing fifteen, or more, miles before it reached us.

17 I moved from High Pt. to Riverside this morning—leaving a negro in charge of the things we left behind. My storeroom in the round tabby[8] was completed to-day.

18 Sunday. Slept to-day.

19 Rode out to Big Marsh and South end. Plowing corn & hoeing cotton in "New Ground."

20 Hoeing corn in Big Marsh. Spent the day there & in "New Ground." Light showers.

21 Plowing corn in Big Marsh—hoeing corn in house field. Light showers.

22 Thursday. Finished first plowing in Big Marsh. Plowing third time in New Ground.

23 Rain late this afternoon. Miss Jessie & John McQ. McIntosh arrived this evening on Str. *Lizzie Baker.*

24 Rain this afternoon, which ran me home from the field.

25 Sunday. Literally a day of rest with me after a fatiguing week in the fields.

26 Tom started work on Bourke's cowpen at the South end this morning—taking Bermuda with him. A great deal of rain.

27 More rain. Been busy to-day putting my new room to rights—placing furniture &c.

28 Wednesday. Went fishing this morning, but had poor luck— only catching a mess. My sister has been sick all day. No rain to-day.

29 Went with Carl McK. to Little Sapelo fishing.

30 Went to High Pt. to get two bbls. crackers off the steam boat. Rained on me nearly all the way back. Charlie Bass returned from Valdosta. He reports that on the 27th inst. near

8. The former Spalding sugar cane grinding structure at Riverside. Actually octagonal. This area on Barn Creek, referred to as Riverside throughout the *Journal,* appears to have been the industrial center of the Thomas Spalding antebellum plantation; the sugar production facilities, the gin, and a barn were located here as well as an overseer's house. When the McKinleys and the Spalding boys returned after the war they first lived in the barn. See Juengst, *Sapelo Papers* and the Ella Barrow Spalding letter in this volume.

Valdosta, lightning killed Tom's grey mare Sallie & stunned him (Charlie), Bourke & the latter's mare.

JULY

1 Heavy rain this morning.
2 Sunday. Nothing doing.
3 Hoeing corn in New Ground. Have stopped all our plows but one. No rain to-day.
4 I have been working to-day on Bourke's cow pen at the South end. No rain to-day. Eight years ago to-day Genl. Pemberton surrendered Vicksburg to Genl. Grant. Sallie has been sick all day.
5 Wednesday. I have been working all day on Bourke's cow pen at the South end. When sheltered from the sea breeze, it has been the hottest day, I ever felt. It makes me sick.
6 Rode down to the South end. Finished Bourke's cow pen this morning. Afterwards went over to the light house, where we found Capt. Dean, a pilot, who gave Tom, Car-lyle McK. & myself a sail across the Sound to Wolf Is. in their sail boat, the *Sapelo*. Sound very rough. This day is the 24th anniversary of my Mother's death.
7 Hands been hoeing corn in "New Ground" all day. We "laid by" the corn in that field to-day. Bourke arrived at Darien, with his cattle to-day. Tom went up this morning to meet him.
8 My hands, with one exception, took holiday to-day. Dry & exceedingly warm.
9 Sunday. Dry & warm.
10 Went down to the South end to meet Bourke & his cattle, but he did not come. Warmest day so far.
11 The tug *Starlight* arrived at the light house at 1 o'cl. with 3 flats loaded with cattle & 1 with horse & books. Bourke lands 99 head of cattle. Dry.
12 Wednesday. Tom brought down yesterday two White Chester hogs. We heard a day or two ago of the killing on the 3d inst. of Lewis H. Kenan by Jno. R. Strother. I ex-changed my Westwood gun to-day with Tom for his Manton gun. Dry.

13 The hands hoeing cotton in New Ground. Dry & warm. Bourke returned to-night from Darien, where he had been to return the flats that brought down his cattle.

14 Rode down with Bourke this morning to look at his cattle & at the same time we carried my red bull "Ah Sin" (so called from Bret Harte's poem the "Heathen Chinee"), to put him with the herd. Hoeing cotton in New Ground. Dry yet.

15 Hoeing cotton in New Ground. The crops are beginning to suffer for rain.

16 Sunday. Very warm & very dry.

17 Went fishing this morning. Went to South End in afternoon & helped Bourke to pen his cattle & to haul a load of lumber. A severe storm at 10 o'cl. P.M. Vivid lightning.

18 Plowing cotton. Nothing else of interest going on.

19 Wednesday. My sister Sarah & Miss Jessie McIntosh are learning to swim.

20 This morning just after day light Bourke killed an alligator 9 ft. 3 in. long, in the creek in front of the house. Two very good rains to-day.

21 Rode down to South end & helped Bourke to drive his cattle out to pasture.

22 Bourke sick with an attack of fever. Finished plowing cotton in New Ground.

23 Sunday. A cool N.E. wind blowing.

24 Commenced plowing corn in Big Marsh. The mercury at 5 o'cl. A.M. stood at 68°. Bourke has hired a white boy named Jno. Fraser, to mind his cattle. He sets in to-day.

25 Finished plowing our crop to-day, except one plowing to give our young corn in Big Marsh hereafter. Mr. Bass went to Darien to attend Masonic meeting. Wind has been N.E. since Sunday, with thermometer 68° to 74°.

26 Wednesday. Bourke has been sick with chills since Saturday. Tom went deer hunting this morning. He jumped ten deer & killed none. Jno. McQ. McIntosh returned from Mainland yesterday. Wind N.E.

27 Still hoeing cotton. Dry weather yet.

28 Charlie Bass & our servant boy Cato had a fight this afternoon. The latter quit afterwards.

29 We gave our hands holiday to-day. Cato returned to his
   work. Tom & I went to High Pt. for corn. A light shower
   this afternoon.
30 Sunday. Island Sabbath. Rains in sight, but we get none
   except sprinkles.
31 Commenced pulling fodder in the barn field this morning.
   Charlie & Carl McK. started for the Ridge at 12 o'cl. Wm.
   Nightingale arrived to-day with two hounds for a deer hunt.

AUGUST

1 Went deer hunting, both drive & jump hunting. Carl McK.
  killed one the former way & Tom killed one in the grass. As
  it was Carl's first deer, we bloodied him. Killed them in Bell
  drive and Cotton savanna.
2 Wednesday. My nephew Tom Cobb's third birth-day. Been
  shooting at a porpoise this morning. First open cotton found
  on 29th ult. Went hunting this afternoon & in the upper
  pine barren drive on the stand toward the seaside; I killed a
  doe. No rain for three days past.
3 Our party went hunting again this morning & Bourke killed
  a doe in Drink Water drive. Our cook left us this morning—
  a woman named Rachel Brown.
4 My colt, Sallie is two years old to-day. Willie Nightingale
  left for home this morning. Jno. M. McIntosh did the same
  this afternoon, and a young man named McQueen McIntosh
  arrived.
5 Light rain nearly all the afternoon. Sallie has been sick all
  day. Still pulling fodder.
6 Sunday. Sent to High Pt. for a load of corn.
7 My week in the field. Finished pulling fodder near the
  house & put all hands to hoeing cotton in "New Ground."
8 To-day we bought, for $150 payable 1st Jan. next, from the
  pilots, the sailing yacht *Sapelo*. Tom & Bourke brought her
  around from the light house this morning, and then we all
  took a sail down the river. She was brought out in 1867, by
  J. N. A. Griswold of N.Y. Finished hoeing cotton in New
  Ground. First open boll in our cotton to-day.

9   Wednesday. Bourke, Carl McK. & myself went to Darien in the *Sapelo*. On account of light wind, it took us seven hours to go. Caught by a storm coming back & spent most of the night at Doboy. Richard Cogdell, an old citizen of Darien, died suddenly yesterday.

10   Cloudy all day & raining most of it. We commenced digging a canal for a boat house to-day.

11   Still at work on the dock for our boats. Weather cleared off.

12   Went to High Pt. for corn & other movables. Bourke & all the rest (Tom & myself excepted) went to the Ridge. Carl McK. fell overboard. Still working on the dock. Breaking up land to plant turnips.

13   Sunday. Somewhat cloudy and wind shifting from N.E. to S.E., indicating rain.

14   This morning between 3 & 4 o'cl. A.M. we had a tremendous fall of rain. Afterwards it rained most of the morning. The boys went out this evening & killed twenty four night hawks.

15   We all, except Mr. Bass, went in our sail boat the *Sapelo* to Moses Hammock fishing. Caught 40 fish averaging about 18 inches & fourteen crabs. We had a very pleasant sail of about 14 miles.

16   Wednesday. Bourke & Carl McK. went to Darien last night—returning to-day at 4.15 P.M. Commenced pasturing our horses yesterday. Rachel Brady set in as cook to-day. Wind N.E. Heard to-day of the death on 30th ult. of my cousin Charles Archibald McKinley. Bought 10 bus. corn.

17   Wind N.E. strong & weather cloudy. Bourke, Tom & Carl McK. went to Mary Hammock to shoot gannets. They killed two.

18   Raining all day long. During the morning the wind blew almost a gale from N.E. The rain destroys some fodder for us in New Ground.

19   A good deal of rain. From mid-night last night until this morning we had quite a gale from N.W. Our servant Cato has been sick since Thursday.

20   Sunday. Helped Bourke to pen his cattle this afternoon. He also carried our colts out and put them to pasture with the cows.

21 Bourke & Charlie went in the *Sapelo* to Col. Chas. Spalding's, to put down a pump. A letter this evening from Father about a Military & Agricultural College being located at Milledgeville.

22 Wind this morning N.W. & cool. Began raining about 8 o'cl. & has continued steadily all day since—the wind gradually shifting to S.E. & blowing very hard. The negroes are working the roads.

23 Wednesday. Weather clear, wind S.E. Bourke & Charlie returned from Col. Spalding's this afternoon. The boys have been shooting at porpoises. I have been sick.

24 The boys went to Little Sapelo at day light to shoot curlews;[9] they killed six. On their way back they got a porpoise which they killed yesterday. He was a small one, weighing only 188 lbs.

25 My sister & Tom expected to start for Savannah this afternoon, but on account [of] rough weather had to postpone their departure. McQueen McIntosh has gone to High Pt. expecting to take the Steamer to-night. The wind N.E. & gradually increasing in force since mid-day.

26 The wind increased yesterday so that from 9 till 1 o'cl. last night it blew a gale. Keeping me up until the latter hour. My sister & Tom left for High Pt. at 10½ o'cl. A.M., to take boat for Savannah.

27 Sunday. The High Pt. party, which should have taken Steamer Friday night, did not get off until 8½ o'cl. to-night. Wind almost died out.

28 Big rain at 10 o'cl. A.M. Put a new mast in our sail boat, the *Sapelo*, to-day & greased it with porpoise oil. Bourke brought 4 of his cows up to milk. Showery all day with wind N.E.

29 Hunted deer in the beach marsh & on Cabareta island. I had a shot at a fawn, but did not kill it. A negro in the party afterwards killed it.

30 Wednesday. All the boys went to Darien before day light in the sail boat & returned about 2½ o'cl. P.M. I went fishing, but caught only a few small ones. The first bright day we've had for two weeks. Wind West.

9. The White ibis, *Eudocimus alba*.

31 Took our canoe out of the water this morning. Its bottom was a mass of barnacles. We also fixed a mooring for our sail‧ boat. Finished turning down corn.

SEPTEMBER

1 We took our sail boat out this morning & scraped the barnacles off her bottom—putting her back to-night. We also made a buoy of a vinegar keg. We bought about 800 lbs. fodder & stacked it. Wind N.E.
2 All the family, except Mrs. Spalding & Mr. Bass, went to the Ridge in sail boat. I, with the other men, walked into Darien. May Holmes returned with us. Sound was rough. Wind N.E. I bought a pair of boots from Crumbley for $13.00. Had my Mother lived to-day would have been her fifty third birth-day.
3 Sunday. Have been sick all day. Wind N.E.
4 Wind N.E. & cool. Took our skiff out and turned her up to dry, preparatory to overhauling & repairing. Tom's old canoe, lost over a year ago was recovered to-day.
5 Wind N.E. with some rain. Bourke commences work on another cow pen near Hog hammock this morning.
6 Wednesday. Wind N.E. with heavy rain before & after day light. We started to Darien, but on account of rain, we turned back. This is my wife's twenty seventh birth-day.
7 Carl McK., Bourke & myself went to Darien for freight & returned at 9 o'cl. P.M. A good deal of rain. Just received from Savannah a fine felt saddle cloth. Gave W. R. Gignilliat a note belonging to Dr. Case & on H. Huntington for collection.
8 Mr. Bass has been building a paling fence around the garden to-day. Carl McKinley left for Doboy this afternoon to take Steamer there to-night for Savannah. With a high North wind they sailed very fast. I commenced a shrimp net to-day.
9 The Steamer for Savannah did not come along last night, so that Carl McK. and the other boys returned from Doboy at 10½ o'cl. this A.M., after a very risky sail there & back. An

exceedingly stormy day, with high wind & hard rain from N. & N.W.

10 Sunday. Between mid-night & day this morning the wind shifted from N.W. to N.E. & for a short time blew a fierce gale. Wind N.E. all day.

11 Wind N.E. all day. Bourke has hired a white boy named Alfred Summersell & old Billy Williams to mind his cattle, and has built a new pen near Hog hammock. His former cattle minder, Jno. Fraser, we have all hired to take charge of our horses. He sets in to-day.

12 Rain, rain with wind N.E. Our hands have been picking cotton between showers. Received a letter this morning from Sister Sarah written from Milledgeville.

13 Wednesday. Wind still N.E., but a comparatively bright day. Some of the family went to Little Sapelo fishing & caught 67 very nice fish.

14 Had new spokes put in my wagon wheel. The brightest day we have had for a long time. Bourke shot at a buck at the old gate & run him to Cabareta & then off it, but lost him after all.

15 Carl McKinley left this morning at 10 o'cl. A.M. for Darien, there to take Str. *Nick King* for Savannah. Bourke brought down a load of corn.

16 Thomas Spalding's twenty-fourth birth-day. Went to Little Sapelo fishing, but caught only a few. Hear to-day of the killing of Seaton Grantland by his father-in-law, Dr. W. W. Carr.

17 Sunday. Very warm, with light Westerly breeze, and towards afternoon showers with thunder.

18 Commenced pulling corn, but the ground was so wet & boggy that we could not haul much. Also picked some cotton. Weather clearing up. Mosquitos are dreadful.

19 Commenced a dock for our sail boat, just in front of the house. A cloud from S.W. at 9 o'cl. to-night & rain nearly all night. Padded my saddle.

20 Wednesday. Showery all day. Rode with Bourke out to his cowpen. One of his cows had a calf last night—the first calf of his herd. We commenced a shelter for our colts this afternoon.

21 A good deal of rain & very stormy all day. Wind N.E. Charlie went to Darien with a negro boat. Bourke started, but turned back.

22 Wind North & cool enough for fire & to make us all put on winter clothing. Bourke killed his first beef out of his herd to-day—a two year old steer, weighing 146 lbs. nett.

23 Been working on our colt shelter. Helped to wash out our sail boat, the *Sapelo*. Weather fair, but wind still blowing from N.E.

24 Sunday. Wind N.E.—cloudy & raining. My bull, Ah Sin, got out of the pen last night & we found him this morning in Big Marsh. My mule colt Ditto getting sickly, I am keeping her up & feeding her.

25 Raining most of the day with wind N.E. I gave my Skye terrier Norry to Fraser.

26 The girls & Charlie went chinquepin hunting & brought back about five thousand. Bourke went to Doboy for bacon, as we were entirely out. My mule colt is nearly dead—down & can't get up & yet I can see nothing the matter with her. Wind S.E.

27 Wednesday. Clear cool weather at last with wind from N.W. Mr. Bass, May Holmes, Bourke & Charlie went to Darien this morning. Hands picking cotton in New Ground.

28 The boat returned from Darien this afternoon. Letter from Sister Sarah. A decidedly cool, Autumn day—necessitating the first fires of the season. Wind N., weather clear.

29 Commenced repairing our skiff to-day. Most of the family went chinquepin hunting. We had to put my mule in a standing position by means of a derrick.

30 Went deer hunting. Bourke killed a fawn at the head stand of Bell drive. After white leading our skiff yesterday, we put the first coat of white paint on to-day. Wind N.E. Pulling corn near the house.

OCTOBER

1 Sunday. Weather beautiful, with wind N.

2 Been painting our boat. Hands pulling corn. Mule colt still very bad off. Wind S.E.—clouding up.

3   Been painting the skiff again—also greasing & painting the
    mast of our sail boat. Weather cloudy & calm all day, but
    wind blowing N.E. to-night.

4   Wednesday. Heavy rain all day. Wind blowing hard from
    N.E. all day & at present (9 o'cl. P.M.) blowing a gale. Hands
    been shucking corn to-day.

5   The gale last night lasted until mid-night. Put a third coat of
    paint on the outside & the second on the inside of our skiff.
    Wind E., with some rain. Still shucking corn.

6   Rigged an old mast on a tabby wall, to put a weather cock
    on. Been painting the skiff again. Hands picking cotton. A
    great tidal wave predicted for last night did not put in an
    appearance at the time. Weather clearing up. Wind gone
    South West.

7   The sail boat went to Darien in the morning. Brought up
    one of Bourke's cows & calves & built a calf pen. Wind gone
    back N.E., but the weather clear. Fixed a saddle rack in my
    room. Picking cotton.

8   Sunday. The boat returned from Darien this morning—
    having staid all night at Doboy for lack of wind. Wind to-day
    N.E. & rising rapidly.

9   Pulling corn in the barn field. Helped to fix a rudder iron on
    sailboat. A lot of groceries from Savannah arrived yesterday.
    Wind N.E.

10 We have hauled our sail boat up into the dock to scrape the
    barnacles off. She is very full of them. Finished pulling corn
    in the barn field. My mule colt is very bad off. Wind S.E.
    Very warm.

11 Wednesday. My brother William's twentieth birth-day. The
    day has been very warm. Rain with thunder & lightning just
    after dark. My mule colt died last night. I could see noth-
    ing the matter with her, but she fell off in flesh & strength,
    eating the meanwhile ravenously, rapidly. Wind S. to S.W.

12 Been scraping barnacles off our boat. Helped to weigh in
    over a thousand pounds of fodder. Bourke & I went dove
    hunting—he killed eight & I two. The weather cleared off
    cold. Wind N.W. this morning & N.E. this afternoon.

13 Carried our canoe on the wagon across to Raccoon Bluff,
    where we caught forty-five fish. I caught the largest bass—
    about 2½ feet long. Wind N.E. & clouding up.

14 Wind still N.E. Some rain this afternoon. Most of our hands took holiday to-day. Mrs. Spalding went up to the Kenan place & got a few oranges.

15 Sunday. Rode down this morning to Oakdale. Weather very warm with wind E. & S.E.

16 Hands picking cotton. Weather very warm. Wind S.E.

17 Commenced pulling corn in New Ground. Weather very warm with wind S.E. Two squalls, each accompanied with very heavy thunder.

18 Wednesday. Bourke & I went to Darien in our sail boat this morning. We had a moderate N. wind & made a very pretty run—making the trip in two hours and thirty five minutes from the mouth of the little creek.

19 Been busy all day having corn pulled & hauled from New Ground. Weather bright with wind N.

20 Miss Jessie McIntosh, Mr. Bass & Charlie left for Darien this morning to take Str. *Nick King* to-night for Savannah. Pulling corn in New Ground. Wind N.E. but weather beautiful.

21 Still pulling corn in New Ground. Bourke returned from Darien at 10 o'cl. last night. Wind N.E. Weather a little cloudy & warm.

22 Sunday. Wind N.E., but weather clear.

23 Went deer hunting on Cabareta Is.—jumped two & Bourke killed one—a large doe. We launched our skiff this afternoon. My cow, Spot, gave birth to a calf to-day. Wind N.E., weather clear.

24 Woke up this morning by a heavy rain. Wind S.E. this morning & N.E. in afternoon. Went fishing at Andrew's landing & caught a few. Finished my shrimp net (commenced Sept. 8th) all but putting the balls on.

25 Wednesday. Finished pulling corn in New Ground this morning. I went this morning with Bourke to put his cattle on Cabareta Island. Wind N.W.

26 I went fishing with Bourke to-day. We caught a great many small fish, but he caught a Channel bass 3 feet 6 inches long. Weather very warm. Wind N.W. this A.M., but N.E. most of the day.

27 Hands picking cotton. Weather clear with wind from nearly every point of the compass. Two wagons gone to High Pt. to meet the steamboat.
28 Been busy gathering oranges at the Kenan place. We got nearly 1000—a small yield. Mr. Bass & Charlie returned from Savannah last night. Wind from North most of the day and cool.
29 Sunday. Weather rather cool with wind N.E.
30 Wind N.E. with some rain. Weather warmer. Been engaged all day having the barn cleaned out to receive cotton. Bought 392 lbs. fodder. I neglected to state in the proper place that on Sunday (29th) Tom's setter, Bly, gave birth to five puppies, by an imported retriever called Jack.
31 Went to High Point with two wagons to meet Tom Spalding & my sister, who expected to come out on Str. *Nick King*, but she was laid up & they had to come out on Str. *Morgan*, arriving this morning. Wind N.E. Some rain.

NOVEMBER

1 Wednesday. Went deer hunting. Bourke killed a young buck at Shady Oak. We jumped two large ones in Sea Marsh, but did not get them. Wind S.E. Weather very warm.
2 We went to Darien this morning in the sail boat & returned at 8 o'cl. Wind N.E.
3 Had my cow & calf driven up home this morning. Weather cloudy & cool. Wind N.E.
4 Went to the Kenan place in the sail boat & brought back a bedstead & some lumber. Sallie went with us. Heavy rain this A.M. Wind W. & N.W., clearing up.
5 Sunday. Wind N.W. this morning—N.E. this evening. Weather cleared up quite cool.
6 Went with Bourke to Bourbon, McCoy & Drisden Point to get the amount of land planted there. The rent on those fields amounts to 3213 lbs. seed cotton. Bourke killed a small doe in King Savanna on our return. Wind N.W. this A.M., N.E. this P.M.

7 Bourke & I went to Moses Hammock & Chocolate to take the measurement of the land planted. It amounted to forty-three acres. Wind W. & S.E.

8 Wednesday. I have been doing nothing to-day. Tom has been receiving his rent cotton. Bourke brought his cattle back from Cabareta. Weather warm—wind S.W.

9 Cloudy & warm all day, with wind S.W. to S.E. Tom still engaged taking in rent cotton.

10 Been busy all day helping to mend a wagon body. Tom still taking in rent cotton. Wind W. & a little cooler. The Str. *Lizzie Baker* made her first trip out to-day, after being laid up several months for repairs.

11 Wind N.E. & cool. Nothing doing.

12 Sunday. Wind N.E. & warmer. Out of kerosine oil & using lightwood instead.

13 Wind N.E. & raining. The sail boat started for the Ridge, but wind failing, she came back & was hauled up for repairs. Tom started his engine preparatory to ginning. Wind S.E. & blowing a gale to-night.

14 Wind blew a gale all last night. This morning blowing stiff from S.W. & clearing up. Find worms eating our sail boat badly. A regular winter evening—a tremendous wind blowing from W.

15 Went deer hunting with Tom—he killed a doe in Bell & I killed a peg horn buck above Beaver Dam. Bourke went to Darien in the skiff, returning at 5 o'cl. P.M. Thermometer 42° at 8 o'cl. A.M. The first real cold day. Wind W. & clear.

16 The mercury at sun rise stood at 36°, but too windy last night for frost. Been cleaning the sail boat. We cut & banked to-day 3715 stalks seed cane. Wind W.

17 Wind N. and cold. We had our first frost this morning. Been painting our sail boat to-day.

18 Been painting the sail boat. Borke brought his cattle to the house field this afternoon. James Dunwoody arrived this evening. Wind N. & clouding up.

19 Sunday. To-day is the fifth anniversary of my Marriage. Charlie Bass & Jas. Dunwoody went to the Ridge. On last Tuesday (14th) I hired a girl named Patsy Bailey for $1 per month, to attend to my room. Wind N.

20 Commenced hauling cotton with four horses from Bourbon.
Hauled 1222 lbs. at a load. Charlie B. & Jas. Dunwoody
returned this morning. Wind S.E. & warm.

21 Hauled 1296 lbs. rent cotton from Bourbon. Bourke has
two more calves. Weather warm. Wind N.W. to S.W. Later
(9 P.M.) the wind went W. & blew a gale nearly.

22 Wednesday. Clear & cold. Wind W. Hauled 1328 lbs. rent
cotton from Bourbon & Chocolate.

23 Wind N.E. most of the day. Hauled 1314 lbs. rent cotton.
Tom, Charlie Bass & Jas. Dunwoody went to the Ridge
yesterday & all came back tight last night. The latter killed a
deer to-day.

24 Heavy rain this morning. Wind S.E. & warm. Rode up to
High Pt. this afternoon to meet the boat.

25 Hauled 1284 lbs. cotton from Moses Hammock—this
making 6444 lbs. rent cotton received thus far from the
North end. Wind N.E.

26 Sunday. Charlie carried Jas. Dunwoody to the Thicket this
morning.

27 Went to High Pt. with the wagon to meet the Steamer.
While I was gone Wm. Nightingale arrived. He brought two
hound puppies, about two months old, one of which Tom
has given me. Wind South—weather very warm.

28 Went hunting to-day. I killed a doe in Hog hammock
drive—had to pull her down with dogs. Tom started his gins
yesterday. Wind S.E.—very warm, with some rain.

29 Wednesday. We launched our sail boat yesterday & rigged
our sail to-day, after which the boys took a sail to the Sound,
bringing back a load of cotton from Little Sapelo. Wind
N.W. & a little cooler.

30 This is my Father's sixty-second birth day. Before day this
morning the wind shifted to North & the weather clouded
up & turned very cold. Bourke, Charlie & Willie Nightingale went to Darien.

DECEMBER

1 A cold bleak day. Wind from the North—thermometer 40°, and raining nearly all day—making us keep indoors by fires all day. Exceedingly stormy.

2 Thermometer 33°. Went deer hunting & Bourke killed a doe at the Patch of Pines in Bell drive. A large buck ran out at an unoccupied stand. Wind N.E. & blowing very hard—rain after dark.

3 Sunday. It rained nearly all last night. Wm. Nightingale left for home this morning. Some rain.

4 A little rain in the morning—afterwards blowing off cold with a high West wind. Bourke has been making a pump for the sail boat.

5 Been burning off the savannas around big marsh for winter pasturage. The coldest day of the season so far—thermometer 25° this morning—ice plentiful. Wind N.W.

6 Wednesday. Coldest day yet—the mercury standing at 23° this morning at seven o'clock. Wind N.W. this A.M. but shifting to S.E. this P.M.

7 The weather has moderated greatly. Bourke has made & put in a pump in the sail boat. Wind S.W.

8 Went to Doboy to meet cousins Clara & Nellie Barrow, who were expected on the *Lizzie Baker*, but they did not come. The wind failed us coming back & we had to send for the skiff. Wind S.E.

9 Went with Tom to take an account of the plowed land on the Kenan place.

10 Sunday. Weather pleasant. Nothing occurring.

11 Wind S.W. & cool. Nothing occurring.

12 Been busy most of the day taking in Mrs. Kenan's rent. Tom & I weighed in to their barn 5040 lbs. We have been living on the Island one year this evening. Wind S.W. & cool.

13 Wednesday. Went with Bourke & Charlie dove hunting. We killed fifteen birds. Wind S.W.

14 Wind North, raining & stormy. Bourke & Charlie went to Darien & returned at sunset, drenched with rain.

15 Went to the Kenan place bird hunting. The whole party killed thirty partridges & eleven doves. Wind N.W., cloudy & cold.

16 Went with Bourke & Charlie to Darien in the sail boat, to get a load of groceries. Weather clearing up & very cold. A little wind from N.

17 Sunday. Weather warm. A most delightful day.

18 The skiff went to the Ridge. Mrs. Spalding went in it to stay several days. Weather warm—wind E. Hammie Wylly arrived this evening in our boat.

19 Weather warm & nothing doing. Wind S.W.

20 Wednesday. Wm. Wylly arrived this morning at 1 o'clock. We all went hunting, but got nothing, though a deer ran almost over Hammie Wylly's stand without being shot at. Wind N. & very cold.

21 We all went hunting again to-day, but got nothing. Wind N. with thermometer marking 25°. The boys killed 4 English Ducks.

22 Went hunting again to-day, but got nothing. Tom, Charlie, Willie & Hammie Wylly all having missed shots. Got a gallon of whiskey from Savannah for Christmas.

23 Went hunting again this morning. Started to gin the North end rent cotton on the 21th. Killed no deer, Wind S.E. & warm.

24 Sunday. Willie & Hammie Wylly left for the Ridge. Mrs. Spalding returned to-night about 10 o'clock.

25 Christmas. We all went bird hunting & killed altogether thirty three doves & partridges. Foggy in the morning & somewhat cloudy—from 12 to 3 o'clock showery—clearing up later in the day. Wind S.W.

26 Weather very warm—thermometer marking 75°. I have not had fire in two days. Partially cloudy, but sun shining all day. Wind S. to S.E.

27 Wednesday. Partially cloudy all day, but sun shining—clearing up at dark. Wind W. Capt. Crane of schooner *Welcome Return* took off 10 bales of Tom's cotton to market.

28 Wind N. early this A.M. N.E. clouding up & turning cold after 9 o'cl. this A.M. Began ginning again to-day. Schooner *Welcome Return* got off with difficulty this morning. Ran a line across the Island for a fence, it was 1902 yds. long.

29 Clear until noon, with N.W. wind. Afterwards cloudy with E. wind, but no rain.

30 A dense fog all last night & to-day—so much so that I fear our mail boat cannot return to-night from Darien. Wind N.E. & warm. To-day is my sister, Mary Cobb's twenty seventh birth-day.

31 Sunday. The fog lifted about ten o'clock this morning, after which we had a very pretty bright day with only a few scattering clouds. Wind S.E. The mail boat returned last night without bringing my mail.

1872

JANUARY

1 Monday. Weather bright & pretty all day with only a few
   scattering clouds. Oppressively warm. Went deer hunting—jumped six deer. Tom missed one doe in Bell drive
   & Bourke killed one near the cypress. All but two of our
   negroes quit yesterday.

2 Three of us went to Big field bird hunting. We killed in all
   19 partridges & 16 doves. Cloudy all day with N.E. wind &
   much cooler. Hired a girl named Patsy Bailey this morning
   at $5.00 a month.

3 Wednesday. Cloudy & damp all day. Wind N. Sent our skiff
   to Camber's Island to carry dogs. Stopped ginning until we
   can get some bagging.

4 Weather cleared off early this morning with cool Westerly winds. Hired a white boy this morning, named Alfred
   Summersell, for $6.00 a month.

5 Bourke & I went to Darien in the sail boat—got becalmed &
   didn't get there in seven hours. Brought Mr. R. L. Morris,
   who was drunk, as far as Myhall Mill on our way back.
   Weather clear & bright. Wind S.E.

6 Rode up to High Pt. with Tom to look after things. Griswold
   rents us the North end again this year for $500 due 1st Jan.
   1873. Clouding up. Wind S.E.

7 Sunday. The negro preacher came last week and they have
   been preaching I believe most of the day.

8 Started the gins at 2½ o'clock P.M. Weather clouding up
   with wind N.E.

9   Went bird shooting to Little Sapelo, but did not find many birds. Walked over most of the Island. Charlie killed a very large raccoon. Wind N., cloudy & cold.

10 Wednesday. Cleared off cool with N.W. wind. Busy ginning North end rent cotton.

11 Weather clear & delightful—thermometer 42°, which is about the coldest weather since Christmas.

12 Weather clear & nothing happening.

13 Went hunting to-day. Bourke killed a very fat, fine doe at the upper end of Cotton Savanna. We afterwards killed thirty-six partridges near Moses hammock. If my sister Caroline had lived, she would have been thirty two years old to-day.

14 Sunday. Island Sunday.

15 Started very early this morning to Darien in our sail boat. The wind died out & we had to row most of the way there & back. I received from Milledgeville $212 rent for my house there.

16 Left the Island with four bales of cotton for Doboy, to wait for Str. *Lizzie Baker*.

17 Wednesday. The *Lizzie Baker* got to Doboy just before day. Shipped my cotton (North end rent) & got aboard, arriving in Savannah at 10 o'cl. after a rough trip outside. Weather very cold.

18 Attended to my business in Savannah, stopping at the Pulaski House. Took 7 o'cl. P.M. train for Macon.

19 Arrived at Macon at 5.15 o'cl. this morning—left at 6.30 o'cl. A.M. on the Macon & Augusta R. R. arriving in Milledgeville at 8.15 A.M.—At my Father's. Some rain.

20 Went into Milledgeville. Saw the men who bought my Walnut Level place about the last payment on it.

21 Sunday. Attended Presbyterian Church.

22 My Walnut Level men do not come up to time as promised. Weather very cold.

23 Went into Milledgeville. Vaughan still does not pay for Walnut Level. Father left for Savannah yesterday.

24 Father returned this morning. Went to Walnut Level to see Vaughn. He promises a meeting tomorrow.

25 Thursday. Vaughn (the purchaser of Walnut Level) came to see me to-day but brought no money. Weather cold—commenced snowing about 5 o'cl. P.M. & still falling (6½ o'cl.), ground white.

26 Clayton Vaughn came up this morning and paid me $100 on his debt. The snow continued to fall up to 11 o'cl. last night. This morning we have three inches of snow on the level. I left Milledgeville for Savannah at 2½ o'cl. this afternoon.

27 Reached Savannah at 5.30 o'cl. A.M. Rain commenced last night at midnight & has continued with little intermission all day. Been busy making purchases. I collected $119.65 from sale of North end cotton & took up my rent note ($507.64) due J. N. A. Griswold for his plantation.

28 Sunday. I am stopping at the Marshall House. Rain nearly all morning—afterwards cleared up & I walked out to the Park & called on the McIntoshes also.

29 Left Savannah at 10 o'cl. A.M. on the *Lizzie Baker*, reaching High Pt. at 4.20 P.M. Boat crowded with yankees.

30 Been sick all day with severe cold. I neglect to state in the proper place that on the 15th inst. I moved into the old overseer's house, which I have bought from Tom.

31 Wednesday. I bought a pair of large heavy boots in Savannah on the 27th inst. I put them on for the first time to-day. Bourke has had a pair made and put them on for the first time yesterday. Been having some locks put on my doors. My coffee, bacon & hams arrived last night. Weather intensely cold yesterday & to-day—ground frozen, pump frozen & ice in my bedroom.

FEBRUARY

1 Went partridge hunting with Tom & Bourke to New Ground, Oakdale & Long hammock. In all we only killed fourteen birds. We had a light sleet this A.M. At dark rain set in—high wind.

2 Rain nearly all night last night and a good [one] this morning. Cloudy all day with wind N.W. Been clearing up my new yard.

3 High blustering W. wind, but cloudy & cold. The boys went to Darien in the sail boat & brought back some chestnuts sent by Howell Cobb—they also brought 20 bus. corn for me.

4 Sunday. Read my bible & spent an island Sunday.

5 We all went deer hunting and jumped two in the first drive, but owing to bad behavior of one of our dogs, they got away. I afterwards killed a young buck in Bell Marsh. Wind N.E. & warm.

6 Washed out my gun. The negroes have been annoying me very much, trying to get money due them for ginning the North end cotton. Weather warm with high S.E. wind, which culminated this afternoon in a heavy thunder storm from N.W.

7 Wednesday. I have been suffering all day with a rheumatic headache. Weather cloudy & cold. Wind North. To-night is one of the stormiest I ever knew. Heavy rain.

8 A stormy, wet day. Necessitating indoor work. Wind N. & cold. I have been sick all day.

9 Weather clearing up. We went bird shooting in New Orleans & Big fields. We killed thirty three.

10 We went this morning to Moses Hammock to shoot birds. We killed forty partridges & 13 doves. Weather very warm & cloudy.

11 Sunday. Emphatically an island Sunday. Weather warm— raining at night.

12 Started to splitting rails to make a calf pen in Oakdale. Cesar Sams paid his last year's rent (fifty dollars) for Jack's Hammock, to-day. Weather warm & Springlike but cloudy. Wind S.W.

13 Dr. Spalding Kenan arrived last night on the *Lizzie Baker*. We sent our boat to Darien this morning, but her negro crew got drunk & got to fighting & lost several of our things. Received a letter from W. O. Tuggle of LaGrange Ga. in reference to the Street land. Weather warm & wind S.W.

14 Wednesday & St. Valentine's day. We all went hunting. Tom & Bourke killed a small deer between them. High West wind & very cold.

15 Weather moderating—clear & pleasant. Wind S.W. Been cutting & splitting rails nearly all day, around Oakdale field, for our calf pen.

16 Went deer hunting again to-day, but as our dogs insisted on hunting rabbits only, we jumped no deer. Wind S.E.— raining this afternoon, but clear to-night. Dr. Kenan dined with us.

17 Set out some orange trees. Dr. Kenan, Bourke & Charlie went in the sail boat to Bruro. Weather Springlike—wind S.W.

18 Sunday. A pleasant, bright & Spring-like morning, but cold & cloudy afternoon, with a little rain.

19 Wind W. to N. & clearing up moderately cool. Bourke and Charlie returned from Bruro at 12.20 o'cl. P.M.

20 We altogether split & cut 325 rails & poles to-day. Our man Fraser cut his foot badly with an axe. Wind N., weather clear & Springlike.

21 Wednesday. We have all been busy cutting & building a brush fence around part of Oakdale field. Clouding up with some rain. Warm. Wind E.

22 Started at our brush fence again this morning, but I cut my foot with my axe & I had to stop. Tom started his gins again this morning. Weather clearing up, but pleasant. Wind N.W. The new knives which Tom got for his gins do not work well—much to his disappointment.

23 Bourke Spalding's twenty-first birth-day. We all took dinner with him at Riverside. Sallie has started to raising chickens—she now has a young brood about two weeks old & another hatched yesterday.

24 We started to dig holes & plant posts for our long pasture fence to-day. My white boy Alfred has been sick since 21st. Clouding up. Wind S.E., some rain.

25 Sunday. Weather warm & delightful.

26 At work again on our pasture fence. We dug 135 post holes—that putting us within 70 feet of New Orleans creek. Hauled 30 posts. Delightful weather.

27 Busy hauling & burying posts, and digging holes—all for our pasture fence. Weather warm—wind S.

28 Wednesday. We dug 76 post holes to-day & stopped. Weather cool—wind N.E., cloudy with some rain. My boy Alfred being sick left this morning for his home on the main land, to get well.

29 This being leap year this month requires one more day. We finished digging the holes for our pasture fence a little after 12 o'clock. Wind S.W. Warm & clear.

MARCH

1 We (Bourke, Charlie & I) started for the Ridge shortly after day light. We had a very pleasant sail up but on our way back a wind & rain squall struck us off Heard's Island & we stopped there all night with Capt. Aiken.[1] Just a succession of wind & rain squalls until midnight. Wind N.E. & very heavy.

2 Between midnight & day the wind got N.W. & blew a most terrific gale—rocking Capt. Aiken's house like a leaf. Left Heard's Island at 2.11 o'cl., making the Sound in 27 minutes—crossing it in 9 minutes & making the whole trip in one hour & forty minutes. Weather clearing up cold.

3 Sunday. Spent the day in visiting the other house, reading the Bible, one of Dr. Blair's sermons &c.

4 Been amusing myself by cleaning up a patch to plant in corn. To-night I wrote off a bond for titles for Mrs. Spalding.

5 Rode up to Moses Hammock this morning to get a bag of shot left there on the 10th ult. This afternoon Tom & I went partridge shooting & killed nine. Bourke & Charlie went to Darien this morning. Simpson Hillery, an old negro man aged 96 years, died to-day. Wind N.E. & cool.

6 Wednesday. Bourke & Charlie returned from Darien last night, bringing with them Dr. Kenan. Been working on our pasture fence to-day. Wind N.E. I have been setting out young orange trees to-day.

1. Herd's Island (sometimes spelled Heard's by McKinley) is between Sapelo Island and the Ridge (see Map). Isaac M. Aiken operated a sawmill there.

7 Rather an idle day with me. Wind east.
8 Have done a heavy day's work—Mr. Bass, Charlie & I
   having buried 180 cedar posts on our new fence line. We
   hear to-day of an underhanded attempt by Dr. Kenan to
   entice away our negroes. Wind S.E. & stiff.
9 A strong S.E. wind all morning—gradually clouding up.
   About 1 o'cl. the rain began, accompanied by thunder &
   lightning, & has continued until now 7 P.M., the wind in the
   meantime boxing the compass—it being now N.E. Charlie
   gone to the Ridge.
10 Sunday. Took dinner at Riverside.[2] Tom & Bourke started for
   the Ridge at 9.20 o'cl. P.M. to get a warrant to arrest a Capt.
   Morrison of the British bark *Jno. Campbell*, for stealing live
   oak. Wind S.W.
11 About sunrise Tom & Bourke overhauled Capt. Morrison
   just in the act of leaving the Port. They went aboard, but
   instead of arresting him, they allowed him to blarney them
   until his vessel passed the outer buoy, when he claimed
   them as his seamen & ordered his sailors to tie them & it
   was only by showing a bold front with cocked pistols leveled
   that they were enabled to return at all—he insisting on
   carrying them & one of their negro boathands to Europe.
   Wind W.—cloudy. Been building a chicken coop most of
   the day.
12 Took dinner at Riverside & spent the day there. Sister
   Sarah, Tom Spalding & Spalding Kenan left this afternoon
   for High Pt. to take the Steamer *Lizzie Baker* for Savannah—the first & last named on their way to Milledgeville, &
   Tom for Savannah. Weather very cold—wind N.W. & stiff.
13 Wednesday. Tom & my sister left this morning on Str.
   Nick King. Spalding Kenan came back & went to Doboy
   to take the *Lizzie Baker*. I have been busy burying fence
   posts across Hog hammock marsh, where I killed two rattle
   snakes. Weather warmer—wind N.E.
14 Been working at my orange trees & chicken coop, which last
   I finished. Weather warm—wind East.

2. Riverside was the name for the area on Barn Creek on the west side of
Sapelo where the McKinleys and Spaldings lived. See Map.

15 Had a hard day's work at the South End, piling plank which Bourke hauled to our new fence. Weather warm & clouding up—wind S.W.

16 We hauled a load of lumber to the fence & a load of wood to the house, but got very wet in a cold driving North rain— wet all day.

17 Sunday. The rain recommenced about 3 o'cl. P.M. & continued far into the night.

18 Weather clearing up—wind N.W. in A.M. S.E. in P.M. Nailing up plank on our fence this morning. This afternoon we went to Doboy in the sail boat to meet Tom—he did not come though, and we brought back a load of freight, reaching home about 10 o'cl. P.M.

19 This the seventh anniversary of my last battle—Bentonville N.C. Busy all morning nailing plank on our fence. Wind West.

20 Wednesday. I left the Island, with Bourke & Charlie, at 7½ o'cl. this morning for Myhall Mill, where we made a raft of lumber & started back at dark. At night a stiff N.W. wind sprang up & drifted our raft on the wrong shore, so that when it got to Rock Dunder river we could not keep it out. After going down it about two miles the raft ran aground, when we anchored it & all got in the sail boat & come home.

21 We hauled two loads of lumber from the house to the new fence. Bourke & Charlie have gone to Doboy to meet Tom, who is expected out on the *Lizzie Baker*. Yesterday morning we put six of our hogs on Little Sapelo. Wind N.W. to N.E.

22 Been nailing plank on the pasture fence most of the day. Wind commenced this morning to blow from N.W., then worked around to N.E., then to S.E., from where it blew almost a gale to-night.

23 Heavy rain last night—some this morning. Bourke & I went cattle hunting toward Raccoon bluff & Kenan's house— found 41 head. On the round we killed 7 snipe and about 14 partridges. Wind N.W. & clearing.

24 Sunday. Weather cool for some days past. Wind S.E.

25 Weather getting warmer. A high S.E. wind blowing till about 4 o'cl. P.M. when we had a S.W. thunder cloud. Bourke took 3 more hogs & 7 pigs to Little Sapelo.

26 A dark, rainy day with wind from N.W. & North. There is more water now on the Island than there has been at any time during my two years residence on it. All the ponds are overflowing—the roads, rows & every thing else is full of it.

27 Wednesday. Hauled two loads of wood with Kate. Bourke & Charlie went to Myhall Mill last [night] in a large boat & returned this afternoon with a load of lumber. Weather clearing—cool—wind N.W.

28 Been hauling & nailing up lumber on the pasture fence & tore down the garden fence & put up another. Wind N.E. & warmer. Clouding up.

29 Been hard at work nailing plank on the fence. I planted a few rows of corn this morning. Wind N.E.

30 Working on our fence. Charlie went up to the Ridge & on his return brought Jack Barclay with him. Wind E. Weather very warm.

31 Sunday. This being Mrs. Spalding's forty-ninth birth-day, my wife & I took dinner & spent the day with her at River-side. Wind S.E.

APRIL

1 My Sister Sarah's twenty-fifth birth-day. I have been work-ing on our fence. I hear that a small rattle-snake was killed in the garden at Riverside. Weather warm—wind N.W. Myriads of sand flies.

2 We finished our pasture fence at 4.20 o'clock this afternoon. Weather cooler. Wind N.E.

3 Wednesday. Wind N.E.—raining. Went cow hunting. We turned 94 head into the pasture & got thoroughly drenched with rain. Took dinner at Riverside. Miss Mary Ann Cobb, of Athens, gets married to-night.

4 We went out this morning and gave some finishing touches to our fence. Wind N.E. and cool—so much so as to make fires comfortable at night.

5 I plowed my garden & tried to list some corn land, but the ground was too wet for the latter. Afterwards fixed up my garden & planted okra, snap beans, seewee beans & spinach. Wind N.E. & cool as yesterday.

6 We planted a patch of sugar cane to-day. Turned our extra horses & colts into the pasture. Wind E. & towards night beginning to rain some. Cool. Between 8 & 10 o'cl. P.M. a very severe gale from S.E.

7 Sunday. A thunder squall about day break. At about 9 o'cl. this morning it commenced to rain & continued heavily without cessation till nearly dark—flooding every thing. Wind S.E.

8 I went with Bourke around the pasture. We counted 98 head of cattle. More water on the Island than I ever saw. Wind still S.E. & blowing stiff.

9 Wind still S.E. A little rain & thunder. Went crab fishing & had some for dinner—the first of the season for us. Very warm to-night.

10 Wednesday. Been busy nearly all day, planting sugar cane around the gin house & down at Riverside. Wind S.E.— clear & warm.

11 Been gardening & planting corn & watermelons. Planted a banana in my garden. Wind N.E.—clear & warm.

12 Feeling unwell most of the day. I have done nothing but put all my axes in complete order. Wind S.E.

13 Have had a negro man plowing corn ground for me all day. I have now about three acres ready for planting. Weather charming. Wind S.E. Bourke went to Darien to-day. Charlie has just brought us a dish of fine mullet.

14 Sunday. Went with Bourke to look after the cows. We found 96 head, counting yearlings, of old cattle & 25 head of suck- ing calves. We afterwards went on the beach. Wind N.E. & cool.

15 Had a hard day's work building a calf pen at Oakdale. Wind S.W.—a clear and exceedingly warm day.

16 We finished our calf pen about noon. Charlie Bass carried his friend Jack Barclay home yesterday morning. Wind E. Millions of sandflies. Weather warm.

17 Wednesday. Went with Bourke, to see him mark, brand & castrate his calves. I have nearly three acres of corn planted. Wind E. Warm in the day.

18 With the exception of a little gardening it has been an idle day with me. Very warm.

19 Went with Bourke in the sail boat to the light house to see
    one of the pilots, but missed him. A high, flarry West wind.
    Myriads of sand flies.

20 A good rain about 4 o'clock this afternoon. Wind S.E.
    Cloudy, cool & pleasant.

21 Sunday. We had green peas & irish potatoes for dinner
    to-day for the first time. Wind N.E. Warm.

22 I worked most of the morning in the garden at Riverside.
    Bourke went to Darien. Two thunder squalls this afternoon,
    with heavy rain & hail.

23 A cold wind blowing from N.E. Weather cloudy. After
    Bourke returned from Darien this afternoon, we dismantled
    our sail boat, the *Sapelo*, and hauled her ashore, preparatory
    to coppering her.

24 Been pretty busy working on our boat and working in
    my garden. Wind still N.E. & cool, but getting gradually
    warmer.

25 Thursday. I have been hard at work nearly all day plowing
    (listing ground for corn) & am very tired. Wind N.E. and
    weather warmer.

26 Went with Bourke & Charlie to High Pt. where we met
    Tom, who arrived on Str. *Nick King*. He brought me a
    hound from Milledgeville. There is a ship & a bark loading
    with timber in Sapelo Sound.

27 We all rode around the pasture, to the South end and the
    beach. Wind S.E. & somewhat warm.

28 Sunday. Weather very warm. Wind S.E.

29 We turned the sail boat over to copper her. Fog this morn-
    ing—clouds this evening. Wind N.E. Cool. Planting corn.

30 Worked over my garden. Finished planting corn. The boys
    gone to Doboy to get freight from Steamboat. Wind N.E.
    Weather getting warmer.

MAY

1   Went down to Riverside this morning to see them unpack
    their freight. Tom brought me a horse collar, pair trace
    chains, two curd presses, two boxes gun wads, set wagon

hubs & some axle grease. Some rain last night. Wind N.E.
Weather warm. Planted some "Tahiti" cotton seed in my
garden.

2 Thursday. I got ready to start to Brunswick to-night at
10 o'cl., but the boat hands failed us.

3 This morning Bourke & I started to Brunswick to attend a
boat club meeting. After a pleasant trip we arrived at
Cambers Island, on our way, for dinner. There we picked
up Campbell & Wm. Wylly & at night we all started for
Altama, Mr. Couper's plantation, on the Glynn Co. side of
the river.

4 From Altama we all took a buggy & drove into Brunswick,
arriving there at 4 o'cl. A.M. After breakfast Bourke & I
went to Mr. P. M. Nightingale's. In the afternoon we had
a race between our old race boat & one just built for us by
Mr. Forman—the latter boat winning twice. In the evening
the Club was entertained magnificently by Mr. Forman.

5 After walking & driving around Brunswick we left Mr. Nightingale's about 5 o'cl. P.M. for Altama—stopping a few minutes on the way at Mr. Jno. K. Nightingale's, the latter
drove with us as far as Altama where we took boat & reached
Camber's Is. on our return at 10.45 o'cl. P.M.

6 Monday. This morning Mr. A. C. Wylly, Bourke & I left
Cambers for Darien. Bourke & I then walked out to the
Ridge with Charlie Bass, where I got a pair of boots just
made for me. We then took boat for Sapelo, where I arrived this afternoon after an exceedingly pleasant trip all
round. Weather charming for a week past. Wind to-day E.
[*Marginal note:* Got my Crumbley boots.]

7 Commenced work on our sail boat—having coppered the
centreboard. Weather beautiful. Wind S.E.

8 Wednesday. Busy all day coppering our sail boat. Been sick
to-day. Weather beautiful. Wind S.E.

9 Had to suspend work on our boat on account of being out of
tar & copper tacks. Weather warm—wind S.E.

10 Been having my corn plowed out to-day. Weather warm.
Wind N.E. Went fishing yesterday, but caught almost
nothing.

11 Good rains to-day, which were much needed. Wm. Night-
    ingale arrived to-day. He came to Doboy last night on the
    Steamboat. Wind N.E.

12 Sunday. This morning Bourke & Wm. Nightingale, while
    riding around the pasture, found my mare Fanny dead.
    Cause of death unknown. Wind S.E. Spent the day at
    Riverside.

13 Been helping Tom to measure & sack cotton seed. Wm.
    Nightingale, Bourke & Charlie went in the skiff to Broad-
    field for Jno. Nightingale & Jas. Dent.

14 The boys returned last night, but brought no one with
    them except Jas. T. Dent. Been sacking cotton seed most of
    the day.

15 Wednesday. We all went deer hunting. I wounded a large
    doe in Bell drive, which Bourke afterwards killed.

16 Went hunting again this morning—only jumped one deer &
    did not kill him. To-day is the ninth anniversary of the battle
    of Baker's Creek in which I was wounded.

17 The party did not hunt to-day because the dogs wanted
    rest. A slow rain this evening & night—a very fine one for
    the crops.

18 Some of us went hunting this morning. We jumped one in
    Big Marsh, but he & the dogs both got away. Wind S.W. to
    S.E.

19 Sunday. Weather warm. Stiff breeze from S.W.

20 We all went hunting to-day. Jumped one deer in the pine
    barrens, but he got away. Mr. Dent afterwards killed one in
    New Orleans field. Cow flies are more numerous than I ever
    saw before.

21 We all went hunting again this morning. Wm. Nightingale
    missed two deer in Gum pond. I missed one & killed one
    large buck at the same place. We launched our sail boat
    this afternoon after coppering her & painting her green.
    Weather very warm.

22 This morning at 9.30 o'clock Mr. Dent, Wm. Nightingale,
    Thos. & Bourke Spalding, Charlie Bass & myself started
    in our sail boat for Brunswick—on our way to Cumberland
    Island. We encountered three thunder storms before reach-

ing Buttermilk Sound—then lost our way & did not reach St. Simons Sound before mid-night, where after sticking on two or three sand banks, we anchored & slept till day light.

23 Thursday. We had just started from our anchorage this morning when the boom struck Wm. Nightingale & knocked him overboard. After taking him aboard, we ran pleasant up to Brunswick, which place we reached about 5 o'clock this A.M. We here gave up our idea of going to Cumberland Is. & spent the day in Brunswick. Wind S.W.

24 We left Brunswick & our visitors at 5.35 o'clock this A.M. on our return home with a light S.W. breeze, and made the trip in 7 hours & 50 minutes. On the way we landed at the old town of Frederica on St. Simon's Is.

25 Been trying to make up sleep lost on the trip to Brunswick.

26 Sunday. Nothing of interest occurring.

27 This is my thirtieth birth-day. Thank God I have been allowed to see it in perfect health. Been engaged this evening in taking Mr. Bass' interrogatories in a lawsuit in Savannah.

28 Been an idle day with me. Wind S.E. & dry.

29 Wednesday. Nothing of interest occurring.

30 Had part of my corn plowed to-day. My hound bitch gave birth last night to eight puppies, six of which I save & drown two.

31 Finished plowing my corn the first time, to-day. A Ship Capt. at High Pt. sends us notice this afternoon that he has imported English pointers, retrievers & terriers for sale.

JUNE

1 We all went to New Orleans creek this morning for clams. The whole party got about a bushel & a half. Weather partially cloudy & a strong N.E. wind blowing.

2 Sunday. Started for Darien in our sail boat with Bourke & Charlie, about 10 o'cl. P.M.

3 Reached Darien a little after sun rise & left there 8.40 o'cl. A.M. I have suffered from heat more to-day than ever in my life. A light shower & heavy blow from W. late this evening.

4 A light shower of rain this afternoon.

5 Wednesday. This is my niece Katie Taylor's eighth birth-
   day. Tom & Bourke started a new kitchen. Been hoeing
   some young corn. Wind N.E. & cooler.

6 Still hoeing my corn. Weather warm & dry.

7 Our stallion, "Ku Klux," that we bought in March 1871, died
   this morning. The flies had prevented his feeding enough to
   keep up his strength—got down & couldn't get up.

8 Charlie, myself & a negro man went to Little Sapelo fishing. We caught 30 scale fish & 15 cat fish. Wind W. to S.W.
   Weather warm.

9 Sunday. Weather very warm & so dry that the crops are
   suffering for want of rain.

10 Finished hoeing my young corn this morning. Still no rain.

11 The boys at the other house went to Herd's Island Mill in
   the sail boat & brought 500 feet of lumber. Still no rain.

12 Wednesday. Been busy mending harness. Rain in sight, but
   none here yet.

13 Sister Kate Taylor's thirty-fifth birth-day. I went fishing
   this morning, but caught only a few. No rain yet & corn
   crops burning up. This entry completes the third year of my
   journal.

14 No rain yet. Been occupying myself in reading Mad. Tus-
   saud's Memoirs of the French Revolution.

15 I started this morning with Bourke & Charlie, to Darien—
   arrived there at 10 o'cl. P.M. We all three joined a volunteer
   company called the "McIntosh Guards,"[3] Jos. Hilton, Captain. On our way back had to put into Doboy from a thunder
   squall.

16 Sunday. Got home this morning before day & been making
   up sleep since.

17 Went with Tom & Bourke to Herd's Is. Mill for lumber.
   Brought about 500 feet. On our way back, had to put into
   Doboy again from a thunder squall. Got home about mid-
   night. Light shower on Sapelo.

3. James M. Smith, governor of Georgia from 1872 to 1876, established
two white militia companies to control black unrest. See Introduction.

18 Been making up sleep again. My boy of all work is sick & I have to stay around the house.

19 Wednesday. Doing nothing to-day. Tom & Bourke went to Darien to give in their taxes. They had a fine N.E. wind & had to take a reef.

20 Wind N.W. & rain from same quarter—a regular September spell of weather. Very high tides.

21 We, Tom, Bourke & myself, rode up to High Pt. to meet the Livingstons, who are moving down. Mr. & Mrs. Livingston, Mollie, & Lewis [4] came on Str. *Nick King*. They will live in Kenan's house.

22 We all sailed around to the Kenan place to show the Livingstons the house. Sallie took sick to-day—is threatened with bilious fever.

23 Sunday. Sallie has been quite sick down at Riverside all day, but came home in the evening.

24 Went deer hunting this morning, but killed nothing. Had quite a good rain this afternoon, but not quite enough of it. Tom went up to High Pt. this afternoon to take Steamboat for Savannah, to meet his wife there next Thursday.

25 Been plowing corn to-day, and am broke down to-night. Good rains to-day.

26 Wednesday. Still plowing corn & very tired. Bourke & Lewis Livingston went to Darien.

27 Having finished my plowing yesterday I am resting. Lewis L. & I went fishing this morning at Andrew's landing & each caught a large school bass.

28 Sister Sarah & Tom returned this afternoon on Str. *Nick King*. The former brought me the 2d quarter's rent for my Milledgeville house.

29 Nothing of interest occurring. Very dry weather.

30 Sunday. The crops are again suffering for want of rain.

---

4. Lewis and Elizabeth Bass Livingston, originally of Columbus, Ga., she the sister of Mrs. Randolph Spalding. They came to be caretakers of the Kenan Place. Their daughter, Evelyn Elizabeth, had married Dr. Spalding Kenan. A son, Charles Lewis, appears frequently in the journal.

JULY

1 I went to Darien with Bourke & Lewis L. It took us nearly all day to get there. We towed back to Doboy behind the tug *Starlight*, where I had a ham stolen. The sparks from the engine set fire to our sail & burnt five holes in it. Reached home at day break.

2 Been suffering all day with headache. Weather still dry & crops burning up.

3 Wednesday. To-day is the sixth birth-day of my little nephew, Willie Cobb. Went fishing & took Sister Sarah & Mollie with us. I caught a large School bass & some Drum & Sheephead.

4 Been hoeing my corn to-day. The crops are suffering for rain very much. Killed a black snake in my back yard.

5 Nothing of interest occurring.

6 We all went to Little Sapelo fishing, but caught few. Twenty five years ago this evening my Mother died in Lexington, Georgia.

7 Sunday. We took dinner at Riverside, where we ate the first watermelon of the season. One of their banana trees is just out of, & another just in flower.

8 We all went over to the beach & spent a pleasant evening. S.E. wind with occasional light—very light—showers. Crops burning up.

9 To-day is the eighteenth anniversary of my Sister Caroline's death. Tom, Bourke & I rode to the N. end to get our contract signed, but the negroes all refused to sign, but agree work up to the same verbal contract.

10 Wednesday. The caterpillar has appeared already on the Island, not withstanding the unusual dry weather.

11 All of us men, Mr. Bass excepted, went to Oakdale creek to fish for bass. The Sound was rough. Caught only a mess of trout & these in the river.

12 The sail boat has gone to Darien. Laid by my little corn crop. Good rains in sight, but none on the Island.

13 We are beginning to enjoy the figs from the trees in my yard. Bourke put a new pump in our sail boat.

14 Sunday. We heard yesterday of the nomination on 9th inst. of Horace Greeley for President by the Democratic Convention at Baltimore.

15 Put a new bottom rudder iron on our sail boat this morning. Tom & Bourke have gone to Blackbeard to see about getting some drift timber off the beach for Jas. E. Holmes. A very light shower yesterday—none to-day.

16 Mr. Alex. W. Wylly,[5] who married my wife's aunt, died at his home on the morning of the 13th inst. All of us without exception went in the sail boat to a pic-nic at Brighton, but on hearing of Mr. Wylly's death, none of the family participated in the amusements. We ran, or beat, down the Sound by moonlight & in very rough water—a scary sail with the ladies. Mollie Livingston & Charlie Bass remained on the Ridge, visiting friends.

17 Wednesday. Spent the morning at the Kenan house. Tom & Bourke took the hound puppies I gave them home this evening.

18 All hands have been at work to-day moving the cowpen from Oakdale to the corner of the pasture nearest "Behavior."[6] Bourke went to the Ridge to-night for Mollie Livingston.

19 A light shower this morning. I name my home to-day "Ballibay" after the town of my ancestors in the North of Ireland. A good rain at 2 P.M. Continuing several hours. Mollie L. returned, accompanied by May Holmes.

20 Nothing unusual going on.

21 Sunday. Read one of Henry Ward Beecher's[7] sermons—

5. Alexander William Wylly (1801–72). Patriarch of the Wyllys who appear in the journal.

6. Behavior (sometimes spelled Behaviour) was the primary slave settlement of Thomas Spalding on the west side of Oakdale Creek on the south end of Sapelo Island. All that remains today is the cemetery, also called Behavior, located on the road from Riverside to Hog Hammock (see Map). The settlement was located to the south and east of the cemetery. In 1872 there was no settlement at Hog Hammock. Legend has it that Spalding chose the name to encourage good behavior among his slaves.

7. A liberal Congregational minister who was one of the most influential Protestant spokesmen of the time. He was emphatic in opposing slavery but after the war supported a moderate Reconstruction policy for the South. At this time he was minister of the Plymouth Church, Brooklyn, N.Y. Brother of Harriet Beecher Stowe, author of *Uncle Tom's Cabin*.

good. Some unknown one has sent me a year's subscription to them.

22 We started a bathing house at Riverside. I am cutting most of my corn stalks & saving them for fodder.

23 Took Mollie L. up to the Kenan house this morning, where she found a great deal to be dissatisfied with. Needing more rain.

24 Wednesday. The boys are still working on their bathing house. Charlie & Lewis L. went to Darien for lime & shingles.

25 Fodder pulling has commenced on the Island. Owing to the long drought, the corn crop has been cut off fully one half, and now we are expecting that the caterpillar will sweep the cotton crop.

26 Charlie & I took Mollie & May Holmes fishing this morning. Had poor luck—the whole party only catching 32 scale fish.

27 On the night of the 23d inst. Tom's setter bitch Bly gave birth to ten half pointer pups. He saved only four of them & gave me a white one which I call "Don." Bourke's fine mule colt (Nellie's colt) died this afternoon from what we think was "stomach staggers." Rode round the pasture to-day with Bourke. A very good rain this afternoon.

28 Sunday. First dog-day. A very good rain.

29 Been covering the bathing house with palmetto. A sprinkle & a very heavy blow from N.W.

30 This morning at 2.30 o'cl. we all started for the pilot boat near the light house. A little after 3 o'cl. A.M. we hoisted sail on the pilot boat (*Ada*) & stood out to sea, intending to go out to the blackfish banks, but on getting to the sea buoy, so many vessels hove in sight that the pilots could not spare the time to go fishing. We therefore cruised most of the day 25 or 30 miles out & off St. Catherine's Island. We were entirely out of sight of land & were told afterwards that we could have seen Tybee light house. Robt. Scott arrived at the other house.

31 Wednesday. Bourke & Charlie gone to Darien for corn. Good rain last night.

AUGUST

1 My servant boy, Carr, left me yesterday after raising a row. Bought a sack of corn @ $1.20 per bus. Just heard of a big row between whites & blacks in Savannah last Monday, over the question of riding to-gether in Street cars.

2 My little nephew Tom Cobb's fourth birth-day. A very heavy rain this afternoon. McQueen McIntosh arrived at the other house to-night.

3 May Holmes left for the Ridge this morning & got caught in a heavy rain.

4 Sunday. My bay filly (Kate's colt) is three years old to-day. I want to break her this fall.

5 Mr. & Mrs. Lewis Livingston moved up to the Kenan place to-day. The boys went fishing & caught enough shrimp to eat at both places.

6 Mollie Livingston moved to the Kenan house to-day. Sallie went up to help them fix. Went deer hunting, but killed nothing. Jessie McIntosh arrived at Riverside this afternoon. A light shower about 2 o'cl. P.M.

7 Wednesday. I have been busying myself in chopping up grass & cleaning my yard generally—its getting too snaky.

8 Wind N.E. Still cleaning my yard and also pulling some fodder. No rain to-day.

9 Wind N.E. Cleaning my yard & working my banana plant. Mollie Livingston came down on a visit to us this afternoon.

10 Wind N.E. We got the last of the peaches off our trees this morning.

11 Sunday. Rode up to the Kenan place this afternoon with Mollie Livingston. They are getting fixed up there very comfortably.

12 I went to Darien with the boys in our sail boat—pleasant sail. Wind N.E. Robt. Scott went up on his return to Savannah.

13 Hired a boy named Gib Carter yesterday, at $5 a month. Am suffering with head ache.

14 Been sick most of the day. The boys have been working on the roof of the bath house. Wind E. Somewhat cool & partially cloudy.

15 Took Sallie to pay a visit to the Livingstons'. Mollie came
back with us to spend the night. Bourke, Charlie & McQ.
McIntosh gone to Darien for corn. The negroes are working
the roads on the Island.

16 We all, i.e. the men, went by water to the Livingstons' to
put their piano in the house for them. Weather cloudy with
high S.W. winds for several days, but no rain.

17 The long drought having dried up most of the water in
the pasture, Tom, Bourke & myself went out & dug a cow
hole—a hard job it was too.

18 Sunday. Caterpillars appeared in Mr. Bass's cotton to-day
& are eating the leaves off rapidly. The chicken cholera
appeared among my chickens to-day—killing one. Very dry.

19 Wind N.E. Chickens dying fast, from cholera, six or eight
having died to-day. Mollie Livingston, who came down
on Saturday, returned home this morning. Needing rain
very much.

20 Wind N.E. Been pulling fodder. I ate, this morning, the
first hominy made of my new corn.

21 Wednesday. Wind N.E. Bourke & Charlie gone to the
Ridge to bring Capt. C. S. Wylly & his wife to Riverside for
a visit.

22 Capt. Charlie Wylly, wife & daughter & Jas. Dunwoody
arrived at Riverside yesterday afternoon. We all went fishing, but caught only a few.

23 We went deer hunting this morning & jumped three deer,
but did not get a shot. My gun snapping lost Bourke a deer.
Charlie Bass gone to carry Capt. Wylly & Jas. Dunwoody to
the "Thicket."

24 Went out this morning to help Bourke kill a beef. He killed
a young steer—weighing 266 lbs.—half of which he gives
the negroes for digging cowholes. Yesterday & to-day the
hottest of the year so far.

25 Sunday. Sallie, Bourke & myself spent the day with the
Livingstons. Mollie came back with us & spent the night
here.

26 I, together with Bourke, Tom & McQ. McIntosh, went to
Darien in the sail boat. We had very little wind either way
& had to row most of it. I found in the Ordinary's a bond

of F. L. Gué on the estate of R. Spalding, dec'd, which we have been trying to get. Charlie Wylly returned with us.

27 We all, at this place & Riverside, man, women & children, went round in the boat & took dinner with the Livingstons & spent the afternoon.

28 Wednesday. All the men at Riverside (Mr. Bass excepted) & myself went to Blackbeard Is. to-day, where we arrived about 3 o'cl. P.M. We went in the sail boat, outside of Sapelo Is. where we had some large swells & some trouble in finding Cabaretta inlet.

29 Some of the boys tried to sit for deer last night, but had to give it up on account of mosquitos. The rest of us tried to fish, but did such poor business at it, & the mosquitos were so bad, that we started home at 1½ o'cl. on the inland route. On account of squalls & loss of tides we have a long & tedious passage.

30 We reached home, tired & worn out, at 1½ o'cl. this morning, having made the entire circuit of Sapelo Is.—about 40 miles. I find mosquitos very bad at home too.

31 Wind N.E. & rising. Having heard of a rattle snake den in the pine barren, we went out to it this morning and unearthed it & killed thirteen rattle snakes—one large one and twelve smaller ones about one foot long. I bring my half setter, half pointer pup "Don" (Bly's puppy by Bell whelped on 23d ult.) home this morning.

SEPTEMBER

1 Sunday. Wind N.E. & blowing quite hard. Cool in the wind, but very warm out of it.

2 This would be my Mother's fifty-fourth birth-day if she were living. Charlie Bass carried some of the visitors to Darien & returned this afternoon. Jas. Dunwoody returned home. Wind N.E. & blowing quite fresh.

3 Mollie Livingston came down on a visit this morning.

4 Wednesday. Charlie Wylly & his wife took dinner with us to-day.

5 Nothing happening worth recording.

6   My wife's twenty-eighth birth-day. Tom & my sister took
    dinner with us. Charlie Wylly went to Darien—leaving his
    wife & child at Riverside.

7   Mollie returned home this afternoon. So far it has been
    the driest September I recollect ever having seen. In fact
    we have had but one good heavy rain since 1st of May.
    McQueen McIntosh left for Savannah yesterday.

8   Sunday. Passed the day in sleeping, visiting and reading the
    Bible & Henry Ward Beecher's sermons.

9   Wind N.E. with a light shower this morning. We took din-
    ner at Riverside. As my mare Kate, will soon have a colt, I
    had her brought up to-day so that I could take better care
    of her.

10 I drove up to High Point this morning to store away the
    smaller articles in the house. I brought back a bedstead, a
    matress, a chair & a rolling pin. My mare Kate last night
    gave birth to her second colt—a mare, which promises to be
    sorrel with one white hind foot & blaze in forehead.

11 Wednesday. Been helping to work on our skiff, which we
    propose repairing. Call my colt "Surprise."

12 Weather showery until 3 o'cl. P.M. Wind S.E.

13 Went fishing with Bourke this morning. We caught very few
    fish and enough shrimp for a small mess. Mollie L. came
    down to-day.

14 Bourke went out this morning & killed a buck & a doe.
    Wind gone N.E. Very high tide.

15 Sunday. Wind N.E. Between midnight & day light this
    morning, had heavy rains.

16 Thomas Spalding's 25th birth-day. We took dinner at River-
    side to-day. I helped Mr. Bass to pick cotton this morning.

17 All the men except myself went to Darien and returned
    about dark. A light drizzling rain most of the day. After dark
    a N.W. rain storm.

18 Wednesday. Wind N.E. Have just seen a statement of the
    timber business of Darien for the 1st half of this year. She
    shipped nearly forty million of feet in that time.

19 All the men, except Tom & myself, gone to Mr. Livingston's
    to help him shingle his house.

20 Wind N.E. Some of Bourke's cattle broke into the negroes' crops last night. Mollie L. came down this afternoon.

21 We went deer hunting (jump) this morning. We jumped twelve deer & only killed two—they by Tom & Lewis L. As it was the latter's first deer, we bloodied him. Wind N.E. Weather clear & warm. We found not a drop of water in the savannas.

22 Sunday. Wind N.E. Heard yesterday of my brother William going into business in Atlanta.

23 Wind N.E. Drizzling rain most of the day. Been knitting on Lewis L.'s shrimp net.

24 Wind N.W. & much cooler. Nothing of interest happening.

25 Weather warm again. Wind shifting.

26 Tuesday. Been laid up with head ache all day. Weather very warm & mosquitos by the thousand.

27 Doing nothing of importance. Weather very warm & mosquitos dreadful.

28 Heavy rain & violent thunder storm between 3 & 4 o'cl. P.M. Went deer hunting. I killed a very large buck at the head of Bell drive. Bourke killed a small one in Hangman hammock.

29 Sunday. Nothing of interest occurring. A stiff breeze from S.E. & very warm. Mosquitos by thousands.

30 This morning before day we had a very violent thunder storm from S.E., after which the wind went N. & turned a little cool. The first day of the season at all like Autumn.

OCTOBER

1 A decidedly cool morning & pleasantly cool throughout the entire day—necessitating winter clothing. Wind N.W.

2 Wednesday. All the men, except Charlie Bass & myself, went to Darien this morning to attend an election for Governor & members of the legislature. Weather cool.

3 We went fishing in the sail boat. Caught about thirty pan fish & Bourke caught a bass about 3½ feet long. Mornings & evenings quite cool.

4 We all expected to go deer hunting, but were disappointed in getting our horses from the pasture. Weather moderating. Sand flies & mosquitos troublesome.

5 Went deer hunting this morning. Bourke killed a good sized buck out of the grass in Bell marsh. Weather turned very warm. Wind N.E.

6 Sunday. Received a registered letter with $25 this morning from Father.

7 Left Sapelo this A.M. for Darien, on my way to Milledge-ville. Bourke, Lewis Livingston & Jessie McIntosh go with me. The first two to Milledgeville to help move Dr. Kenan to Sapelo—the last goes home to Savannah. After waiting all day in Darien, we got aboard the *Nick King* Steamboat at 7 o'cl. P.M.

8 We did not reach Savannah until 12 o'cl. to-day. Stopped at the Marshall House.

9 Wednesday. Left Savannah on the C. R. Rd. at 8.40 o'cl. this A.M. & at station 16 we met my Father returning from Wilkinson County Court. Reached Milledgeville at mid-night.

10 Went into town, where I received the last payment ($1118.80) on my Walnut Level place. Weather cooler than on Sapelo.

11 Willie McKinley's twentyfirst birth-day.

12 The first frost of the season in this section [*illegible super-script note*] this morning.

13 Sunday. Frost again this morning. Attended Church to-day for the first time since last January.

14 Julia, Bourke & myself left Milledgeville this morning, the two first for Atlanta & I for Athens, which place I reached at 5 o'cl. P.M. & found Sister Mary & family all well.

15 Had their first killing frost here this morning. Called on Cousin Lucy Cobb & her sisters Clara & Nellie Barrow.

16 Wednesday. Called on Mrs. Gen. H. Cobb & family. Mr. Lipscombe & wife called here.

17 Called on my Cousin Claud Thomas & Mr. Lipscombe & family. Spent most of the day down town with Howell.

18 Took dinner at my cousin Lucy Cobb's, where I met D. C. Barrow, jr.[8] & his brother Henry. I forgot to state that my brother Andrews is here at College.

8. David Crenshaw Barrow, Jr. (1852–1929), a first cousin of McKinley. Later he became longtime chancellor of the University of Georgia (1906–1925).

19 Left Athens this morning at 9.30 o'cl., accompanied by Sister Mary & her youngest child, Howell. Reached Milledgeville about dark.

20 Sunday. Attended Presbyterian Church. On my return to this place, I find that Father is in Atlanta, attending Supreme Court.

21 Spent the day in Milledgeville. My Sister Julia returned from Atlanta. Weather very warm.

22 Howell Cobb & two children and Clara & Nellie Barrow arrived at Father's this evening. Weather warmer.

23 Sister Kate & Julia, Katie Taylor, Clara & Nellie B. & myself started to Savannah this evening, on our way to Sapelo. We have to wait 5½ hours at Gordon, on the way. Bourke Spalding & Lewis Livingston started for Darien, overland, this morning with Dr. Kenan's horses & wagon. [*Pasted here is the following newspaper clipping:*]

HOTEL ARRIVALS

Pulaski House

C. E. Barrett, Pomeroy Snedair Opera Company; G. W. Ely, New York; A. Kummer, Baltimore; Thos. E. Twohoff, Rotterdam; Mrs. Taylor and child, Miss McKinley, Milledgeville; Miss Barrow, Miss Nellie Barrow, Athens, Ga; A. C. McKinley, Sapelo Island; J. G. Miller, city; W. T. Kelly, Jacksonville, Florida; Ira Jeler, Roanoke county, Va.

24 Thursday. After a comparatively pleasant ride all-night, our party reached Savannah this morning at 7½ o'cl., where we met Tom Spalding. Busy buying household supplies all day. Wind N.E., with an occasional shower of rain.

25 Our party left Savannah this morning at 10.30 o'cl. on Str. *Nick King.* After a pleasant trip outside, reached High Pt. about sunset & home at 8.30 o'cl. P.M. Wind W. & weather cleared.

26 Been resting from my journey. Nellie Barrow & my Sister Julia are staying with us.

27 Sunday. Spent the day at Mr. Livingston's.

28 Tom & Charlie went to Darien to pay taxes & get our groceries from the warehouse. I went partridge hunting, but killed nothing. Weather cool.

29 Brought a load of wood. Went partridge hunting—killed
four birds out of five shots. Weather cloudy with a cold,
bleak N. wind. Finished a one-stall stable on my lot this
morning. Tom & Charlie returned with a load of groceries—
were detained at Doboy all night & to-day by stress of
weather. Charlie has secured a clerkship at the store of
Wilcox & Churchill in Darien & leaves us tomorrow. A light
frost here on the 16th inst.

30 Wednesday. Charlie Bass left here to-day to go to his new
place. Cold N.E. wind. Weather cloudy.

31 I set out to-day 43 sweet orange trees, 3 lemon trees, two
sweet shrubs & five Malaga grape vines. Tom & I went partridge shooting—he killed ten birds out of eleven shots & I
killed seven with eight shots. Weather cold—wind N. with a
little rain.

NOVEMBER

1 Been busy nearly all day putting a "Keeny drive in well"
down. We finished late this afternoon & in two hours had
excellent water—almost entirely clear of sand. I am just
starting to break my three year old, three quarter Morgan
filly—Sally.

2 Been busy paying off servants, and fixing my pump. A little
rain this evening. Wind S.W.

3 Sunday. Took dinner at Riverside & heard some delightful
sacred music.

4 Before breakfast, I rode with Bourke over the pasture.
Afterwards we all went to the beach in the wagon. Bourke
driving four in hand.

5 Went to Darien to vote in the Presidential election—Horace
Greeley conservative candidate, U. S. Grant radical & Chas.
O'Connor ultra-democrat. Had a very pleasant sail there &
back. Wind N.E.

6 Wednesday. Been sick to-day. Bourke killed a doe in Cotton
Savanna. Wind N.E. some rain.

7 All of [us] (ladies included) went hunting in the wagon.
Jumped one in pine barren but he run back. Took the hound
puppies out for the first time.

8 Been indoors most of the day. Wind N.W., cloudy—some rain & very warm.

9 I drove up to High Point with Mollie Livingston & brought down from there a bedstead & lounge. Tom returned from Darien with a horse power to run his gin with. Wind N. heavy rain this A.M.

10 Sunday. Took dinner at Riverside. Cloudy.

11 Tom, Bourke & I took the ladies fishing, but caught very few. Afterwards sailed as far as the Sound. Weather clearing up.

12 Tom & Bourke went deer hunting this morning. The former killed two & the latter one—all in Big Marsh. Bourke & I started to Darien at 11 o'cl. P.M., but our rudder iron broke and we had to return home after getting to the Sound.

13 We men all went to Darien to-day. Towed up by the tug *Leon*. Took supper at Capt. Tom Wylly's. Wm. Wylly returned with us. Having no wind, we pulled to this shore of the Sound then anchored & all went to sleep.

14 Thursday. We reached our landing at 5 o'cl. this morning. Heavy rain from S.W. soon afterwards. Every body, excepting Sister Kate & myself, gone to spend the evening with the Livingstons.

15 Cleared up before day with a high cold wind from the W. Our first Winter day on Sapelo. Dr. Spalding Kenan & family arrived on Str. *Nick King*, to settle permanently. Wm. Wylly left on same boat for Darien.

16 Very cold. First heavy frost of the season. Julia McKinley & Bourke Spalding gone horseback riding. Wind N.W. [*Marginal note:* 1st killing frost.]

17 Sunday. A boat load sailed up to Kenan's place. Sallie & I walked to the same place. Very cold. My pump was frozen up this morning. Ice plentiful.

18 Very cold yet. Been helping Tom to attach his gin to a horse power.

19 The sixth anniversary of my marriage. Went deer hunting—Tom killed two & Bourke one. In all, we jumped thirteen—mostly in Kenan's marsh. Weather moderating, but cold still.

20 Wednesday. We all got ready to go to Darien to see a tournament, but as it was postponed, we didn't go.

21 Took the ladies, in the sail boat, first to Doboy & then to the light house. I saw the lamp there for the first time myself. Had a delightful sail. Indian Summer.

22 Been most of the day at the barn where Tom & Bourke have been fixing a gin. Weather much warmer.

23 I went with Bourke to Darien, in the sail boat. Sallie, Mrs. Spalding, Nellie Barrow & little Katie Taylor went with us. Weather pleasant.

24 Sunday. Spent the day at home. Weather warm.

25 Weather very warm with wind East.

26 Commenced hauling rent cotton from Bourbon. Brought 1274 lbs. Weather very warm. A light rain.

27 I did not go with them for cotton to-day. Bourke killed a deer on the way. I went for partridges but did not find one. Weather very warm.

28 Been busy hauling wood most of the day. Tom has a man named Abeel here to fix up his engine. To-night five years ago my first and only child was born and died. Weather still very warm.

29 Friday. Bourke & I went hunting to-day. We did not jump a deer & killed only six partridges. Weather very cold. A cutting W. wind.

30 My Father's 63d birth-day. Been hauling wood & strained my back severely lifting a log of wood. Bourke's cattle in the fields for the first time. Intensely cold. Thermometer at 8 o'cl. A.M. 25°.

DECEMBER

1 Sunday. Nothing of interest occurring. Weather moderating.

2 We tore down the pasture cow pen to-day & moved the rails, to build it closer home. Weather warm.

3 Went deer hunting, but did not jump one. Weather almost as warm as Summer.

4 Wednesday. This morning about 5 o'cl. Sister Kate, little Katie Taylor, Sallie, Sister Sarah, Julia, Clara & Nellie Barrow, Tom, Bourke & myself went to Darien in our sail boat—returned about 9.30 o'cl. P.M. Pleasant trip.

5 Helped Bourke this morning to drive his cattle to this side of the Island. He has built him a pen in the garden.

6 Nothing of interest occurring to-day. Weather warm.

7 We all went dove shooting. The party killed about forty doves & a few partridges. Weather warm.

8 Sunday. My brother Andrews' 19th birth-day.

9 We took Tom to Darien on his way to Savannah. Had a rough & stormy trip. Weather turning cold.

10 We had a visit from three Ship Captains, lying at Doboy. They are anxious to get beef & we at last hope we see our way towards making money in that line. Put new halyards & main stay on our sail boat to-day. Started to Doboy (Bourke & myself), but met the Ship Captains & returned. Weather cloudy, wind N. & very cold.

11 Wednesday. We killed a beef to-day & started to Doboy with it, but the weather was so rough that we turned back. Wind North—raining most of the day, exceedingly cold & stormy.

12 Still stormy, but prospects of clearing up. Bourke took three quarters of beef to Doboy & sold them readily at 9 cents per pound.

13 Killed another beef this morning. In the afternoon drove up to High Pt. to meet the Steamer. Tom Spalding, Sister Mary Cobb & her three boys, Willie, Tom & Howell came out on it.

14 Carried ¾ of a beef to Doboy for vessels lying there. Afterwards went to Darien & got there after dark. Cold & no wind.

15 Sunday. Towed down from Darien this morning behind the tug *Starlight*.

16 Killed another beef this morning. Carried it to Doboy & delivered to the vessels.

17 Left the Island at 2 o'cl. A.M. with Tom, Bourke, Dr. Kenan, Lewis Livingston, Mollie Livingston, Sisters Sarah & Julia, Sallie & Clara & Ella Barrow. All to attend a boat race in Darien. Bourke came near having a fight with a negro there & thereby causing a riot. Had a pleasant dance at the Court House in the evening. Warm.

18 Wednesday. Our party left Darien at 2.15 o'cl. with a splendid wind—made Doboy in one & three quarter hours,

but the wind died then and we did not get home till about 7 o'clock.

19 Killed two beeves this morning, weighing 312 & 400 lbs. A damp cloudy day. Wind N.

20 The beef which we killed yesterday, we took to Doboy and sold to-day without difficulty. Warm & squally.

21 We all intended to go to Darien to-day, but having left our boat at Marsh landing yesterday, when we got there this morning the boat was turned over. Bourke went to Doboy in the canoe & from there to Darien in the Tug *Starlight*.

22 Sunday. Nothing of interest occurring.

23 We killed three beeves to-day. Butchering them was a pretty hard day's work too. On the 21st we collected $31.05 for beef from the bark *Viscount Canning*—British.

24 Took 885 lbs. of beef to Doboy & sold it for about $80. Before we got home the wind had risen to a very stiff one from N.E.

25 Christmas. Wednesday. A cold, wet, stormy day, compelling people to stay within doors.

26 Went out this morning to drive up beeves. We killed one in the pen, but another got away after being shot & ran nearly to New Orleans field before he was killed.

27 We ought to have carried beef to Doboy this morning, but our boat was in the dock & the tide did not rise high enough last night to float it. Wind W. & exceedingly cold.

28 Carried two beeves to Doboy & sold them to-day. Our sail boat is leaking very badly, in consequence of thumping on the rafts at Doboy. Weather cold.

29 Sunday. We all with the exception of Sister Kate went to the beach & afterwards, to the South end of the Island, to show it to Sister Mary. I rode my new mare Little Sallie, that I raised & which was foaled 4th August 1869, & was very much pleased with her.

30 Sister Mary's twenty-eighth birth-day. She spent it with us—with her three fine boys. We killed three beeves to-day. Afterwards I worked on our sail boat & at last got her dry.

31 Bourke & I carried 993 lbs. of beef to Doboy to-day & sold it at 9 cents. We were becalmed & were out until 8½ o'clock at night.

1873

JANUARY

1 The sail boat, with Tom, Mr. Bass, Mr. Livingston & Lewis L. went to Darien this morning to the election of county officers.

2 Thursday. We killed two beeves to-day. Wind S.E.—foggy, showery & warm.

3 Carried beef to Doboy—Bourke & I. The weather was so warm last night that some of it was tainted, but we sold it all. Second anniversary of Sister Sarah's wedding.

4 Bourke & I went to Darien to collect the beef bills from the Ship *Orwell*, Capt. Young & the bark *Araminta*, Capt. Mosher, amounting to $171.90. Had a very pleasant trip. Wind N. to N.E.

5 Sunday. Commenced to rain early last night & continued till late this morning with high winds from S.E.

6 Killed & butchered two more beeves to-day. Weather warm & delightful. Wind N.W. & light.

7 Tom & Bourke carried the beef to Doboy, while I drove to High Pt. to meet my brother-in-law Howell Cobb, who arrived there on the Str. *Lizzie Baker* about 7 o'cl. P.M.

8 Wednesday. We all went bird shooting, but had poor luck. Tom started his gin a few days ago. Capt. Wm. Brailsford arrived this afternoon in his yacht *Rainbow*, a beautiful boat by the way.

9 We all (men) went to Darien to collect money for beef— returning about 11 o'cl. P.M.

10 The other men went rabbit hunting—killing twenty rabbits.

11 We all went deer hunting at the South end, but killed nothing.

12 Sunday. Dined at Riverside.

13 My deceased Sister Caroline's birth-day. If living, she would be thirty-three years old.

14 Howell & Tom went deer hunting in the grass. The former had a shot & missed—the latter killed it. The rest of us went sailing to Dr. Kenan's house.

15 We all sailed to the light house yesterday, to show it to our visitors. Howell Cobb & myself called on the Kenans & Livingstons.

16 Thursday. Went deer hunting in the pine barren. Howell killed a young doe & we bloodied him.

17 Bourke went to Doboy to take Str. *Nick King* for Palatka, Fla. to buy beef cattle for us.

18 Went deer hunting—jumped one in Hog hammock, but he would not run so as to give any of us a shot. Our hound puppies ran beautifully.

19 Sunday. Took dinner at Riverside. Intensely cold. Thermometer 17°. A negro that we sent to Darien yesterday got frost bitten on his return.

20 We left for High Pt. this afternoon, with our visitors to take Steamer for Savannah.

21 Steamer *Nick King* did not come last night or to-day. All of us at High Pt. waiting for it.

22 Wednesday. Str. *Nick King* arrived this morning about 10 o'cl., when Howell Cobb, wife & three children, Sister Kate & daughter, Sister Julia, & Cousins Clara & Nellie Barrow left for their respective homes.

23 Having sat up most of two nights, Sallie & I have been resting ourselves. I hear that my cow Spot has another calf.

24 By a boat just from Darien we learn that the small pox has broken out there.

25 Broke my little wagon again yesterday. I rode my mare "Little Sallie" down to the South end to see about building a butcher pen. I am delighted with my young mare.

26 Sunday. Rode out to & down the beach, at my leisure & enjoyed it very much.

27 We hear to-day that the Steamboat *Nick King* going up to Darien on the night of the 24th inst. ran into an old wreck & sank in a short time just in front of Darien.[1] This is a sore disappointment to us, as Bourke is in Florida waiting to bring a drove of beeves on this boat. Tom went to Doboy.

28 Went to Little Sapelo with the whole party except Mr. Bass. We caught 3 hogs & sailed home in a driving N. rain. Ladies & all were thoroughly wet when we got home.

29 Wednesday. More or less rain all last night & to-day. Wind N.E., cold & disagreeable.

30 A cold, disagreeable day. Wind N.W. to N. Cloudy with some rain. Have had a quarrel with our man Jack.

31 Another dull gloomy day. Tom went to Darien in the sail boat, taking with him two bales of his cotton & 1 bale of hides weighing 304 lbs.—the latter belonging to all of us. All to be shipped to Savannah.

FEBRUARY

1 The Sun shone out to-day for the first time since last Monday.

2 Sunday. Bourke returned from Florida this morning without having bought any beef cattle. The Cuba market keeps that country drained of good beef.

3 This evening on returning from a bird hunt I found a telegram from Father saying that Sister Kate was sinking rapidly. Sister Sarah, Sallie, Tom & I will start for Milledgeville in the morning.

4 As we afterwards found, Sister *Kate McKinley Taylor* died between 4 & five o'clock this afternoon, of consumption produced by chills & whooping cough. She was thirty five years, seven months and twenty two days old—having been born on the 13th of June 1837. On January 7th 1863 she married Capt. R. D. B. Taylor of Athens, Ga. On the 4th

1. The *New York Times*, January 27, 1873, reported "The steamer *Nick King* bound to Florida, struck a snag near Darien, Ga., on Friday night. The passengers and crew were saved." The steamer was not salvaged.

of June 1864 her first and only child (a daughter) was born
& in a few days her husband died. She was Father's & *my*
Mother's first born & since we were left motherless in 1847,
we had learned to look up to her as a second mother. She
only left us on Sapelo three weeks ago after promising to
return in May. She died a most peaceful death, literally
going to sleep—sleep being the thing she most craved.
Her last words were—in a family group around her bed-
side—"I haven't the breath to talk but that will make me the
better listener." In a minute she was dead.[2] We took Str. *San
Antonio* at 11.45 o'cl. this morning in Long Reach & arrived
at Savannah at 3 o'cl. next morning.

5 Wednesday. Left Savannah at 8.45 o'cl. this morning.

6 Reached Milledgeville at 1.30 o'clock this morning, when I
first heard positively of poor Sister Kate's death on the 4th
inst. Her funeral was preached at the Presbyterian Church
at half past ten o'clock this morning and we buried her in
the Milledgeville Cemetery. The last of my poor, loved suffering Sister—though, thank God she died as peaceful &
easy a death as mortal man could. My Father came very
near dying from excessive grief during the funeral & is now
very ill indeed.

7 My Father some better to-day. All of his children have
gathered here to our Sister's funeral.

8 I have been staying close at Father's to nurse him. He is not
so well to-day.

9 Sunday. Most of the family staid at home—not going to
Church.

10 Sister Mary, Howell Cobb & my brother Andrews left
for Athens to-day. Father, Tom Spalding & I rode out to
Midway.

11 Tom Spalding left for Sapelo this afternoon. Father a little
better & insists on going back to his business at his office.

12 Wednesday. Clara & Ella Barrow left for Athens this morning.

2. Here McKinley drew a long horizontal line. His meaning is unclear,
perhaps despair or grief.

13 I spent the morning in Milledgeville. Father insists that I shall not go back to Sapelo yet, but spend some time here with him.

14 Valentine day. Willie & Guy were the only ones of the family who got any.

15 Guy's fifteenth birth-day. He is the only one of Father's children who was born at this place.

16 Sunday. Heavy rains yesterday & this morning. River rising rapidly.

17 This morning the river covered all the low ground. I crossed in a batteau & spent the day in town. Father left for Savannah this evening, to attend a bankrupt court, and was very unwell indeed.

18 Crossed the river in a batteau again this morning & spent the day in Milledgeville.

19 Wednesday. Drove down to the river expecting to drive across, but found it rising. Walked to the depot & met Father on his return from Savannah. He is much better. The river has fallen a few inches.

20 The river has fallen enough this morning to admit of a carriage being driven across the upper embankment.

21 Spent the morning in Milledgeville. The river still falling.

22 No news worth recording.

23 Sunday. Most of the family attended Church this morning— I did not.

24 Baldwin county Superior Court met this morning, Judge Geo. T. Bartlett of Jasper county presided for his first time.

25 Attended Court. The people are not pleased with their new Judge.

26 Ash Wednesday—recognized by Catholics & Episcopalians. Sallie gone to Church.

27 Attended Court to-day.

28 Superior Court adjourned this evening until the fifth Monday (31st) of March.

MARCH

1   Walked into Milledgeville this morning.
2   Sunday. Very stormy. Too wet for anybody to attend Church.
3   Cleared up last night. High W. winds & very cold.
4   President U. S. Grant will be inaugurated for a second term, to-day at Washington City.
5   Wednesday. Nothing worth recording.
6   Sister Sarah left for Athens this morning to nurse Sister Mary through her confinement.
7   Sallie & Grace went out to Scottsboro to-day to call on Mrs. DuBignon & Mrs. Furman.
8   Sallie & I left Milledgeville this afternoon for home. We went to Macon & at 9.50 o'cl. P.M. took the Savannah train.
9   Sunday. Arrived at Savannah about 9 o'cl. this morning—an hour & a half behind time. Stopping at Mrs. McIntosh's. A great deal of rain.
10 Spent the day in Savannah shopping.
11 Took Str. *Lizzie Baker* at 10 o'cl. A.M. Arrived at High Pt. at 3.40 o'cl. & home about 8 P.M.
12 Wednesday. Been ailing most of the day & have done little or nothing. The meningetis is prevailing on the Island & killing a good many negroes. Charlie Bass down with measles.
13 Went hunting this afternoon on Cabareta island. Tom got shots at two deer, but missed.
14 The horses at the gin broke down to-day & we have to rest them. Tom rode his young stallion hunting yesterday. The first time he ever was ridden.
15 We went hunting again to-day—jumped four. Tom & Bourke both had shots & both missed.
16 Sunday. Mrs. Spalding taken sick to-day with the measles. Livingston Kenan also.
17 Been working most of the day at the South end. We are going to fix a butcher pen & room there of a part of the old tabe homestead. Ships &c. arriving at Doboy rapidly—five this morning. I am alone to-night, Sallie staying with her mother. Cloudy and a cold, damp N.E. wind blowing.

18 Still working at the South end. I took up my quarters at Riverside to-night.

19 I went with Bourke to Darien to-day, to get Dr. Kenan to see Mrs. Spalding. I came back sick.

20 Thursday. Sold one beef at Doboy—weight 269 lbs. at 10 cents. Tom's mare Lou died to-day of colic.

21 I had a chill this morning & have been more or less sick ever since. Mrs. Livingston went home to-day & Mollie came down to nurse the sick.

22 Been working nearly all day at the South end, on our butcher pen. Tom carried five bales cotton to High Pt., to ship to Savannah.

23 Sunday. Letters received last night inform us of the birth of Sister Mary Cobb's first daughter, named Mary Ann.

24 Butchered three beeves to-day—one for Doboy @ 10¢ & two for Sapelo Sound @ 12¢.

25 I carried one of the beeves butchered yesterday to High Pt. this morning. On the way I was overtaken by a thunder storm & got wet. Tom took another one of the same beeves to Doboy. Wind S.E. Weather warm & damp.

26 Wednesday. Went to the South end in the forenoon & worked on our butcher pen. In the afternoon we butchered two beeves. High N.W. wind with very cold weather.

27 The two beeves killed yesterday were taken this morning to Doboy by Bourke. This afternoon we all went to the South end & worked on our butcher pen. Weather very cold.

28 We worked at the South end till afternoon, then butchered a beef for High Pt.

29 Tom carried the beef to High Pt. & the rest of us worked at the South end.

30 Sunday. Rode with Mollie to the Livingstons'. After dinner Bourke & I got up a beef to kill tomorrow.

31 Butchered one beef & sent it to Doboy. Bourke & I have been busy getting up cattle & putting them in pasture. Mrs. Spalding's fiftieth birth-day.

APRIL

1 Been busy most of the day driving cows into the pasture. In the afternoon we got an unexpected beef order from Doboy & had to go out & drive them up. Tom & I got caught in a shower & got very wet. Very tired indeed. Sister Sarah's twenty-sixth birth-day.

2 Butchered two beeves this morning & Tom took them to Doboy. I have been white leading our skiff. Bourke was taken down yesterday with measles, & I hear that Sister Sarah also has them, in Athens.

3 Thursday. Gave the skiff one coat of white paint & afterwards butchered a bull—weight 470 lbs.

4 Tom & I took the beef to High Pt. this morning. Rested this afternoon.

5 Been rest day with me & done nothing.

6 Sunday. Another fatal case of meningetis to-day at Behavior. Taken yesterday & died to-day—a negro boy aged about 14 years.

7 Rode up to High Pt. this morning to get some beef bills signed, but was unsuccessful. The sailors and negroes have gutted Mr. Griswold's house up there. Very warm.

8 I went to Darien on beef business—returned about 11 o'cl. P.M. Capt. Scott of the British Bark *Viscount Canning*—a man whom I like returned from England on Sunday—his second trip this Winter. Bad state of feeling between whites & blacks in Darien.

9 Wednesday. Been suffering from a severe head ache all day.

10 Butchered two beeves at the South end this morning— the first time we have used that pen. Sallie attacked with measles to-night.

11 Sallie broken out thick with measles this morning. Showery.

12 I gave our skiff an inside coat of paint & spent the rest of the day nursing Sallie.

13 Sunday. Sallie was very sick last night, but better this morning. To-day is Easter—observed by Episcopalians & Catholics.

14 Sallie a little better this morning.

15 Sent two beeves to Doboy this morning, weighing 652 lbs.

16 Wednesday. My friend Capt. Wm. Scott of the Bark *Viscount Canning* from Applebord, England came to visit me to-day.

17 Butchered two beeves weighing 586 lbs. for Doboy to-day.

18 Friday. We launched our skiff to-day & in the afternoon took her around to the South end to keep there to carry beef to Doboy in. I rowed all the way round—the first long row with sculls.

19 Carried beef to-day to Doboy. Left Tom there to get bills made out & Bourke & I kept on to Darien. Wind ahead & a very hard pull. Found a drowned man in Long Reach. We came back as far as Doboy with Capt. Scott.

20 Sunday. Capt. Scott met us at the Marsh landing & took us down to Capt. Chilcott's ship (*Great Britain*) down below the light. There we took dinner & afterwards went in Capt. S's sail boat to his bark (*Viscount Canning*) & there home—a pleasant day.

21 Butchered a beef for Doboy early this morning. Afterwards Capt. Scott, Capt. & Mrs. Chilcott came ashore & took dinner.

22 Butchered two beeves for Doboy this morning. Bourke's hound Sable was snake bitten this afternoon.

23 Mollie Livingston having been called home by the sickness of her mother, I alone am left to nurse Sallie. I am also resting, for I am tired.

24 Thursday. Most of the people from Riverside & the Livingstons are gone to take dinner on the ship *Great Britain* with Capt. Chilcott. Bourke bought a magnificent Newfoundland dog from the British ship *Thoraldsen* for $12.00. On their return from the ship, the dining party missed their road on the beach, getting home 11.15 P.M.

25 My Father arrived this morning, having come on Str. *San Antonio* & landed at High Pt. at 9 o'cl. A.M.

26 Took my Father down to the South end to see us butcher two beeves for Doboy.

27 Sunday. Took Father out for a drive on the beach. The Livingstons and Kenans went with us. My step-Mother's fifty eighth Birth-day.

28 Butchered one beef for Doboy. Since noon the weather has been quite showery—the first rain in almost a month.

29 My Father having to leave to-day, Tom & I with two hands took him in our skiff to Doboy after dinner, to take Str. *Lizzie Baker* for Savannah via Brunswick. The Sound was very smooth—quite a contrast to what it was when he crossed it six years ago. Weather showery.

30 Butchered two beeves & spent most of the day on Doboy—taking dinner on board the *Viscount Canning* down the Sound with Capt. Scott.

MAY

1 Spent the day at home. Heavy rains last night. The wind has shifted from N.E. yesterday to a stiff southeaster to-day. Cloudy with thunder.

2 Friday. We went deer hunting to-day—jumped one in the Pine barren & I got a shot at Riley Camp, but not knowing the stand I had to shoot too far. Jack's dog bitten by a rattlesnake, but not killed. Wrote to Father on important business.

3 Butchered one beef, weight 257 lbs., for Doboy. After dinner worked in Mr. Bass' garden.

4 Sunday. Got letters last night from Father saying that he had reached Savannah safely.

5 We started to Darien this morning, but the weather looked so threatening that we turned back & before I got home a N.E. rain commenced which lasted nearly all day. I see by the newspaper that Clayton Vaughn, who bought my Walnut Level place, is dead.

6 Butchered two beeves this morning & Bourke took them to Doboy & from there went to town. Finished a sail for the skiff last night. Mollie Livingston has been staying with us since Saturday evening. A very heavy rain at sunset, lasting into the night.

7 Wednesday. Hunted a wild cow all the morning. When I got home I found Capt. Scott here. We went out deer hunting. I shot a doe in Big hammock. Jack shot the same deer.

8 Went hunting again this morning, but killed nothing although we had two long runs. Went to Doboy this evening.

9 Butchered two beeves for Doboy to-day & Tom took them over—weight 590 lbs.

10 Eleven years ago I assisted in raising our company for the Confederate army. Been helping Bourke to mark & castrate his calves. He marked 13 heifer & 9 bull calves—all this year's calves.

11 Sunday. Literally a rest day with me.

12 By appointment we went to Doboy & received from Jas. Abeel $849 for 8490 lbs. of beef sold him—paying out of it a bill of $236.30 for Tom & Bourke & one of $43.48 for myself.

13 Killed two beeves this morning & sent them to Doboy by Bourke, who then went on to Darien.

14 Wednesday. Bourke returned from Darien this afternoon. A good rain later in the afternoon.

15 My little colt "Surprise" has an ugly swelling on her hock, which seems to be a snake bite. It disables her very much. We drove up beef for tomorrow & got caught at the South End by a heavy thunder storm.

16 All the cattle we penned last night were out & gone this morning and we had to get them up again. Butchered two beeves & Bourke took them to Doboy. This evening we all three went to Doboy to try to raise a loan, to enable us to carry on the cattle business, but were unsuccessful. I killed a worthless hound I had to-day. This is the tenth anniversary of the battle of Baker's Creek in Mississippi.

17 Drove a wild cow into the pasture this morning. This after-noon while deer hunting Bourke had his mare "Bess" snake bitten.

18 Sunday. Rode out to the pasture to look after my snake bitten colt. She is getting better. Bourke's mare worse to-day.

19 Worked most of the morning in my little garden. We went out this afternoon & caught two little alligators for Capt. Thomas a British ship Capt. Good rain this evening.

20 I went up to Darien in the skiff this morning with Bourke.
Towed up behind the tug *Keebler* & lost my hat in a squall.

21 Wednesday. We staid all night in Darien & came home this
morning. Slow rain nearly all the afternoon.

22 Butchered two beeves this morning & sent them to Doboy.
This winds up our beef business for this season—we having
killed & sold since the 11th of last December up to this time
fifty six head of cattle.

23 We went to the beach this morning & caught five dozen
crabs. Two Norwegian ship Captains came over to buy a live
oak tree from Tom, which he sold them for $7.00.

24 Tom reshipped to Savannah this morning a horse power he
bought last October and which has proven a failure. Bourke
gone to Darien. I went fishing this morning for the first time
this season—caught two, drum & whiting.

25 Sunday. A boat from the bark *Energie*, Capt. Horn, of Bre-
men came over to-day with two bottles of wine & one of gin,
from the Capt.

26 Worked most of the morning in the garden at Riverside.
Discharged my boy Gib this morning. We took our sail boat
out this evening.

27 My thirty-first birthday (May 27, 1842). We have all been
enjoying it on 1 bottle of imported Martel brandy & two
bottles of imported Claret wine. Busy most of day making
out beef accounts.

28 Wednesday. We have been busy all day settling the beef
business & arranging a division of the cash. Bourke gets
only $84.68 & I get $352. It would have been much more
but our private bills were deducted. We invested $900 &
have made on that since last December $662 net profit, or
73⅝ per cent.

29 I went with Tom & Bourke to Doboy & afterwards aboard
the German barks *Arracan* & *Energie* where the Capts.
(Horn & Rossini) treated us sumptuously—brandy in abun-
dance.

30 Been about home all day with somewhat of a headache from
yesterday's work.

31 Been busy most of the day in my garden, transplanting
okra, pepper & mint. Wind N.E. & weather showery. This

evening & night a regular September gale blowing. Tom & Bourke gone to Darien.

JUNE

1 Sunday. Hammie Wylly & Jas. Dunwoody came down with the boys to-day. After blowing a gale last night the wind is still N.E. & strong & weather very cool & showery.
2 Wind still strong from N.E. A good deal of rain has fallen too to-day. For three days we have had a genuine spell of September weather.
3 Helped Bourke butcher two beeves this morning. Weather moderating. Went out to drive for deer this afternoon. Jas. Dunwoody & I both missed one & Tom's gun snapped at another.
4 Wednesday. Weather very warm. Went driving for deer again this afternoon. Bourke killed a buck in Gum Pond drive.
5 My little niece's (Katie Taylor) ninth birth-day. Bourke & Jas. Dunwoody started for Savannah this morning on the tug boat *Leon*.
6 Set out 13 okra plants this evening. Light shower. I hear that Capt. Thomas & wife of the British barque *Monarch*[3] was wrecked & drowned off the Ga. Coast a few days ago.
7 Helped Bourke to butcher one beef for High Pt. He returned from Savannah this morning. Heard to-day of the death of Mr. William Dunwoody, a lawyer of Darien.
8 Sunday. Last night old Carolina's house caught afire & came very near burning the old negroes (himself & wife) up as neither one could walk. The house burnt down, though they were saved being burnt very seriously however.[4]

3. *Lloyd's List*, June 18, 1873, reported "The master (Thomas) of the MONARCH, from Doboy to Newcastle, which went ashore 31 May in St. Andrew's Sound, is reported to have been lost, together with his wife, mate and four men."

4. Refers to Carolina and Hannah Underwood, listed in the 1870 census as both being 95 years old. They died shortly after the fire. See Ella Barrow Spalding letter in this volume.

9   Helped Bourke butcher a beef for High Pt. Afterwards
    worked in my garden.
10 Drove to the beach this afternoon & got a load of driftwood.
    Bourke took Dr. Kenan to Darien this morning & returned
    about 3 o'cl. P.M.
11 Wednesday. Hammie Wylly went home to-day with Tom
    & Bourke. The two latter went to Darien to attend a meet-
    ing of our cavalry company. Heavy rains on the mainland
    this morning. Slow rain here since about 5 o'clock (now 8½
    o'clock).
12 Tom & Bourke returned from Darien. The latter was elected
    3d Sergeant of our cavalry company. On their way back a
    British Capt. gave them a magnificent liver colored pointer
    dog from Scotland, which they gave me.
13 This would have been poor Sister Kate's thirty-sixth birth-
    day had she lived. The pointer dog which the boys gave me
    yesterday went mad this morning & in self defense I had to
    shoot him. He was the first rabid dog I ever saw. Tonight
    completes the fourth year of my journal.
14 Shortly after day light Capt. Brailsford's boat arrived with
    himself & crew, Mr. Maxwell of St. Catharine's Is., B. B.
    Ferrill & F. O. O'Driscol of Savh. on board—all drink-
    ing, except Mr. M., pretty freely. Hunted most of the day.
    Mr. Maxwell killed a fine buck in Bell drive. Came home
    drenched to the skin.
15 Sunday. The party started for home this morning Bourke
    going with them. Tom & I started to go with them as far as
    High Pt., but after getting there I concluded to go on with
    them. Capt. B. very drunk & sick. After an all days sail with
    a poor breeze, it died out entirely at night & we had to row
    the last ten miles. Reached Capt. Brailsford's place about
    10 o'cl. P.M. thoroughly worn out. I should mention that we
    came in his sloop *Rainbow*.
16 We were so tired that we spent the day resting. The party
    all sobered down.
17 Bourke & I walked over Capt. Brailsford's place with him
    & in the evening the whole party took a ride with him—
    returning at 10 o'cl. P.M.

18 This morning we all sailed down to St. Catharine's Island on a hunt. A young man named Elliott from Savh. killed a fine buck. Capt. B. & myself each missed a deer. Dined with the owner of the Island—a Cuban named Rodriguez—a very nice gentleman.

19 Thursday. Our party, with the exception of Bourke & myself, returned with Brailsford this morning. We stay on the Island to take Steamboat for Sapelo in the morning.

20 Took Steamboat *San Antonio* this morning about sun rise, & reached home about 10 o'clock.

21 Bourke & Lewis went to Darien last night & returned about 12 o'clock to-day. Weather intensely warm. Rains all around, but little here.

22 Sunday. Nothing of interest occurring. Warm.

23 Helped Bourke to butcher his last beef this morning. He sold it for fourteen cents. Afterwards Tom & I went to Little Sapelo & caught three pigs and carried them on board the barque *Arracan*, Capt. Rossini, lying in the Sound, where we sold them for $6.00 and bought three boxes of cigars for $8.00.

24 Drove down with Bourke to Marsh landing. He went to Darien in the skiff by himself. I afterwards drove up to the Livingstons.

25 Wednesday. Been busy most of the day hauling & packing cow hides for shipment. Packed forty-nine hides. Tom has been packing seed cotton to sell in Darien. Bourke has not yet returned & we are uneasy.

26 I have been somewhat sick to-day. Bourke returned to-day. A raft ran into our skiff in Darien & stove in her bow, which detained him, (B).

27 For the past two days we have had another September spell of North East wind & rain. Been setting out millet plants.

28 Wind still N.E. Went hunting on Carbareta Island where we jumped three deer, but they all ran so as to give nobody a shot. Dr. Kenan brought our skiff down to-day.

29 Sunday. A stiff South Easter blowing with an occasional shower.

30 Been busy working on my shrimp net—trying to finish it for this fishing season.

JULY

1 Most of the men from the Island have gone to-day to Darien to attend a special election for county officers. The vessels are nearly all gone from Doboy now—the business season being about ended.

2 Wednesday. The boys returned from the election in Darien this morning.

3 Tom, Bourke & myself went in the skiff this morning to Wolf Island to see the light keeper there & get him to repair our sail boat.

4 We went fishing at Sand Patch (a river between Doboy & Patterson rivers) this morning, but with no luck except one turtle caught by Bourke. I came back home overpowered by hard rowing & heat.

5 Been laid up all day by yesterday's exertion. I bought yesterday one case of [*phonographic alphabet*] Irish [*phonographic alphabet*].[5] Sent 50 cow hides to Savannah to sell.

6 Sunday. Twenty six years ago this afternoon my Mother died. Thunder storm with heavy rain this morning between 12 & 2 o'clock.

7 Tom & Bourke with a hired hand towed our sail boat down to Wolf Island this morning to have her put in good order once more.

8 Tom sent a boat load of short staple & stained cotton to Darien. The same boat brought back 1920 shingles for me. A thunder squall & very heavy blow from N.W. this afternoon.

9 Wednesday. Nineteenth anniversary of the death of my Sister Caroline. I received to-day the first copies of Frank Leslie's Illustrated Newspaper.

10 Tom sent another load of cotton to Darien to-day—or rather he carried one himself.

11 Finished a shrimp net this morning. Mrs. Spalding left on Str. *Lizzie Baker* for Savannah, Tom for Milledgeville & Bourke for Athens.

---

5. The second set of symbols decodes to "whsk"—whiskey. As noted in the Preface, McKinley used the phonographic alphabet occasionally in his journal, presumably for the few things he wished others not to read. This example of *whiskey* is the only one I have been able to interpret with any certainty.

12 Heavy rains both to-day & yesterday. Wind N.E. to-night. Been making estimates for lumber to repair my house.

13 Sunday. Lonely by ourselves. Nothing to record.

14 Been fishing at the landing, but caught very few. Also been hoeing millet.

15 Sallie, Mollie & I went fishing this morning. As Mollie threw her hook in the water it caught in her finger & we had to send for Dr. Kenan to cut it out. We started work this morning on our new vegetable garden.

16 Wednesday. The hands got back from Doboy to-day, bringing me a raft of about 4000 feet of lumber to repair my house with.

17 Went fishing this morning in the skiff to a point just above Little Sapelo. Caught twenty-two very nice pan fish & one bass about two feet long, and more shrimp bait than I could use.

18 Nothing worth recording. I have been busy making me a chair. A very good rain late this afternoon.

19 Finished my chair about dinner time. We are beginning to enjoy our figs & peaches now—though our chickens get most of them. A tolerable shower this afternoon.

20 Sunday. Charlie Bass came down from Darien last night on a visit to us.

21 Charlie's twentieth birth-day. He returned to Darien to-night. We went fishing this morning at Little Sapelo & caught 50 or 60. The twelfth anniversary of the first battle of Manassas. Heavy rain this morning.

22 The ninth anniversary of a big battle near Atlanta in which I was engaged. Commenced repairs on my house yesterday.

23 Wednesday. Been busy most of the day building two pig pens. Wind N.E. with heavy & long continued rains.

24 Carpenter progressing very slowly on my house.

25 Hauled a load of posts for my piazza, from Shell hammock. Mollie Livingston went to Savannah this afternoon.

26 More rain. We hear from Darien that Charlie Bass has lost his clerkship. Got my piazza posts up. Got a lot of garden seed from Philadelphia. Dr. Kenan came down.

27 Sunday. Rode around the pasture to-day. Saw all the horses & about 75 head of cattle. Yesterday a hound puppy arrived

from St. Catharine's Island—sent by William Brailsford to Bourke.

28 Doing nothing but watching the carpenter work on my house.

29 Began shingling my piazza this afternoon & consequently I had to sleep at Riverside.

30 Wednesday. Finished shingling my piazza about noon. Am enjoying some fine watermelons raised by Mr. Bass.

31 Finished shingling the West side of my house to-day. I hear from Milledgeville to-day that my brother William is very ill—threatened with consumption.

AUGUST

1 Went fishing this morning, but caught only six scale fish. Bourke returned from Oglethorpe County, where he had been to visit Ella Barrow to whom he is engaged to be married, this morning.

2 We went to Wolf Island this morning to see about our sail boat, but found that the carpenter had barely begun to work.

3 Sunday. All the men except myself have gone to Mr. Livingston's.

4 Went fishing at the landing—caught about 30 nice fish with the rods. My mare Sallie is four years old to-day.

5 Went fishing at the landing this morning & caught a nice string of fish. Went with Bourke this evening to High Pt. to meet Tom but he did not come—got back home at 12.40 o'cl. last night. Heavy rains this evening.

6 Wednesday. Amuse ourselves fishing at the landing.

7 Hauled another load of piazza posts from Shell hammock, & my shingles from the landing.

8 Went with Bourke to High Point this morning to meet Tom. There we got a message that he would be out on another boat. We came home & afterwards heard that he did come to High Pt. He reached home this afternoon.

9 Went deer hunting this morning. Bourke killed a large buck & a small one. He killed them both in the grass. The first

of the season killed that way. The large one had beautiful horns, which were in velvet.

10 Sunday. Nothing unusual occurring. Weather dry.

11 Tom & I went to the beach this morning to get some sill timber for my house. In afternoon we & Bourke went to Little Sapelo to kill gannets. Bourke killed five. Weather dry.

12 Hear to-day of more cotton caterpillars on the Island. Tom busy making a windmill.

13 Wednesday. Tom, Bourke & Charlie went to Doboy this afternoon & just returned (9 o'cl. P.M.).

14 Nothing unusual occurring to-day. Weather dry still.

15 Tom, Bourke & Charlie went to Wolf Island this morning to see about the sail boat & to carry some more copper to put on her. The carpenter has had her nearly six weeks and has done almost nothing with her.

16 The same crowd with Mr. Livingston went to Darien in the skiff this morning.

17 Sunday. The boys returned from Darien on the pilot boat this afternoon.

18 We went with the pilots this morning at day break in their new schooner *Young America*, to look for the blackfish bank, but could not find them—having gone to the North of them. Spent a very pleasant day indeed—going fifty two miles out. On our return met a squall about twenty miles off Sapelo Sound. Fine wind all day & plenty of swell.

19 Mollie Livingston returned from Savannah this evening.

20 Wednesday. The boys went to Darien this morning before day, in the skiff,

21 and returned last night. My family last night had a light attack of Cholera Morbus. Mollie L., here on a visit, sickest of all. My new bed room, opening on South piazza, nearly finished & I moved in to-day & expect to sleep there to-night for the first time.

22 Went up to High Pt. with Bourke this morning to meet Carl McKinley, whom we expected on the boat, but he did not come. Showery in the early part of the day.

23 Planting Ruta Baga turnips in our market garden this morning. The hottest day of the Summer so far. Light sprinkle of rain this evening.

24 Sunday. Spent island Sunday—reading the papers &c. Wind N.E. for the first time this month.

25 The boys went to Wolf island to look after the sail boat. I paid the carpenter $58.80 for work on my house. So far the house has cost me $146.45. Wind E. to South east.

26 I drove up to High Pt. this afternoon to meet Carl McKinley who came on the Steamer *Lizzie Baker*. Driest weather of the Summer.

27 Wednesday. Tom, Dr. Kenan & Bourke went deer hunting (grass hunt) this morning. Each killed a deer. This afternoon we went to N. Orleans creek for clams & got about a bushel.

28 Nothing unusual occurring to-day.

29 Early this morning Tom was surprised by a visit from Bob Gignilliat, A. S. Barnwell & Sandy Duncan. I took Steamer *Lizzie Baker* at High Pt. at 10 o'cl. P.M. for Savannah.

30 Arrived at Savh. this morning at 10 o'cl. & left for Milledgeville at 1 o'cl. Arrived there about midnight. Stopping at the hotel. Bought a suit of blue flannel in Savh. for $18. Suffering with headache.

31 This Sunday morning I took breakfast at the hotel & then sat out in front & saw my Father's family enter Church, after which I took possession of their carriage & rode out to his house & sent the carriage back for them. Having heard nothing of my coming, they were perfectly [*page bottom eroded*].

SEPTEMBER

1 Found my Father needing rest very much & I was tired so we spent the day at home resting & talking.

2 Spent to-day like we did yesterday. This would have been my Mother's fifty-fifth birth-day if she were living.

3 Wednesday. Drove into Milledgeville this morning with Father. Met several old acquaintances, who seemed glad to see me. Have almost succeeded in selling my house & lot in Milledgeville for $2500.

4 Spent the day in the country, free & easy.

5 Received letter from home (Sapelo) this morning containing bad news, viz. that Tom & Bourke have sold ourselves to work for Bob Gignilliat for $600 a year for six years. At least they have made a beef trade with him that amounts to that.

6 My wife's twenty-ninth birth-day to-day. I drove into Milledgeville with Father.

7 Sunday. We all got ready this morning to go to Church, but it was so late that we were afraid of being laughed at & did not go.

8 I expect to leave on the R. Rd. this evening on my way home via Savannah. Left Milledgeville about six o'cl. P.M.

9 Arrived (with my brother Andrews who is going home with me) in Savh. at six o'cl. this morning. We started on Str. *Lizzie Baker* at 11 o'cl. A.M., but owing to bad tides & high N.E. wind, up to mid-night, we have not reached Sapelo.

10 Wednesday. We reached High Pt. at 1 o'cl. A.M. where we found that the negro who had come to meet us had got scared & gone home. We had therefore to walk as far as Kenan's through rain & wet grass. Find all well at home.

11 I find our sail boat at home once more & looking very pretty though she leaks rather badly. Sallie bought in Savh. a toy barometer or weather house, for $2 & we set it up yesterday. Weather clearing up. Arny seems to be enjoying his visit. Bourke put a wheel on the sail boat, to steer with, to-day.

12 All of us but Tom went in the sail boat first to the Livingstons', then to Doboy (where I bought a case of Irish Whiskey), then on board the Br. bk. *Recovery* of Liverpool, where we had a very good smoke & a drink.

13 Helped Bourke to kill a beef this morning, which he sold to the ships at an average of 11 cents.

14 Sunday. Dressed up & played the gentleman while sleeping[?].

15 During the night the wind shifted to about North, with a good deal of rain.

16 Tom's twenty-sixth birth-day. All but him & Charlie went to Darien. Sailed the entire distance in three hours. Bought a pair of martingales.

17 Wednesday. Got back from Darien this morning at 1 o'clock. Shortly after our return the wind freshened from N.E. & a good deal of rain fell during the night & day.

18 Went out to the beach for a load of timber to build a wharf with. Very warm.

19 Commenced our wharf this morning. Went to the beach for another load of timber. Wind blowing a gale from S.E. all the afternoon, with a good deal of rain.

20 Went to Little Sapelo fishing, caught thirty scale fish. My brother Andrews had a chill on the way.

21 Sunday. We all went in the sail boat to Dr. Kenan's. Wind N.E., stiff & rising.

22 Wind still N.E. & stiff. All the boys, except myself & Arny, went to Doboy to build a raft. Just as much wind as the sail boat could well carry. Arny pretty sick all day.

23 Went to Doboy with the others and helped to make rafts of lumber all day.

24 Wednesday. Went to Doboy again to-day to work on rafts. Bourke & I [*phonographic alphabet*] Sapelo.

25 All the young men, except myself, went deer hunting in the pine barren. My brother Andrews killed his first deer in the upper drive. First fog of the season this morning.

26 We took my cousin Carlyle McKinley over to Doboy this evening to take Str. *Lizzie Baker* for Savannah. It rained on us most of the way.

27 Our boat went to Darien to-day. The party spoken of on the 5th inst. released us from the contract to-day, not being able to raise the money.

28 Sunday. Having been released from the contract mentioned yesterday, the question now is, what are we to do next?

29 Having decided that, as Father had sold my Milledgeville house for $2200, it was best for me to be near a telegraph office. Bourke, Charlie Bass, Andrews & myself left the Island this morning at 9 o'clock in our sail boat for Brunswick. We had very little wind and most of the way tide against us, but at 11 o'clock at night we anchored about three miles below Brunswick and slept the rest of the night.

30 Ran up to Brunswick this morning at 9 o'clock & spent most of the day in telegraphing & receiving answers. Took dinner

& spent the night at William Nightingale's. Heavy rains this afternoon & night.

OCTOBER

1 We reached Brunswick yesterday and this morning at 5½ o'clock I parted from my company, I on my way to Milledgeville & they to Sapelo. After a tedious ride all day I reached Macon to-night at 8 o'clock, & stopped for the night at the Brown House.

2 Thursday. Left Macon about six o'cl. this morning & reached Milledgeville at 8.15 o'cl.

3 Walked into Milledgeville this afternoon. Very warm.

4 Sold my house & lot in Milledgeville this morning for $2200 payable in thirty days by Chauncey M. Wright, P. M. Compton security. Collected three months' rent ($62.50) from T. T. Windsor.

5 Sunday. All the family went to Church except my Father & myself.

6 Walked to town this morning. Left Milledgeville about dark on my way home. Father travelled with me as far as No. 13 on the Central R. Rd.

7 Reached Savannah about day light and went down to the Str. *Lizzie Baker* at 9½ o'cl. but owing to a high West wind the Capt. would not start till about 4 P.M.

8 Wednesday. Reached Doboy at 1 o'clock this morning & got a negro to put me across to the Island in a canoe, reaching home at day light. Landed at Marsh Landing.

9 While in Savannah I bought a two gallon water keg for use in the sail boat.

10 I went to Darien with some of the others in the sail boat. Had no wind & had to row all the way, reaching there after midnight. Strained my right wrist in rowing.

11 My brother William's twenty second birth-day. Reached home about 9 o'cl. at night.

12 Sunday. A little excitement over Tom's recovery of a dirk stolen from him by a negro man named Jim.

13 Tom & Bourke went hunting—the former killed a doe. I have been picking my garden cotton. Been suffering with my strained wrist.

14 All the young men except myself went to Darien this afternoon. Wind N.E., but the weather is exceedingly pleasant.

15 Wednesday. The boys returned from Darien last night. I brought my mare Kate up to-day to fatten her—get her ready for hard work. Bought 50 bus. corn from Lewis Livingston, at $1 per bus. payable in 30 days.

16 Took a long ride nearly all over the pasture to-day. Tom busy taking the measurement of his land in cultivation this year. Wind N.E. but dry.

17 Tom & Bourke went hunting but did not even see a deer. I have been writing letters about cattle &c. Wind N.E., but still clear weather.

18 Lewis Livingston delivered 20 of the 50 bushels of corn I bought on the 15th. Bourke & Charlie returned from Darien, where they went last night. Wind still N.E. Weather clear & warm. Fished at the landing.

19 Sunday. Warm all day. Wind S.W. After dark a good deal of rain, followed by high W. wind.

20 Weather clear this morning with very high W. wind & very cold—making fires necessary to comfort. Thermometer 42°, but no frost on account of wind. [*Marginal note:* First fire of the season]

21 We all went deer hunting this morning, but for the first time in many months we did not even jump a deer. Weather clear & cold.

22 Wednesday. Been making a rack to haul fodder in. A slight frost this morning, but the weather has moderated, as regards cold, since then.

23 On the water & at Doboy all day, helping to bring a raft of lumber over, which we made a month or more ago.

24 We unloaded our raft this evening—dirty work it was too. Arny & Tom been making a wind mill. Weather warm.

25 The mate of a ship lying in Sapelo Sound came down this evening, looking for beef.

26 I went with Bourke aboard the ship *Thorwaldsen* at High Pt. Spent the morning there.

27 Monday. Killed a small beef this morning. I took it to High Pt. this afternoon. We are selling it there at 12¢ per lb. The other boys went to Doboy to look after a ship Capt. who stole some live oak yesterday.

28 Went to Darien in the sail boat. Towed up behind the tug *Staples*. Got there about 10 o'cl. P.M.

29 Wednesday. Started home this morning against the flood, but our mast broke in N. & S. reach & we had to put back to town and cut it down. Got home about 11.30 o'cl. at night. Weather clear & very cold. Wind N.

30 Killed a beef this afternoon for Doboy. Weather cool & pleasant.

31 Charlie & I hauled lumber & posts to the South end for our butcher pen, Tom went to High Pt. to engage beef & Bourke carried yesterday's beef to Doboy. First killing frost of the season.

NOVEMBER

1 Got up before day & helped to butcher a beef at the South end for High Pt. Tom & I then went out to look up cattle said to have gotten out of the pasture.

2 Sunday. Been enjoying a rest day after hard work.

3 Arny & Tom hauled posts from Shell hammock, Bourke & Charlie drove cows from Raccoon Bluff & I added two wings to our slaughter pen. Made an arrangement with Billy Hillery for one of his boys to give me two hours a day of his time at $1.00 per month.

4 All the men except Mr. Bass & I went to Darien & carried a beef to Doboy at the same time.

5 Wednesday. An order for beef to High Point came unexpectedly last night & as no one was here to fill it but me, I had to hire hands & butcher to-day & carry the beef up. It rained on me all the way going & coming. The boys have not returned yet.

6 The boys have not returned from Darien yet. Weather cloudy & threatening. Wind N.E.

7 The boys returned at 2 o'cl. this A.M. having been caught
   last night in a tremendous rain, wetting everything in the
   boat. They report a terribly hard trip all round. Butchered a
   beef for Doboy this evening.

8 Tom gone to Darien. Bourke, Arny & I butchered a calf for
   Doboy shipping this morning. B. & I went to Blackbeard to
   see Capt. Brailsford and returned at 10 o'clock tonight.

9 Sunday. I took the Steamer *M. S. Allison* at High Pt. about
   10 o'clock this morning on my way to Savh. Reached there
   12½ o'cl. at night.

10 Expected to have found some money at the Express office,
   from Father, but was disappointed. Took dinner with
   Jno. M. McIntosh.

11 Met Sister Sarah, Katie Taylor & Lizzie White at the
   depot—on their way to Sapelo. The former brought me the
   money for my house in Milledgeville. Took Steamer *Lizzie
   Baker* & all got off at Doboy at 7.30 o'clock. Tom met us
   with the sail boat there.

12 Wednesday. Butchered a beef this afternoon for Doboy.
   Weather blown off this evening quite cold.

13 Tom & Charlie carried the beef we killed yesterday to
   Doboy this morning. Very high West wind.

14 We started to Darien to-day, but on account of no wind, the
   tug *Starlight* towed us & the pilot boat up to town.

15 We slept aboard the pilot boat last night & got supper &
   breakfast there. I got my groceries that I bought in Savannah the other day. Tom having heard that the man who
   treated him so badly on March 11th, 1872 was in Savh.,
   he has put the case in the hands of a lawyer. Towed down
   behind the *Starlight*.

16 Sunday. We all (except Sallie & Mrs. S.) & Lewis &
   Mollie L. went to the beach. On the 14th I paid Lewis
   Livingston $50 for corn bought on the 15th Oct. Some rain
   after dark.

17 This morning at 1.30 o'cl. had heavy thunder storm accompanied by almost a hurricane from S.W. Clearing up to-day
   with exceedingly high W. wind & cold. Killed a beef to-day
   for bk. *Howard*, but the wind was too strong to carry it over.
   Tom by mistake killed the calf of his fine milk cow.

18 Tom & Charlie carried the beef to Doboy. Wind very strong. My colt "Surprise" came up this morning with her whole right breast torn off by a snag. Tom found this evening that he had not killed his pet calf.

19 Wednesday. To-day is the seventh anniversary of my marriage. It has been an exceedingly blustering & cold day with N.W. wind. Notwithstanding the cold however, I saw a black snake out this morning.

20 Very cold indeed last night & to-day. This morning the mercury marked, in my dining room at 7 o'clock, 18°. Bourke returned from Bryan Co. to-day, bringing with him four goats.

21 Weather moderated a little & clear. This morning the thermometer in my dining room marked 35°. Went hunting on Cabaretta, but jumped nothing.

22 Went early this morning with Tom & Bourke & hauled two loads of wood. This afternoon we killed a beef for home consumption.

23 Sunday. All of them at the other house went up to the Livingstons'. Some rain.

24 All of us younger men went to Blackbeard this morning to meet Capt. Brailsford & hunt. We had 15 hounds & ten standers, but the incessant hard rain broke up the hunt. Only Lewis killed a deer. With rain & wading ponds we returned thoroughly drenched.

25 Bourke & I started with three hands, to Darien for a flat. Put a stove in our sail boat, which added much to our comfort.

26 Wednesday. Left Darien with the flat about 2 o'cl. P.M. Lost the tide at Doboy & had to tie up & sleep all night in the flat.

27 Left Doboy about day break & reached home about 12 M. It commenced to rain about 11 o'cl. last night & has continued without cessation till dark to-day, with a cold N. wind. I was in it all night & half to-day & so got another thorough drenching—Bourke also. Carr (the Darien hotel Keeper) came down with two friends to hunt on the Island.

28 Butchered two beeves & went hunting with the men spoken of yesterday, but jumped nothing.

29 Went hunting again to-day—jumped two but killed none.
Our visitors left this afternoon. Carr is a very clever man,
but the other two are "pizen" Yankees.[6] Cloudy, cold &
wind North.
30 Sunday. My Father's sixty fourth birth-day. Everybody
from the other house, except Mrs. S. and Mr. Bass, went to
Church on the Ridge to-day.

DECEMBER

1 Been hard at work to-day building a cow pen and driving up
cows. Weather very pretty with N.E. winds.
2 Tom has been driving up cattle all day, the firm having
bought Bourke's stock. He drove up 64. I have to go to
Darien to-night to attend Superior Court tomorrow, as a
petit juror.
3 Wednesday. Arrived in Darien early this morning & attended Court. Did not need a jury on the civil docket all
day. We got Bourke excused & he started to Valdosta for
cattle.
4 The judge commenced the Criminal docket to-day, but I
was not needed.
5 I had to sit as a juror to-day on the case of a negro, Joe Des-
verger, charged with stealing a cow—found him guilty &
sent to the penitentiary for two years.
6 Court adjourned this afternoon till the 3d Monday in January. Tom & I came home with Caesar Sams.
7 Sunday. Reached home at 3 o'clock this morning & rested
to-day.
8 Killed two beeves for Doboy & one for High Pt. Tom & I
took it to Doboy tonight, returning at about 12 o'cl. This is
my brother Andrews' twentieth birth-day.
9 Nothing unusual occurring to-day.
10 Wednesday. Tom & I with the help of Arny, Charlie, Lewis
& two hired hands took our horses in a flat to Darien to go
after cattle.

6. A deliberately colloquial spelling of *poison*, *pizen* seems to show
McKinley's distaste for Yankees.

11 We staid in Darien to-day.

12 I & Lee Underwood carried three horses to Johnson Station on the A. & G. R. R.[7], to meet Bourke & the cattle. Left Tom in Darien to perfect arrangements for flatting them down.

13 Bourke arrived this morning at the Station with about 106 head of cattle. We drove them out to Mr. Baggs (three miles) to wait for another carload to-morrow. We sent by express to H. F. Grant (Savannah) $50.00 to pay for a double buggy which we have bought. Rain this afternoon, at night clearing off cold.

14 Sunday. Owing to the gross negligence of the conductor, our car load of cattle was carried on to Savannah & I had to leave Bourke to follow them. I with Lee & 2 hired hands left Baggs' at 9 o'cl. A.M. with 100 head, but had to leave two calves that could not keep up with Baggs. We made Mrs. Amos'—15 miles, to-night.

15 Left Mrs. Amos' at 7 o'cl. A.M. & reached Darien about 4 o'cl. Had great trouble from Mallard's to town on account of swamps—the cattle persistently taking to them. My drove of cattle created quite a sensation in Darien. We put them in Dr. Kenan's office lot.

16 Bourke arrived in Darien about 2 o'cl. with 32 head (those carried to Savannah) & 1 that I lost on the road. Got the two herds aboard a tremendous flat 60 × 30 feet & got the tug *J. R. Staples* to tow us down for $40. Left Darien about 8½ o'cl. & reached the South point of beach near 12 o'cl. at night.

17 Owing to the flat gunwales being so high, it was exceedingly difficult to get the cattle out after we landed. We worked nearly all night all day. During the night I had an attack of rheumatism, caused by working in the water, which disabled me entirely almost. During the day we became so exhausted that we had to send home for extra help.

18 Thursday. Killed a beef for High Pt. which I carried up—weight 205 lbs. Owing to the immense size of our cattle flat, we did not get her a float so as to send her back to Darien to-day.

7. Properly, the Savannah, Albany, and Gulf Railroad.

19 We at last got our flat afloat & off for Darien alongside the
    tug. Driving & flatting the cattle to the Island has been
    altogether the most exhausting & tiresome work I ever did
    in my life.

20 Killed one beef for Doboy & Tom & the boys took it over.
    My rheumatism very painful. Bourke went to Darien last
    night on the tug, to pay bill &c. On the 17th inst. we hired
    a white man named Louis Ammon for one month.

21 Sunday. Literally & emphatically a day of rest. Bourke
    returned last night.

22 Killed one beef this morning for High Pt. Wind N.E.
    Weather cloudy & stormy.

23 Nothing unusual occurring to-day.

24 Killed two beeves & sent them to F. J. Wilkinson butcher
    on Doboy. Late in the afternoon got an order for two more
    tomorrow, but could not find the cattle. Most of us went up
    to spend the evening at Dr. Kenan's. Our horses arrived
    from Darien to-night.

25 Christmas. Thursday. Sat up all night long at Kenan's & was
    out by day dawn hunting cattle. Killed two for Abeel. Wet,
    cold and stormy all day & I have been in it all.

26 Went with Bourke & the beef to Doboy. Cold & clear
    with high W. wind. Got an order for three beeves tomor-
    row. Killed two of them this evening. Tired & pretty well
    broken down.

27 We intended to butcher one beef this morning but the
    weather was so bad that we did not. Raining early this A.M.
    High N.W. wind later & blowing off. Bourke & the boys
    came from Doboy in 50 minutes—though they had to lash
    the gaff to the mast. Sound very rough. Took Christmas
    dinner at Riverside.

28 Sunday. I had hoped that this would be a rest day with me,
    but orders for three beeves in the morning deprive me of
    most of my rest—having to drive up cattle this afternoon.
    Arnie went to High Pt. to take Steamer on his way home,
    but she would not send ashore for him & he returned.

29 This morning we found all our cattle out & gone, so we had
    to drive up again. Killed two for Doboy & one for High Pt.
    Got an order for three more in the morning for Doboy &

had to drive up this afternoon. Hard work has commenced
in earnest.

30 Sister Mary Cobb's twenty-ninth birth-day. The sail boat
went to Darien, carrying Mollie Livingston, Lizzie White,
May Holmes, H. C. Wylly, Arny, Lewis Livingston, Charlie
Bass & Bourke. Some returning home and some going
to a Masonic ball to-morrow night. I got a little rest this
afternoon for the first time in a long while.

31 Wednesday. The sail boat returned from Darien this afternoon, bringing from Doboy orders for four beeves tomorrow. I had consequently to mount my horse and go for
cattle. Riding most of the afternoon and then did not get up
all the cattle we wanted. The weather for a week past has
been quite cold. This day ends the year 1873—a year that
has brought its pleasures and its sorrows. In some respects it
has been a very sad year to me. But thank God I have been
permitted to see it through.

1874

JANUARY

1   Thursday. We butchered four beeves this morning & the
    boat took them to Doboy & then kept on to Darien. I have
    been riding all afternoon—looking up cattle. Weather
    moderating.
2   The boat returned from Darien, bringing the party who
    went to the Masonic ball. Drove up beef this afternoon.
3   Killed & sent to Doboy two beeves. This is Sister Sarah's
    third anniversary of her wedding. Weather very warm.
4   Sunday. A good deal of rain, in showers, during the day.
5   Commenced to build a butcher pen around the barn &
    butchered the two first beeves in the barn. Wind N.E., rain.
6   Dense fog. In taking the beef to Doboy this morning we
    had to steer across the Sound by the compass. I started for
    Savh., but the fog was so dense that the Steamer bound
    South could not come. During the morning the Str. *Lizzie
    Baker* came along disabled & towed by the tug *Keebler*.
    I got aboard the former and ran as far as Sapelo High Pt.
    tonight & anchored.
7   Wednesday. The tug is also towing a barkentine disabled
    at Fernandina. We started about 9 o'cl. A.M. & went as far
    as St. Catharine Sound where we anchored. A tremendous
    wind blowing from N.W. Weighed anchor at 9 o'cl. P.M. &
    run about 20 miles.
8   We ran up to Rommney Marsh this morning & then the tug
    dropped the *Baker* & attempted to take the bark through the
    marsh & both stuck. In the evening the Str. *Allison* came
    along & she too stuck in the marsh. I then left the *Baker* and

went aboard the *Allison*. She floated about 9 o'cl. P.M. & we got under way for Savannah.

9   Reached Savannah this morning at 2 o'clock. Left there about 8 o'cl. A.M. on the C. R. R. for Milledgeville, where I arrived about 11 o'cl. at night.

10   Wrote home to my wife & spent the day out at my Father's house.

11   Sunday. Did not go to Church.

12   Got Father to draw up some law papers, on which we want to raise some money from Uncle Frank Upson,[1] & sent them to Darien for signatures.

13   Raining most of the day, so I staid all day at Father's.

14   Wednesday. Wrote home to my wife.

15   Nothing of interest occurring.

16   Spent most of the day in Milledgeville.

17   Left Milledgeville this morning and arrived at Athens about 5 o'clock P.M. Very cold weather.

18   Sunday. Much to my surprise, I find that Howell Cobb is in Macon. Weather intensely cold.

19   Very cold weather still.

20   Weather changed to very warm.

21   Wednesday. Howell returned from Macon this afternoon.

22   Nothing of interest occurring.

23   Went calling with Sister Mary.

24   Spent most of the day down town at Howell's office.

25   Sunday. Went to Church for the first time in about 18 months.

26   Left Athens & got to Lexington this morning. Uncle Frank Upson gave me a check for $5000. We [are] giving a mortgage on Big & Little Sapelo. Cousin Carrie Robinson married Wm. A. Graham of Texas tonight.

27   Left Lexington this morning about 8 o'clock & reached Augusta at 3.45 P.M. Stopped at Planters Hotel.

28   Wednesday. Got Uncle Frank's check cashed at the Ga. R. R. Bank. I meet here my cousin W. H. McKinley. Left Augusta about 8 o'clock tonight for Savannah.

29   Reached Savannah about 7 o'clock this morning & left there at 5 o'clock this evening.

1. Of Lexington, Ga., married McKinley's aunt Sarah Serena McKinley.

30 Reached Doboy, coming on the Str. *Carrie,* at 5 o'clock this morning. Our boat came for me during the day & I reached home about 4 o'clock this afternoon.

31 Rode, with Tom, out to the beach to-day. Saw 58 head of cattle.

FEBRUARY

1 Sunday. Walked down to York landing. Bourke is preparing to build his home there.

2 Raining too much to attend to any outdoor work. Busy bringing up my accounts.

3 Bourke went to Darien to-day in the sail boat. I have been hauling wood.

4 Wednesday. Tom & I, with help, have been driving cattle all day. The former killed a rattlesnake on the beach—eight rattles. It is one year at 4 o'clock this afternoon since Sister Kate died.

5 Killed one beef for Jas. Abeel, Doboy. Bourke took it over, and Tom & I repaired the pasture fence & turned 86 head of cattle into the pasture. Tom sold a live oak tree to Capt. Stoesen of ship *Velox,* for $10.00.

6 Went with Tom to Raccoon bluff for fodder. Bought 504 lbs. from Prince Carter & 290 lbs. from Sally More. Rained on us most of the way home.

7 I had an attack of Cholera Morbus this morning before day & have been quite sick from it ever since.

8 Sunday. It commenced to rain last night about 9 o'clock & rained continuously for over 18 hours. One of the stormiest days I ever saw. The wind blew a gale from N. this afternoon.

9 Weather clearing up. Bourke commenced with his carpenters on his house to-day.

10 Tom & I burnt a good part of Old Marsh and Big Marsh to-day, to make the young grass spring quicker, for the cattle.

11 Wednesday. Butchered one beef this morning for Abeel, which Old Billy carried to Doboy.

12 Been driving cattle a good deal to-day for butchering tomorrow. The Atwoods of Baisden Bluff are selling beef at Doboy.

13 Carried one beef to Doboy & then went with Bourke to Darien, where I filed a sworn excuse for being absent from last Court as a Petit juror. Started back about 8 o'cl. tonight.

14 Valentine's day. Raining most of the day. Tom & I got very wet hauling wood. Bourke has a new tenant on Little Sapelo—a white man named Hooker, with a large family. He moved there yesterday.

15 Sunday. My brother Guy's sixteenth birth-day. Rain most of the day. Weather warm.

16 Tom & I, with Ammons' help, built a bridge on the beach road & hauled a load of wood. Paid Bourke $300 part pay for his cattle.

17 Bourke left for Savannah to-day, via Darien & by the overland route. He goes to pay off some notes we owe for cattle, & to buy things for his own house which he is building at York Landing.

18 Wednesday. Nothing unusual occurring.

19 Went out with Ammons & hauled two loads of live oak stumps for wood to burn.

20 Nothing unusual to-day except some plain talk between [*phonographic alphabet*].

21 Having heard that Capt. Brailsford & a party were on Blackbeard, Tom & I went over & took a hunt with him. The party killed one deer. He (B.) brought us down a double buggy which we bought last December. Bourke returned from Savh. via Darien to-night.

22 Sunday. Nothing unusual occurring.

23 The party from Blackbeard came over & hunted with us. Had 11 hounds in the woods & their cry was magnificent. Brailsford killed two deer & Bourke one. Bourke's twenty third birth-day.

24 Killed one beef for ships at Doboy @ 11¢. The party tried to hunt, but the wind being from the wrong quarter & blowing almost a gale, they went back to Blackbeard.

25 Wednesday. Tom, who carried the beef to Doboy yesterday got weatherbound & returned this morning. Killed two beeves for Doboy.

26 Tom & Ammons took the beef to Doboy this morning &
then kept on to Darien, from whence they returned after
midnight tonight with a load of corn shipped from Savh.

27 Busy this morning hauling wood. Busy most of the afternoon
driving up cattle (Ammons & I) to butcher tomorrow. The
negroes are very busy fencing New Orleans, Abram & Oakdale fields. I had a large hog killed this morning, but since
then the weather has turned warm & I fear that I will lose
most of it.

28 Butchered one beef this morning & Bourke & Tom took
it to the shipping at Doboy—Bks. *Idiria* & *Ottawa*. We
sell there at 11 cents. I planted 311 hills of early sugar corn
to-day. Weather Springlike & very warm.

MARCH

1 Sunday. Weather has turned off very warm & vegetation
is putting on its Spring look very rapidly. Some rain this
afternoon.

2 Tom & I drove up 42 head of cattle from Oakdale marsh.
Bourke brought down some lumber from Herd's Island for
his house.

3 Butchered two beeves for Doboy—one for Abeel & one for
the shipping. Weather warm.

4 Wednesday. Started to killing beeves before dawn this
morning. Killed one for Abeel & 2 for the shipping. Afterwards I went out to the beach & with help, drove up 52
head of cattle.

5 Butchered two beeves this morning for Doboy. Afterwards
we baled 40 cow hides—preparatory to shipping them.
Weather cool & cloudy. Wind N.E. & stiff.

6 Tom & I drove up cattle this afternoon to butcher in the
morning. We sent to Darien to-day by Mr. Hooker's boat 3
bales or 55 dry flint cow hides, to go to Savannah Sunday on
Str. *Carrie.*

7 Butchered three beeves for the shipping at Doboy. Sold 11
quarters of it, but could not sell the 12th quarter & brought
it home.

8   Sunday. Sallie spent the day with the Livingstons & I kept house at home.

9   Tom, Bourke & I went to Darien to collect two beef bills. Engaged 200 head of cattle @ $12 per head, deliverable next month by a man named Fulton. I bought a handsaw.

10   Killed two beeves—one for High Pt. & 1 to carry to Doboy tomorrow. The Legislature has just passed a game law for this county—with a $500 fine or 6 months imprisonment for killing or trapping deer, turkey & partridge between April 1st & October 1st. Sandflies getting very troublesome.

11   Wednesday. What commenced as a pretty Spring day turned out wet & disagreable. Bourke started to Darien but turned back on account of weather.

12   Went with Bourke to the beach & Riley Camp for cattle, had great difficulty in driving them, they being as wild as bucks. Weather cold.

13   Tom carried beef to Doboy & I took some in the buggy to Chocolate to send to ship *Oriental* at Dog Island. Took Sallie and Katie with me. Had a pleasant ride. A decided frost this morning.

14   I went with the boat this morning to deliver beef. We intended going to town but having eight quarters of beef to deliver aboard as many ships, we did not have daylight enough left to finish the trip.

15   Sunday. Mr. Bass & Miss Lizzie White went to High Pt. to take boat for Savh., but no boat coming along they had to return.

16   Butchered one beef for High Pt. & 1 for Doboy this morning & 3 for Doboy this afternoon. Quite a business day with us. High S.E. wind all day. The bark *Viscount Canning*, Capt. Scott, of Bristol, E. arrived in this port this afternoon.

17   Heavy rain with thunder this morning before day light. Tom & Bourke took the beef to Doboy. They started in almost a gale of wind from S.E., but it moderated before they got to the Sound. Sailed under single reef.

18   Wednesday. Hammie Wylly arrived last night. This morning three porpoises came up the creek & we had three shots but did not get one. Butchered two beeves for tomorrow.

19 Went to Doboy with Bourke to deliver beef. The ebb running out against us was the strongest I ever saw. Went aboard the *Viscount Canning* to see Capt. Scott, where we drank three bottles of champagne—the whole party of 5 or 6.

20 Capt. Scott came over & took dinner with me. After he left we butchered three beeves for Doboy tomorrow. Weather warm—wind S.E. & strong.

21 Tom & I took twelve quarters of beef to Doboy but the weather having turned warm, we found it difficult to get some of the Capts. to take what they had ordered. My mare Kate gave birth to-day to a colt which I shall call Mary.

22 Sunday. To-day was enlivened by a visit of the Capts. of the ships *Hamburg, Saturn, Huron* & *Gens Brandi*, to Tom.

23 Miss Lizzie White & Mr. Bass left for Savannah yesterday morning. We butchered one beef for Doboy & one for High Point.

24 I have been busy working on a fence near the barn. Bourke took the beef to Doboy & Tom to Chocolate. Wind N.E. Some rain. Cool.

25 Wednesday. Weather cold, with a slow N.E. rain. Tom, Bourke & I finished our fence, drove up cattle & butchered four beeves by 6.05 o'cl. this evening. Charlie went to town this morning.

26 Charlie not getting back last night, Tom & Bourke had to take the beef over in the *Rebecca*. I carried beef to High Point. Heavy rains and we all throughly drenched. Charlie returned this morning.

27 Butchered two beeves for Doboy to-day. Weather cleared up warm.

28 Tom took the beef over to Doboy. I have been busy all morning writing—agreement with Fulton about cattle. Bad headache compelling me to take to my bed in the afternoon.

29 Sunday. Been sickish all day. My mare Kate brought her colt up home this evening for the first time.

30 We turned the old gin house into a wagon house to-day, putting the engine in too. Finished the fence near the Barn & afterwards butchered three beeves.

31 We all went with the beef to Doboy to-day & staid there
all day waiting for Mr. Bass who came on the *Lizzie Baker*
from Savannah. Bourke went to Darien on a tug to collect
beef bills.

APRIL

1 Sister Sarah's twenty seventh birth-day. Tom & I drove up
and butchered three beeves. Charlie went to Doboy to meet
Bourke. Light rain. Weather warm.

2 Thursday. Tom & Charlie took beef to Doboy & I took some
to High Point.

3 We got up about 100 head of cattle this afternoon & butchered four beeves.

4 I took some beef to Chocolate while the others took more
to Doboy. Sallie & Katie Taylor went with me to Chocolate.
Planted ten rows of okra seed to-day. Weather yesterday
almost cold enough for frost. My mare Sallie gave birth to
her first colt to-day.

5 Sunday. Weather still cool but getting warmer. Wind N.E.
Tom left for Savh. to buy beef cattle. Had six ship Capts.
visiting us to-day.

6 Started out with Bourke soon after breakfast & drove up
about 80 head of cattle. We butchered five beeves in the
afternoon.

7 Started for Doboy with Bourke to carry the beef, before day
light. Staid at & around Doboy delivering beef all day—
getting home at 11 o'cl. at night. [*Phonographic alphabet*]
Capt. Scott. Tom returned from Savannah, bringing with
him six Tennessee beeves, which he left at Chocolate.

8 Wednesday. Bourke, I & our man Ammons went to Chocolate this morning for our new beeves. They are beauties
certain, ranging from 900 to 1177 lbs. on foot. Cost in Savh.
$4.75 per hundred—$4 freight apiece. We butchered the
two highest this afternoon.

9 All but myself went to Doboy with the beef. I hauled hides
& rigged me up a hammock which Capt. Scott had made
for me. Rain from S.E. most of the afternoon. We sell our
Tennessee beef at 12½¢ pr. lb.

10 Killed two of our Savannah beeves this afternoon for Doboy shipping.

11 Tom & Charlie carried the beef to Doboy. I rode up to High Pt. to collect the *Oriental*'s beef bill, but did not see the Capt.

12 Sunday. A day of much needed rest with me. Three ship Capts. came over on a visit.

13 Killed the last two of our Tennessee beeves & two of our old stock besides.

14 Tom & I went to High Pt. to get some beeves off the Steamer, but were disappointed, as they did not come. Bourke took the beef to Doboy & then went to Darien.

15 Wednesday. Killed five of our old stock of cattle to-day. A hard day's work.

16 Tom carried the beef to Doboy this morning. I forgot to say that on the 11th inst. we got our new sail for our boat. We got it made up by the sail maker on the British Bk. *Viscount Canning*.

17 Got up at 1 o'cl. A.M. and went with Bourke to High Pt., hoping that the Steamer *Carrie* would bring us some beef cattle from Savannah, but we were again disappointed. We afterwards drove up 122 head of our old stock & killed six— making 15 beeves killed this week. This is our heaviest week's work yet. Capt. Scott & his friend Capt. McClellan, Bk. *King's County*, came over to-day & bought beef & hides.

18 Went down to the Bk. *Viscount Canning* below the light house & staid till morning & then loaded the boat with beef at the South end. A bright day turned into a N.E. rain. On the 16th inst. I bought Sallie a Brazilian parrot for $10, off the Bark *St. Croix*.

19 Sunday. As the butchers in Savh. can't be trusted to send us beef regularly, Bourke had to go on there to-day to buy some.

20 Killed & butchered six beeves to-day for the Doboy market. On the 18th inst. we turned loose on Cabarita eight head of hogs.

21 Tom carried the beef to Doboy & I went to High Pt. to meet Bourke on the Steamer. He brought out 9 Tennessee beeves. In jumping them off the Steamer, one swam under the wheel & by an untimely turn of it was killed. He cost us nearly $60.00.

22 Wednesday. Killed two Tennessee beeves for Doboy. The Atwoods on the mainland are trying to crowd us out of the market. Shipped to H. F. Grant—Savh.—by sloop *Rebecca Hertz*, Hagan Master, fifty four (54) dry flint cow hides.

23 Bourke and Charlie took the beef to Doboy. I am sick—threatened with bilious fever.

24 I am still sick. Killed three Tennessee & one Georgia beef for Doboy.

25 All the boys went with the beef to Doboy. Shortly after they left, the wind which was blowing rather stiff from S.E., veered around to S.W. & blew almost a gale. They have not returned yet (9 o'cl. P.M.). Later—11 o'cl. P.M. They have just returned after a terrible day of danger.

26 Sunday. Bourke & I went to Doboy this morning to put a letter aboard the Str. *Carrie*, but being a little late we met her near the buoy & just got our letters aboard (by throwing) by the skin of our teeth. We then went to Doboy to get a magistrate to go to Little Sapelo to marry our hired man L. P. Ammons to Ann Hooker. He, the magistrate, however got a steam tug & brought us all over to attend the wedding.

27 Killed two Tennessee beeves & two beautiful heifers of our own stock—the two latter the prettiest beef we killed this season.

28 Went to Doboy with them to-day to deliver beef. Owing to a very high S.E. wind we had a bad & a hard time of it. Got through at 4 o'cl. & when we had got as far as Little Sapelo on our way home, a very violent Westerly thunder squall struck us & we had to lay by, under the lee of the bluff until it was over. Nine Tennessee beeves arrived on the Str. *Lizzie Baker* for us.

29 Killed two of the new beeves & one of our old stock to-day. A real wintry day. High N.W. wind & fire very comfortable.

30 Went with the boat to Doboy. After getting as far as the mill, Bourke & I got out & while Tom & Charlie delivered beef, B. & I negotiated for a butcher shop on Doboy, but did not finish the trade.

MAY

1 Friday. Killed three of our Tennessee beeves. Tom went to Doboy to see Capt. LaRose of the Str. *Lizzie Baker.*
2 Bourke & Charlie took the beef to Doboy & had to bring back half a quarter. Father arrived unexpectedly, having come on Str. *Carrie* to Doboy & from thence in our boat with Bourke.
3 Sunday. Spent the day with my Father. Capt. Rossini of the German Bark *Arracan* paid us a visit to-day.
4 Bourke & I drove up cattle & got caught in a very heavy rain. Afterwards rained the balance of the day. Butchered two Tennessee beeves.
5 Went with Father, Tom & his wife & Kate to meet cattle at High Pt., but the boat passed sooner than expected & we met a negro driving our cattle at the old Spanish fort. We to-day finished the purchase of a butcher shop on Doboy.
6 Wednesday. Killed two Tennessee beeves for Doboy to-day. Had in the pen 127 head of cattle.
7 Took my Father, on horse back over most of our pasture land. He is delighted with it.
8 Butchered two Tennessee beeves for Doboy.
9 Bourke & Charlie carried the beef over. Tom took Capt. Rossini out to show him live oak. Late in the afternoon I took my Father to call on the Livingstons & Kenans.
10 Sunday. My Father left us this morning—taking Str. *Carrie* at High Point for Savannah. His visit has been a great pleasure to me. Tonight Tom & I started for Darien—little wind blowing.
11 Reached Darien about 3 o'cl. this morning. I went up to collect beef bills & succeeded in collecting about $1058.36. One bark (*Jorgen Lorentzen*) shipped out owing $68.47. Reached [home] at 10.30 o'cl. to-night after a very dark sail across the Sound.
12 A regular September day. Rain most of the day & a N.E. gale blowing. The weather has been so bad that we have not been able to send the beef killed yesterday (2 Tennessees worth $150) to Doboy all day.

13 Wednesday. Tom, Bourke & Charlie carried the beef over at day light. It rained on them almost incessantly from the time they started until they returned.

14 Rain, rain. It has done almost nothing but rain now for three days, but towards evening to-day the weather has cleared up.

15 A bright day at last. I went out with Bourke to look up two Tennessee beeves which had strayed off. Found them at the head of cotton savanna. Butchered one of them & he was tremendous—weighing about 700 lbs. nett.

16 Eleventh anniversary of the battle of Baker's creek, in which I was wounded. Tom & Charlie carried beef to Doboy. Thunder squall with heavy blow about dark. Pleasant letter from Father this afternoon.

17 Sunday. Spent the day, or most of it, reading.

18 Killed another very large beef this evening. The ships in port are fast thinning out.

19 Bourke & Charlie carried the beef to Doboy & then kept on to Darien. In afternoon Tom & I drove up to High Point to meet Carl McKinley & his bride—they arriving by Str. *Lizzie Baker*. They married yesterday at 12 o'cl. in Columbia, S.C. Her name was Elizabeth Bryce.

20 Wednesday. The bride & groom are knocked up from their sea sick trip on the boat outside yesterday. Killed our last Tennessee beef to-day.

21 Tom & Charlie took the beef to Doboy—getting back home by 1 o'clock.

22 The ninth anniversary of Sister Mary's & Howell Cobb's marriage.

23 Charlie took the beef to Doboy. The rest of us have been busy marking & castrating calves.

24 Sunday. Spent the day lounging around home. In the evening Tom took Carl McK. & wife down to the South end grove.

25 Killed two small beeves for Doboy. Just at dark we had from the North West the worst thunder storm I ever saw on Sapelo.

26 Tom & Bourke carried beef to Doboy & then kept on to Darien to return taxes, collect bills & buy lumber. I forgot to say that yesterday we had a count of cattle. Spaldings & McKinley have on hand 76 head & Bourke delivers to the firm 43 head—reserving 3—a cow & yoke of oxen. Making in all for the firm 119 head.

27 Wednesday. This is my thirty second birth-day. Thank God I see it safe and in good health & prosperous business.

28 Nothing unusual occurring to-day.

29 We carried the ladies aboard the German bark *Arracan,* Capt. Rossini, lying just below Doboy.

30 Tom, Bourke & myself carried beef to Doboy & afterwards went to Darien, from which place we started Bourke out to buy cattle with $2000 in hand & $3279 in bank. Had a hard return trip.

31 Sunday. Literally & emphatically a rest day. Got home about sunrise. No wind.

JUNE

1 Killed two beeves to-day. I have been suffering with a bad cold. I always heard that a Summer cold was the worst & now I know it. Its as bad as an attack of fever.

2 Tom & Charlie by starting to Doboy at 2 o'clock this morning, got back by 10 o'cl. A.M. Planted one row of millet.

3 Wednesday. Killed two beeves for Doboy. Been suffering with a very severe cold.

4 Nothing unusual occurring.

5 My niece Katy Taylor's tenth birth-day.

6 Carl McK., Charlie & I, with two hands went to Darien for a flat to carry horses up in. We were delayed in town & lost the tide just this side of long reach, where we tied up. A stiff Southeaster also held us back.

7 Sunday. We cast loose & started at 2 o'cl. A.M. The wind blowing from S.W. We made good headway, having to tie up at Doboy & wait on the ebb. Reached home about 10 o'clock.

8 We hauled all our beef hides still on hand home to-day. We have killed so far, to-day included, 174 head of cattle. Our first dish of okra to-day. We only kill one beef to-day—so few ships in port.

9   This morning I with an old sailor name Rose[2] took the beef to Doboy while Tom & Charlie with hired hands took three horses in a flat to Darien. Jno. M. McIntosh & a Dutchman named Swoll came to-day.

10 I killed one beef to-day. The visitors who came yesterday are staying at my house & have been trying to fish, but with poor success.

11 Thursday. My visitors went with me to Doboy to deliver my beef. The weather is so warm that the four ships now in port are afraid to order beef. I having got only 55 lbs. ordered for Saturday. I therefore stop killing for the Summer—having killed in all this season 175 head.

12 I rode with Mr. Swoll down to the South end & to the beach. Afterward he went with Mr. Rose in our boat to Doboy. Got caught by a squall on the way.

13 This would have been Sister Kate's 37th birth-day, if she had lived. I went to Doboy & settled up bills.

14 Sunday. Stiff N.E. wind blowing & weather showery & cool. It is five years to-day since I commenced my journal.

15 Wind N.E. & fresh—so fresh that we could not land our cattle on the beach. Tom & Bourke brought down in four flats 146 head of cattle, which the tug *Staples* brought to Bourke's landing.

16 One flat got away from us yesterday & drifted up to Tom's wharf where we unloaded her. To-day we took her to the Sound against a S.E. wind where the tug met us & took us to Doboy. Tom & Bourke went up for more cattle.

17 Wednesday. Heavy rain at mid-day. Afterwards it rained slowly until late at night.

18 Started to Darien to help Tom & Bourke bring down another lot of cattle, but we met them in the skiff in the Sound. They had bought the cattle (88 head) to be delivered next Tuesday.

19 I have been helping Tom & Charlie work on our calf pen fence most of the day. Shipped all our tallow to-day to Atwoods & Avery of Darien.

---

2. *Rose* should probably be *Rowes*, an old sailor who was employed by Tom Spalding. See *Journal*, August 26, 1874.

20 Most of the young people got up before day & went fishing, but had very poor luck. Worked on calf fence afterwards.

21 Sunday. I rode round with the other partners to look at our cattle. We have 253 head of very fine cattle now.

22 Tom has taken Carl McKinley & his bride out to the beach early this morning. The latter gentleman has a very nice wife, but her two main faults are that she is a great braggart & is very lazy for a poor man's wife.

23 All of us men went up to Darien to meet a lot of cattle we bought from Jno. R. Middleton of Liberty Co. They arrived late this evening—105 head @ $10 per head.

24 Wednesday. After a great deal of trouble got our cattle in the flats, after losing six by breaking out of the pen. Had a good trip down behind the tug *J. R. Staples.* Finished unloading at Bourke's landing at 9½ o'clock to-night.

25 Soon after unloading last night, Charlie Bass & myself returned on the tug to return the flats. Got home tired & broken down 11.45 o'clock to-night. Weather extremely warm.

26 Rested all day. Light rain about noon. Weather cooler afterwards.

27 Resting & posting my books. We are supplying another ship at High Point with beef. Weather very warm. Thunder squall with very heavy blow from N.W. this evening.

28 Sunday. Much against my will I have to write several business letters, as Tom goes to Darien to-night.

29 Some of our cattle that got away from us the other day in Darien have been brought up & Tom went up last night & sold them out at $15 per head. Killed a beef for ships *Melicete* & *Wm. Wilson.*

30 I took beef to High Pt. & Charlie to Doboy. Afterwards went fishing & four of us caught 61 scale fish. Hear to-day that the Steamer *Clyde* was capsized & wrecked in Sapelo Sound by the heavy blow on the 27th inst.

JULY

1 Wednesday. Killed one beef for Doboy & Sapelo—the first of the new stock.

2 We all—ladies too—went out to sea all day on the pilot boat *Young America*. Most of the party were more or less seasick—the two Sallies the most so.

3 Commenced to rain soon after breakfast & has been a wet day. I have been sick to-day—an abcess forming at the root of one of my jaw teeth.

4 Laid up all day with my face which is much swollen. We got from Barrow, England to-day a check from Capt. Zachariason of the bark *Jorgen Lorentzsen* for his butcher's bill while here.

5 Sunday. Suffering intensely with my face. Very warm.

6 My face better to-day. The twenty-seventh anniversary of my Mother's death. Stiff N.E. wind blowing.

7 Nothing unusual occurring. My face has about got well.

8 Wednesday. Killed one beef—partly for Doboy & partly for High Point.

9 I carried the beef to High Point this morning. The ships now in port loading—three of them, are the last expected in this Summer. To-day is twenty years since the death of my Sister Caroline.

10 Bourke returned from Athens this morning. Killed one beef this afternoon.

11 Been helping Bourke to lath his house. A great deal of rain. The lightning struck a tree in about 100 yards of B's house while we were work[ing] there, scaring us badly.

12 Sunday. Tom, Bourke & myself rode over to Cabaretta beach. On the way on Sapelo beach we found a turtle nest with 125 eggs in it.

13 Killed one beef for Doboy & High Pt.

14 John & Wm. Nightingale arrived to-day. They have bought a sail boat which formerly belonged to A. E. Carr of Darien. They gave $50 for it—a good bargain.

15 Wednesday. Went fishing to Little Sapelo, but caught almost nothing. Afterwards killed one beef.

16 We all, in both sail boats, took an excursion to Egg Island reef to fish for bass & sharks. Jno. Nightingale caught a bass & Charlie Bass caught a drum.

17 Jno. Nightingale wanting to go home, his brother, Charlie Bass, myself & their servant took him to "Grantly" on the

Glynn County shore. We afterwards went to Darien, arriving there about midnight.

18 Loaded with laths for Bourke & started to Sapelo. Wm. Wylly came with us. In the Sound we were joined by Capt. Sverdrup, Norwegian Bk. *Tegner*, who came over with us. Arrived at Sapelo about sunset.

19 Sunday. I forgot to mention that Jim McKinley arrived here on a visit last Tuesday (14th). Been making up for lost sleep.

20 Killed one beef to-day. We had 310 head of cattle up in the pen.

21 One heavy shower of rain to-day. Jessie McIntosh arrived at Riverside.

22 Wednesday. Killed one beef to-day. This is the tenth anniversary of the battle I was engaged in at the siege of Atlanta, Georgia.

23 Tom & I went aboard the British ship *Melicete* lying in Sapelo river & bought a lot of clothing. I bought a blue serge suit for $7.50.

24 Killed a beef this evening. This finishes up the two ships we have been supplying & consequently finishes our business for the Summer.

25 Went fishing at the mouth of the river. The party caught some nice fish. Weather dry at last.

26 Sunday. Called on Lewis Graybill at the Livingstons'. Started to Darien at 10 o'cl. P.M. with Jim McKinley on his way to Savannah.

27 Did not reach Darien till about 7 o'clock this morning— rowed nearly all the way. Towed down the river behind the tug *Leon*. Sick this afternoon.

28 Called up at 3 o'cl. this A.M. to doctor our hired man Ammons.

29 Wednesday. I have a hound puppy—a fine one too, born about the 20th last April.

30 Sore jaw from a bad tooth again.

31 Tom left for Philadelphia to-day to buy us a small steam boat.

AUGUST

1 We shipped yesterday by Tom on Str. *Lizzie Baker* 30 cow hides to Savh. I rode round looking up cattle—could find only 233 head.

2 Sunday. All, but Sallie & I, have gone to the beach. My nephew Tom Cobb's sixth birth-day. Excessively warm weather.

3 Weather as warm as ever. Beginning to need rain some.

4 My mare Sallie that is five years old to-day, is just being broken to the plow & takes to it very kindly.

5 Wednesday. Been trying a horse which a negro on the Island wants to sell me.

6 Went to Darien with Carl McK. & Bourke. Got a tow from tug *Leon* part of the way. Reached home about midnight.

7 Weather dry & very warm.

8 Started to look up cattle, but a big rain ran me home. I only had time to find 120 head. More lightning after dark than I ever saw.

9 Sunday. Lewis Graybill & Mollie Livingston dined with us.

10 Two of the Sapelo negroes have carried a case of slander to the Courts. The first time any of them have ever appealed to a Court of Justice.

11 Very warm. We drove up about 150 head of cattle to tread down and manure the garden.

12 Wednesday. Thermometer 100° in my dining room—the warmest day I ever felt on Sapelo. I rode to Chocolate & Bourbon. Dismantled our sail boat to repair her.

13 Attended a picnic of the Darien people at the High Point of Sapelo.

14 Been feeling knocked up all day. For a week past we have had the warmest weather I ever felt on Sapelo.

15 On getting up this morning I saw out on the quarantine ground[3] a full rigged ship, which I afterwards heard was a ship bound from Havanna to New Brunswick & put in here

3. A designated site where ships carrying infections were ordered to anchor by the port physician, e.g., Dr. James Holmes. This quarantine was in the mouth of the Duplin River. Later, in 1880, a quarantine station was established on Blackbeard Island.

last night in distress with Yellow fever aboard. Capt. & 1st Mate dead & others sick. Been at work on our Sail boat.

16 Sunday. This morning the tug moved the Yellow fever ship out of sight down the Sound. Wind N.E.

17 Discharged our hired man L. P. Ammons to-night. Busy repairing our sail boat. Wind N.E. still.

18 Painted one side of our sail boat black. Willie Wylly & Jessie McIntosh left for the Ridge yesterday. Wind N.E. with a little rain.

19 Wednesday. Nothing unusual occurring.

20 After launching our sail boat we found that she still leaked a little near the keel—so we took her out again.

21 Put our boat back in the water again to-day & started with Bourke & Mr. Bass to Darien at 7 o'cl. P.M. Our boat looks very pretty, but she still leaks a little.

22 Got to town just at Day-break. We took up a new centre board to have it ironed & brought a new rudder. Took break-fast & dinner with the Wyllys & staid in town all night on account of a storm.

23 Sunday. Left Darien this morning about half past five o'clock with a very light S.W. breeze.

24 A succession of thunder storms to-day. I should think at least a dozen, but with very little rain.

25 I went to Darien this morning with Bourke. Good breeze all the way. Slept out at the Wyllys.

26 Wednesday. Left town this morning at 8.20 o'cl. Camp-bell Wylly & his wife came down with us—also Jno. McQ. McIntosh. A man named Rowes who has been staying at Tom's for several months, got drunk & impudent & Bourke turned him off and we put him aboard the bark *Tegner* in the Sound.

27 Heavy rain before breakfast. Wind N.E.

28 I left Sapelo this evening on Str. *Lizzie Baker*, intending to meet Tom with our little Steamboat in Savannah.

29 Reached Savannah about nine o'cl. this morning. Am staying at the McIntoshes'. Heavy N.E. rains.

30 Sunday. As I do not expect Tom for a week yet, I concluded to run up to Milledgeville. Took cars on C. R.R. & arrived at Macon about sun set.

31 Left Macon at 6.30 o'clock this morning on the Macon &
Augusta R.R. and arrived at Milledgeville a little after
8 o'clock. I met Judge Bartlett & Col. Lofton on the road
coming to a second week of Court in Baldwin County. Find
my Father well but very busy.

SEPTEMBER

1 Rode into Milledgeville & spent part of the morning there.
2 Wednesday. My Mother's birth-day.
3 Baldwin County Court adjourned this evening.
4 Spent part of the morning in Milledgeville.
5 Did not go into town at all to-day, spent it at my Father's.
6 Sunday. My brother Andrews joined the Presbyterian
Church this morning. I attended & heard the first Sermon
that I have heard for two or three years.
7 Spent all the morning in town expecting a telegram from
Tom & the Steamboat, but did not get it.
8 To-day has been a repetition of yesterday as to my move-
ments.
9 Wednesday. Heard to-day that Tom has got as far as Morehead City, N.C. with the Steamboat & had disabled his
engine. I started for home (Sapelo) this afternoon, bringing
with me my youngest brother—Guy.
10 We reached Savannah about 8 o'cl. A.M. Met Tom here on
his way home. He had blown out one of his flues & had
to lay up and repair. We left Savh. at 5 o'cl. P.M. on Str.
Carrie.
11 Arrived at Doboy a little before day light—got a ship's boat
to put us to Marsh landing & walked up.
12 I find Bourke very sick—threatened with lock jaw from
severe & neglected colds. Wm. Brailsford, Mr. Rinch[?] &
young Rodriguez arrived this afternoon.
13 Sunday. Carl McKinley & his wife took Str. *Carrie* at Doboy
this morning on their way home. They have been here
since May.

14 Bourke was taken down yesterday morning with what we think is an attack of acute rheumatism in the muscles of his neck. Tom sent for Dr. Kenan who is here now.

15 Bourke still quite sick.

16 Wednesday. Tom Spalding's 27th birth-day. Bourke quite sick.

17 Sallie taken before day light with a light case of Cholera Morbus—soon cured her. Bourke so much worse that Tom sent to-night for Dr. Holmes also. We are beginning to feel quite uneasy.

18 Sat up all night with Bourke & consequently am sleepy. Sent Tom for Dr. Baker also.

19 Dr. Baker arrived late this evening. Bourke worse.

20 Sunday. Left Sapelo with Guy for Morehead City, N.C., for our little Steamboat.

21 Spent the day in Savannah & left for N.C. at 7.30 P.M. via Augusta, Columbia, Charlotte &c.

22 Reached Augusta 5.55 A.M. Met Carl McK. & wife at Columbia & reached Charlotte a little after dark.

23 Wednesday. Left Charlotte at 7.40 last night & reached Morehead City 7.20 tonight. I find it will be some days before the necessary repairs are complete.

24 Spent the day aboard our Str. looking at the work going on.

25 The mechanic gives me hopes that repairs will be completed by Saturday. My pilot is over at Beaufort drunk.

26 Completed all repairs on the boiler last night & this morning I & my pilot went up to Newbern. He got drunk & failed to come back with me.

27 Sunday. Beautiful weather & only waiting on my pilot.

28 Wind at day light S.E. & increasing until towards night it blows a terrific gale. Water breaking clear over the R.R. embankment which is all of 15 feet high. Sat up all night to watch my lines which I feared would part.

29 My pilot returned to-night. Wind gone N.W. Am in a bad place for that wind.

30 Got under steam & left R.R. wharf at 8 o'cl. A.M. arrived at Bogue inlet at 3½ o'cl. P.M. (35 miles) where we tied up to wait for the Sea to calm down.

OCTOBER

1 Thursday. All hands busy making things snug for a Sea trip tomorrow, & rigging a sail. The presence of my brother Guy with me on this trip has been a great comfort to me.

2 Lay wind bound in Bogue inlet all day—tedious business too.

3 A repetition of yesterday, but as the wind seems to be dying out, I hope to start tomorrow.

4 Sunday. A bright pretty day. We got steam & started but stuck on a sand bank & had to pay a fisherman $2 to put us in the ship channel—after which it was too late to put to sea.

5 After lying all day yesterday in a very unpleasant rolling sea, we put out to Sea for the first time this morning at 7.20 o'clock. Towards afternoon, the sea becoming quite rough & seeing that we could not make Smithville bar before dark, we paid a fisherman who put out to us, $3 to put us in Barren Inlet.

6 Left Barren inlet at 6 o'clock this A.M. & got off Federal Pt. (Fort Fisher) at 9.30 o'cl. By some unaccountable mistake my pilot ran 12 miles past New Inlet & had to put back the same distance. Arrived at Smithville just before dark. A N. Easter blowing outside, making a very rough sea.

7 Wednesday. Not being able to get coal at Smithville had to run up Cape Fear river 30 miles to Wilmington, where we arrived at about 5 o'clock P.M.

8 Took in two tons of coal & after getting a drunken pilot aboard we ran back to Smithville this evening. I hired in Wilmington to-day a yellow boy named Jeremiah at $3.00 per month.

9 The weather looked so threatening to-day that we were afraid to put to sea & therefore laid at Smithville all day.

10 The tug *Brandt* towed us nearly to the bar & cut us loose at 5½ o'clock this A.M. About 10 o'cl. a S.W. wind sprung up & made a very ugly head, chop sea. My boat being too deeply laden with coal she took in large quantities of water forward. A fisherman boarded us off Little river inlet & carried us two miles up Calabash river to his wharf.

11 Sunday. The wind still being ahead (S.W.) we did not put to sea to-day, having had enough rough water yesterday. We have at last however got to the South Carolina line.

12 Crossed Little river bar this morning at half past 7 o'clock & had a pleasant run all day. Got off the entrance to George-town harbor about an hour after dark. It being too dark to find the buoys we were afraid to attempt an entrance & therefore stood off for Charleston bar. When off Cape Romain light, the wind (N. to W.) increased to a gale & made a fearful sea. We ran all night—making Rattle snake light ship[4] just before & Charleston bar just after day light. There we had to run in the trough of the sea and an awful sea it was too—breaking clear over the top of the boat every time. Anchored under Fort Moultrie at 8 o'clock on the morning of 13th. We ran 24 hours steadily. All hands up all night. No one on the boat expected to survive the night. It was a fearful night and nothing but God's Mercy brought us through it.

13 Stopped at Charleston to-day to get an inside pilot to Savan-nah, which I did this afternoon for $18.00.

14 Wednesday. Left the Charleston wharf at twenty minutes after nine this morning & at half past ten to-night we an-chored near St. Helena Sound—a run of about sixty miles. I at last feel as if I was nearing home.

15 Started about sunrise. Made Beaufort about noon & Port Royal soon afterwards & Bluffton about 6 o'clock. We waited here for the tide to rise to float us through Wall's cut. Got under way again at 9.30 o'clock to-night.

16 Struck the Savannah river about one o'cl. this morn-ing. It being so dark we anchored at Venus point for day light. Started again then & tied up at Savannah wharf at 8.15 o'cl. A.M. Found Tom Spalding there & find a chance to get home on the tug *Staples*. I left Tom in charge of the boat & Guy & I started home. Anchored all night in Romney Marsh.

4. The lightship marking the entrance to the Charleston harbor.

17 After a pleasant run Guy & I reached home about 7 o'cl. P.M. All there agreeably surprised to see us—thought that we were dead.

18 Sunday. Emphatically & literally a rest day with me.

19 I find Bourke very feeble from his sickness. We all took a kind of half hunt. Jumped one deer but did not get a shot.

20 Staid around home to-day and did little or nothing.

21 Wednesday. Tom arrived with the Steamboat to-day about 4 o'clock P.M. from Savannah, having had to go to Darien to put his pilot out at Darien first.

22 After scouring up the Steamboat generally, we all, little & big, young & old, took a trip to Doboy in her & on our return ran up to the Livingstons'.

23 The Steamboat went to Darien to-day via Doboy & took in her first two dollars passage money. Owing to some of the ladies going, Guy, Mr. Bass & myself could not go.

24 Most of [us] hunted deer nearly all day. Toward night Tom shot a large basket horned buck in Sea Marsh & afterwards caught him in the Pine Barren.

25 Sunday. Doing nothing in particular.

26 Killed the first beef of the season for market. Bourke moved into his new house to-day.

27 Ran the Steamer to Doboy & Darien. Got two passengers.

28 Had a bad headache all day. The weather has turned very warm.

29 Carried Bourke (on his way to be married) & Wm. Wylly to Hammersmith landing on the Steamer. Got three passengers from Darien to Hammersmith. Picked up Wm. Nightingale at Cambers Island.

30 Carried over beef to Doboy & went to Darien. Carried two passengers up & three down. Selling beef at 11¢.

31 Tom, his wife, Guy & Charlie went deer hunting—jumped plenty of deer & got shots & killed none.

NOVEMBER

1 Sunday. Nothing unusual going on.

2 Been busy all day nearly putting down pilings at Bourke's bluff to make a Steamboat wharf. Killed one beef.

3 We all—that is the men,—went to Darien to vote in the congressional election. Candidates as follows—Hartridge, democrat, Bryant radical & Wimberly independent radical.[5] A very quiet election.

4 Wednesday. We all went to Doboy in the Steamboat this afternoon to meet Bourke & his bride who arrived on the *Lizzie Baker*. He & Ella P. Barrow were married in Athens yesterday morning.

5 Killed one beef & took him to Doboy. Afterwards went on our regular schedule to Darien.

6 Went deer hunting. Tom killed a peg horned buck in the Pine barren.

7 Went to Darien on regular schedule.

8 Sunday. Called on the bride to-day.

9 Butchered to-day. The cattle we drove up were very wild. Weather very warm.

10 Steamboat went to Darien on regular schedule. Yesterday I took her to Pumpkin Hammock Mill for repairs.

11 Wednesday. Butchered to-day. Weather still very warm.

12 We started to Darien, but the heater in the smokestack commenced to leak & we had to lay at Doboy all day & repair. Rain from N.E. most of the night.

13 Butchered to-day for the first time this season in the barn.

14 Steamboat gone to Darien. I did not go as Bourke & I are going alternately.

15 Sunday. Nothing doing particularly.

16 Tom & I butchered. Bourke took his wife to Darien to show her to Col. Spalding. Sallie went with them.

17 Tom & I took the beef to Doboy in the Steamboat—not expecting to go to Darien, but Capt. Stresen of the Norwegian bark *Roska* being very sick, chartered us to take him to Darien. Two new barks in to-day.

18 Wednesday. Nothing uncommon going on. We butchered one beef for Doboy.

19 To-day is the eighth anniversary of my wedding. We tried our Steamer on towing a raft of 120 logs & were agreably surprised at her ability. In trying a second tow however her heater gave out.

5. Won by Julian Hartridge of Savannah.

20 Tom went to Darien in the Steamer, but she broke down again & we have to lay her up for repairs, if they can be put on, which I doubt. I am afraid that our Steamboat will not be [a] success.

21 I took the beef to the ships in a canoe with two hired hands.

22 Sunday. Rode up to Mr. Livingston's & afterwards to the Pine barren.

23 Tom, Guy & myself butchered while Bourke & Charlie went down the Sound in the sail boat to collect a bill.

24 Tom, Bourke & myself carried the beef to Doboy & afterwards had a settlement with Jas. Abeel, running through 12 months. I paid my bill of $256.15 & had $14.75 due me. The boys lacked $507.96 of paying their bills & gave a joint sixty day note for that amount.

25 Wednesday. We found a large rattlesnake in a hole this morning & Tom, Bourke & Charlie caught him alive & uninjured. I suppose he is very near 4½ feet long.

26 Tom, Bourke & I carried the beef over in the sail boat this morning. We had a fine North wind and made a very early start in consequence of which we had to wait nearly an hour for the sailors to wake up. Weather quite cold early in the morning.

27 Worked on the Steamboat (which is laid up) all morning— afterwards drove up cattle & butchered.

28 Carried beef (Tom, Bourke & I) to Doboy in the sail boat. Lost the tide & had to leave the boat at Marsh landing. Two more vessels in. Weather very warm.

29 Sunday. Hearing of a rattlesnake den in Long hammock we went to try to get them but did not succeed.

30 My Father's 65th birth-day. I went to Darien to help to carry Charlie Bass who is on the Grand jury. Weather very cold. The first really cold day of the season.

DECEMBER

1 Tom & Bourke carried one beef to Doboy in the sail boat. I worked on the Steam boat. Commenced to paint her. Six vessels (square rigged) in port to-day.

2 Wednesday. Worked on the Steamboat in the morning & butchered one beef in the afternoon. Weather moderating.

3 Tom, Guy & I carried beef to Doboy in the sail boat. We had a hard time as we had no wind going. Mr. Livingston went over to Doboy to take charge of our butcher shop there.

4 Killed three beeves to-day for the first time this season— one bark (*Aurora*) ordering a 300 lb. beef to take to sea.

5 I went over with Bourke & Charlie to carry the beef. Coming back had brisk wind from N. & had to reef our sail.

6 Sunday. We hear of the very serious illness of Sister Mary's baby daughter.

7 As vessels are beginning to arrive pretty freely, we killed three more beeves this afternoon. I fear though that we will not be able to sell it all. Heavy wind & rain last night from S.E. Cleared up to-day.

8 This is my brother Andrews' twenty first birth-day. I did not go with the beef boat this morning—it being my "off" day. Sail boat kept on to town. I helped paint the hull of the Steamboat.

9 Wednesday. Killed three beeves for Doboy tomorrow.

10 Went with Tom, Charlie & Guy to deliver beef. On our way back the Steamboat met us at the mouth of the small creek & towed us up. Heard yesterday of the death of Sister Mary's baby, Mary Ann.

11 Bourke & I started this morning in the Steamboat to Darien to have the boiler, or flues, worked on, but not finding the proper tools there, we started for Brunswick about 8 o'clock P.M.

12 After laying by last night for a fog & sticking on a sand bank, we reached Brunswick early this morning & immediately put the machinist to work.

13 Sunday. I came out home with Jno. Nightingale last night & returned to Brunswick with him to-night. The machinists have been at work all day.

14 Jno. Nightingale, Jas. Floyd, Grant Troup, ourselves, dogs, guns &c. left Brunswick on our Steamer between 9 & 10 o'clock A.M. & reached home this afternoon.

15 I carried the beef to Doboy in our Steamer while the others hunted. Flues got to leaking & I got home after dark with great difficulty.

16 Wednesday. Tom undertook to make a trip to Darien in the Steamer, but broke down at Doboy & returned in a skiff. The Brunswick machinist has evidently done his work very poorly. Went hunting but killed nothing.

17 Carried over four beeves this morning but had to bring back two quarters as we overstocked the market. We hunted the South end & Tom & Jno. Nightingale each killed a small deer.

18 Drove up cattle & only killed two beeves this time.

19 Our guests left us for their homes this morning. Tom, Guy & Charlie taking them to Broadfield—delivering our beef on their way up. Went in sail boat. Raining.

20 Sunday. Did nothing but lay around home. The boys returned from Darien this morning under double reefed sail & peak down. Wind S.W. & very stiff.

21 Killed two beeves this afternoon for Doboy. Weather clearing up & wind N.W.

22 I delivered beef with Bourke to-day & had a terribly hard time rowing against tide.

23 Wednesday. Butchered two beeves for Doboy.

24 We all went to Doboy with the beef this morning—thinking that Tom would get into a row there with a displeased[?] Ship Capt., but we were happily mistaken. We brought our Steam boat, which [had] been lying broken down at Doboy, home to-day.

25 Christmas. We spent our Christmas butchering & working on the Steamboat. Ten fights on Doboy. Weather cloudy but dry.

26 Tom, Charlie & I delivered beef. Rained nearly all night. Weather warm.

27 Sunday. Nothing unusual occurring.

28 Guy, Charlie Bass & I started in a dense fog with our Steamboat for Brunswick for repairs, but broke down at Doboy— the boiler leaking so that we could not keep fire going.

29 Being disabled we got the Str. *Carrie* to tow us to Brunswick for $20. Reached there in the afternoon. Weather cloudy & foggy.

30 Wednesday. Clouds & fog. Upset our boiler & the machinists went to work. Sleep on board all of us.

31 Clouds & fog. Big day in Brunswick in spite of rain and bad
weather—John Robinson's Circus & Menagerie having arrived this morning. The boys went to it, but I staid with my
boat. Still at work on it, but hope to finish it to-morrow. It
is very uncomfortable sleeping on board as everything is so
damp. This day ends the year 1874. It finds [us] doing not so
well financially as I could wish, our Steam boat having sunk
a great deal of money for us. I fear it is a bad speculation. I
am opposed to it now and never did advocate its purchase.

1875

JANUARY

1 The new year opens with dark & dismal weather. I hope it does not presage the same kind of fortune [for] us. Upon trying our boiler to-day I find that it leaks as bad as ever, so we have to tear down & go to work again on it. Guy & Charlie return to Sapelo to-night by way of the R. Road.

2 Cloudy & wet. The boys having left me last night, I have been very lonely & low spirited to-day.

3 Sunday. A wet comfortless Sunday for me. Spent the day on board.

4 After working all day the machinist finish[ed] repairs about 10 o'clock to-night, but there was such a dense fog that we could not start.

5 Left Brunswick about day light & after a pretty run reached home in afternoon. Cold & raining.

6 Wednesday. Took one beef to Doboy in the Steamboat & then went to Darien to vote for County officers. The flues are leaking almost as bad as ever. Weather cloudy & damp.

7 Nothing especial doing. Cloudy.

8 Killed one beef. Cloudy & raining.

9 Carried beef to Doboy in Steamer. The machinist arrived to-night & worked nearly all night on the flues. About 3 hours of sunshine to-day.

10 Sunday. Made a trial trip with the Steamer to Doboy. Clouds & fog.

11 Bourke & Nellie, Mrs. Spalding, Katie, Sallie & I, with the machinist, Hertel started to Brunswick at 10 o'cl., got there at 8½ o'cl. P.M. Night intensely dark & raining.

12 At work on the boat. Raining very hard nearly all day.
    Mrs. Spalding is staying with her niece Mrs. Bostwick—the
    rest of us at the Nightingales'.

13 Sister Caroline's birth-day. Left Brunswick about noon,
    broke down, stopped & fixed up. Started again & got
    befogged & had to lay all night at mouth of Broughton
    Is. river.

14 Thursday. Got home through the fog about noon—the ladies
    thoroughly worn out with discomfort & hunger. Killed a
    beef for Doboy.

15 Carried beef in the Steamer. The first bright day for nine-
    teen days.

16 Went deer hunting—hunted all day, several shots fired & no
    deer killed. A bright pretty day.

17 Sunday. Cold N. wind blowing with some rain. Bourke
    went to Doboy in the Steamer to meet his Mother from
    Brunswick, but she did not come home.

18 Killed one beef to-day for Doboy.

19 Tom & Bourke took their wives to Darien—delivering
    beef at Doboy as they passed. At Doboy they picked up
    Mrs. Bryce & her daughter of Columbia, S.C., and brought
    back from Darien Sallie, Lillian & Mattie Wylly & the
    son of the second. The Steamer was crowded & we are
    overwhelmed with company.

20 Wednesday. Bourke & I drove cattle alone and a hard time
    we have of it too. We are now selling beef at 12½¢ & the
    beef is very—very poor too. Tom sick in bed.

21 Our engineer C. V. Archambault left us to-day to return
    to his home in Philadelphia. His absence from my house—
    where he took up—is an unspeakable gratification to me. I
    never had as unwelcomed a visitor in my life. We paid him
    $100 cash & $130.53 by note. After a very little practice
    Bourke & Charlie run the engine better than he did.

22 Tom sick in bed. Had a hard cattle drive. One steer made a
    dash at me on horseback, but I cleared him.

23 Bourke, Charlie & I took the beef over in the Steamboat.
    Both of them sick & Tom confined to his bed. All with
    aggravated forms of bad colds.

24 Sunday. Spent most of the day visiting the sick. Guy & Sister Sallie taken down with same complaint to-day.

25 Tom & I drove up cattle. We butchered one.

26 Left home in the Steamboat at 3 o'clock A.M. Put Mrs. Bryce on the *Carrie* at Doboy & took the Wylly women to Darien, where we found Mrs. Spalding returned from Brunswick. In taking wood on the Steam boat I mashed my toe very painfully.

27 Wednesday. Sick & laid up with my toe. Brought cattle from the beach. They are very fat. Without any company once more.

28 Laid up sick. Tom & Bourke carried beef in the Steamboat.

29 Went after beef in the rain—got them from Hog hammock.

30 Atwood has again commenced to sell beef. Great complaints of our beef being marshy—giving us great trouble.

31 Sunday. Slept most of the day.

FEBRUARY

1 Killed one beef to-day. Nothing unusual occurring.

2 On our way to Doboy this morning in the sail boat, we met Lewis Graybill & Mrs. Bryce returning to Sapelo.

3 Wednesday. Very unexpectedly it commenced to rain last night & continued heavily most of the morning. Went deer hunting & Jack killed a doe in the Pine barren.

4 Mrs. Bryce, her daughter & Guy left Sapelo this morning. They intended to go on the *Carrie*, but were too late—so we took them to Darien & got them off on the *Daisy*. Weather very cold & sleeting most of the day. The first sleet I ever saw in this country.

5 Weather intensely cold—ice plentiful & ground frozen. Left town in afternoon. We have to-day a new engineer (John Priester) on trial.

6 Intensely cold weather yet. Killed one beef & sold half of it at Doboy.

7 Sunday. Weather very cold yet. Tried to make up a hunt on Blackbeard but failed. Mutual visitings all round.

8 Went bird shooting & burning pastures. Jumped six deer but got none. Col. B. W. Frobill—surveying "Great Western Canal"—came here to-day.[1] Bourke, Charlie & I start to Darien to-night to take him to Brunswick tomorrow.

9 We reached Darien a little after sun rise & left for Brunswick about 11 o'clock A.M. & reached there about 4 or 5 o'cl. P.M. Left there about 9 o'cl. to-night. Very dark steering.

10 Reached Darien about 3 o'cl. A.M. & started for home this afternoon.

11 Thursday. Heavy rain last night & this morning. The same party together with two of the surveying party went to Darien this morning expecting to tow their flats to Savannah, but Darien gave a supper to the surveying party & they could not go.

12 Our boiler is leaking so badly that we cannot go to Savannah. After the supper last night some of the surveying party got into a fight with some rowdys & were very roughly handled. Came home this evening.

13 I worked on my yard fence most of the day. Tom killed a deer.

14 Sunday. St. Valentine's day. Spent most of the day at home reading.

15 Drove up cattle from South end, but as they seemed to have been on the marsh we did not butcher to-day. Afterwards burned grass & hunted deer. Tom wounded one at Grassy island, but did not get him.

16 Butchered this morning & sent the beef to Doboy. Continual rain nearly all day.

17 Wednesday. Rain all day & very cold.

18 Went deer hunting. Tom killed a large buck on Cabareta & two does in Shady Oak drive. A good day's sport—for him.

19 Drove up cattle & butchered.

20 Sent the beef to Doboy. Afterwards I hauled wood. More rain to-night.

1. Refers to the Atlantic and Great Western Canal Company authorized by the Georgia General Assembly in 1870 to construct a canal from near Rome, Ga. to Macon, Brunswick, or Savannah.

21 Sunday. Took Sallie to ride on horseback. The first time I ever saw her on a horse.

22 Bourke, Charlie & I rode from 10 o'clock this morning until nearly dark in search of a lot of 70 head of cattle, but did not succeed in finding them.

23 Tom & Charlie took the beef to Doboy. I worked on my yard fence. Bourke's 24th birth-day.

24 Wednesday. The wind being favorable we went deer hunting but had bad luck—losing two dogs & nobody getting a shot. Pretty Spring weather at last.

25 Went deer hunting again early this morning. At the side stand at Hog hammock drive I killed a small doe—the second I've killed at that stand.

26 Butchered one small beef. As the grass begins to spring the wild cattle which have been feeding toward the N. end begin to work back this way. My cow "Spot" has another calf.

27 Bourke & I took the beef over in our sail boat. Four vessels in port, of which number we have two, but to-day got orders from all four. The Harbor Master, Steadwell, is our rival butcher & wants us to raise the price to 12¢, but having acted very dishonorably towards us on the same point already, we refuse to accede to his proposition & continue to sell at 10 cents.

28 Sunday. Nothing unusual occurring.

MARCH

1 Drove up cattle very early this morning & afterwards went hunting. Tom killed two deer. Butchered late this afternoon.

2 Tom & Charlie took the beef over. I finished my outer yard fence.

3 Wednesday. All hands commenced work on a wharf at Bourke's bluff, for the Steamboat.

4 Busy most of the day sinking the pilings for our new wharf.

5 Drove up cattle early this morning & working afterwards on our wharf.

6 Bourke, Charlie & I took the beef over. Rain most of the
   day. We were in most of it & got thoroughly drenched.
   Mr. Livingston fell overboard & had a narrow escape.
7 Sunday. Weather cleared up with very high W. wind—
   colder too.
8 Tom & I rode up to High Pt. this morning & met Capt.
   Brailsford, Mr. Lide Goodwin & Gen. R. H. Anderson of
   Savh. & all went deer hunting. They had nine fine hounds
   and we had five making altogether a splendid cry after
   a deer. Only one deer was killed & that by a negro of
   the party.
9 Tom carried the beef over. The rest of us worked on our
   wharf. Late this evening Jno. & Wm. Nightingale arrived,
   bringing with them their cousin—old Dr. Green.
10 Wednesday. Hunted the pine barren, Shady Oak & beech
   myrtle drives. Jumped nine deer. I killed a large doe in the
   former drive.
11 Hunted again to-day. Jumped five deer. Charlie Bass killed a
   doe at Hog Hammock. Heavy frost this morning.
12 Hunted this morning. Jumped two deer but nobody killed
   any. Butchered this afternoon. A boiler maker arrived from
   Savh. & commenced putting new tubes in our boiler on the
   11th inst.
13 Bourke & I carried the beef over. The Nightingales &
   Dr. Green left this morning.
14 Sunday. The machinists worked all day on our boiler.
   Weather warm & foggy.
15 Bourke carried his Mother up to Darien in the sail boat &
   returned to-night. Hammie Wylly came with him. Tom & I
   butchered. Heavy rain & thunder.
16 A great deal of rain with Westerly thunder squall & very
   high wind in the morning. Tom & Charlie carried the beef
   over in the sail boat late in the day.
17 Wednesday. Butchered one beef. The new grass has sprung
   enough to make the cattle begin to take to the savannas.
   Owing to excessive wet weather the grass is very backward.
18 The steamboat took the beef over this morning—her first
   trip since she was laid up for repairs. She now has a complete set of new tubes.

19   Butchered two beeves—partly for home consumption. My cook Patsy Bailey who has been with us since Jan. 2, 1872 left us to-day. Some rain.

20   Tom, Charlie & I took the beef over in the Steamboat. High S.E. wind. Thunder & heavy rain to-night.

21   Sunday. A beautiful clear Spring day. Sallie & Tom's wife & Katie have gone with Tom to Mr. Livingston's.

22   Hired a new cook this morning named Chloe Handy at $5 per month. Weather clear & cold W. wind blowing— thermometer at 42° in the house. 2 Beeves to-day.

23   My off day, so I did not go to Doboy with beef. Planted 86 hills of okra.

24   Wednesday. Rode most of the day hunting beef, but found only inferior ones.

25   Went with the Steamboat to Doboy. Boarded one new bark below the Light.[2]

26   Had to go to King savanna for beef. Killed two of them.

27   My off day again. After selling the beef the Steamer went on to Darien.

28   Sunday. Heard particulars last night of an awful hurricane at Milledgeville. Been sick all day.

29   Busy butchering for tomorrow's sales. Vessels are beginning to get thicker at Doboy wharves.

30   Tom & I carried the beef over in the Steamboat & afterwards we all loaded a flat, which we towed over, with lumber to make a new butcher pen of.

31   Tom carried the Steamboat to Darien with passengers while Bourke & I drove up cattle & butchered two beeves.

APRIL

1   Thursday. Sister Sarah's twenty-eighth birth day. Tom did not return from Darien last night, so that Bourke & I had to carry beef over in the sail boat. We found the Steamer at Doboy—boiler broke down again. Did not get it home until nearly 9 o'cl. to-night. We to-day concluded a bargain with

2. The Sapelo Island lighthouse.

Steadwell & McKenzie to sell all our beef to them for ten cents per lb.

2 Killed only one beef to-day. I to-day gave Sister Sarah one of my year old colts.

3 Carried round our beef to the ships which had ordered from us. This finishes for the present our delivery to ships.

4 Sunday. Having had a hard week's work, I have done nothing but rest to-day.

5 Got up at 3 o'cl. A.M. & drove up cattle. Butchered four beeves for Steadwell & McKenzie & delivered to them 1113 lbs. beef @ 10¢. Bourke went to Jessup to meet Clara Barrow & took the Steamboat as far as Darien for repairs— also towed a flat up.

6 Tom & I have been working all day upon a new butcher pen fence. He & I did not reach home last night until nearly midnight. Stopped at Marsh Landing.

7 Wednesday. Tom & I got up before day light & went out for cattle. We hired some help & butchered four beeves & then he & I took to Doboy 1071 lbs. beef. My mare Sallie gave birth to her second colt to-day.

8 Tom & I have been hard at work all day upon our butcher pen fence.

9 Tom & I with some hired help butchered four beeves & carried them to Doboy. We have delivered altogether this week 3315 lbs. beef @ 10¢. The Steamboat returned this afternoon.

10 Tom & I finished our new butcher pen to-day. Weather very warm.

11 Sunday. All the whites from the other two houses have gone in the Steamboat to Darien to hear Bishop Beckwith[3] preach to-night. Clara Barrow arrived on the Island last Friday.

12 We all drove up & butchered three beeves to-day weighing 845 lbs. I did not go to Doboy. Carried the beef on the Steamboat. Steady rain all last night & until about 9 o'cl. this A.M.

13 We drove up all the cattle we could find, for the purpose of marking &c. Riding all day & very tired tonight.

3. John W. Beckwith was the bishop for the Episcopal diocese of Georgia from 1868 to 1890.

14 Wednesday. We butchered three beeves to-day & Tom & I took over in the Steamboat 878 lbs. beef.

15 We all took over an extra order of beef to-day—210 lbs. My mare Kate turned up with her fourth colt to-day—a stallion. [*Marginal note:* Kate's 4th colt.]

16 Carried over four beeves weighing 832 lbs. in the Steamboat. The wind was blowing a gale from S.W. directly ahead of us. Had a rough Sound. Got out of fresh water & had to use salt water coming home, which foamed so, we did not get home till midnight.

17 Started to Darien to-day, but owing to our getting home so late last night, we couldn't get off early enough this morning, so gave up the trip. Sallie & Willie Wylly, came down on a visit yesterday. Wind still blowing a gale from S.W. First dish of crabs of the season, from the beach.

18 Sunday. Heard some delightful Sacred music at Tom's house. S.W. gale still blowing.

19 Butchered three beeves. Tom & Bourke took them to Doboy in the Steamer.

20 Charlie Bass & I took the Steamer to Young & Langdon's mill for repairs. Found that the work could not be done to-day, so ran on up to Darien & returned to the mill to-night.

21 Wednesday. The machinist would not work last night, so my boat has to lay up till to-night. Broke up our boat club, (organized 7th April 1870) raffling the boats. Mr. Forman won one boat & Jas. B. Floyd the other. Afterwards we went with a party & staid all night at Cambers Island.

22 Came down from Cambers & started for home in afternoon—reaching there before dark. Heavy N.E. rain all night.

23 Butchered three beeves & Tom & I carried them to Doboy.

24 Tom took the Steamboat to Darien. I have been sick all day—bad cold.

25 Sunday. Have spent most of the day at home. Not very well yet.

26 Butchered as usual to-day. I did not go to Doboy.

27 Drove up cattle for tomorrow's butchering.

28 Wednesday. The Steamboat took beef to Doboy & then carried me on to Darien to attend Court, which meets tomorrow, where I am summoned to attend as a grand juror. Stopping at Dr. Kenan's, brought Sallie in with me.

29 On our way up yesterday Tom, Charlie & myself & Wm. Wylly got into an ugly row at Doboy with a crowd of drunken negroes. Tom received a blow in the face from a drunken negro, that I persuaded him not to kill. This was the only injury we sustained, but we had to draw our pistols to quell the mob. Court convened about noon.

30 Moved to the Wyllys this afternoon. Old T. G. Campbell[4]— a notorious negro, was again indicted for false imprisonment to-day. When the Sheriff attempted to carry him to jail, he was prevented from doing so by a mob of furious negroes, who fired into the posse. Several on both sides were shot, but none seriously. Altogether however there is an ugly state of affairs existing in this County.

MAY

1 Court adjourned this afternoon. Everyone expected a more serious row tonight than we had last night & both sides were fully armed & prepared for it, but luckily by Judge Thompkins' forethought a special Steamboat took the prisoner Campbell off to Chatham County jail instead of the regular passenger boat, at whose leaving the riot was expected to commence.

2 Sunday. Sallie & I went out to Col. Chas. Spalding's this morning.

3 Walked into Darien with Col. Spalding. The boys from Sapelo & their wives & company came up to Darien and attended a ball. We could not attend.

4 The whole party left Darien on the Steamer & reached home all safely before dark.

5 Wednesday. I went with Tom to carry beef.

4. Tunis G. Campbell, Sr., of New Jersey, was a Freedmen's Bureau representative who established colonies of freedpeople on St. Catherines and Sapelo islands in 1865. He was later magistrate, state senator, and representative of McIntosh County. See Introduction.

6 Tom gone on a passenger trip to Darien. Bourke & I drove
up cattle for tomorrows butchering. Weather delightful.

7 Carried over two beeves to Doboy. I did not go, as it was my
off day.

8 Tom made a passenger trip to Darien. His wife, Katie & I
went with him.

9 Sunday. Woke up quite sick to-day. Had a chill produced by
bad cold that night & been in bed most of the day.

10 Sick all day. I neglected to state that on Friday 7th inst.
Capt. John A. Cobb & his family arrived on a visit to
Bourke.

11 The Steamboat started to Darien but broke down at Doboy
& had to lay there all day repairing.

12 Wednesday. Steamboat all right again. I was too feeble from
my sickness to go to Doboy with the beef.

13 Went with Capt. Cobb & Bourke to the South end, Light
house & aboard the pilot boat *Ethel*. Afterwards drove up
cattle in the rain with Bourke.

14 Not having driven up the right sized cattle yesterday, had to
go for them again this morning. Killed three & Bourke & I
took them over in the Steamer.

15 Tom made a passenger trip in the Steamer to Darien, but
did not get a single white passenger.

16 This is the 12th anniversary of the battle of Baker's creek in
Mississippi. A cold raw N. E. wind blowing.

17 Monday. Went to Doboy with the beef.

18 Jno. A. Cobb & myself went to Darien on our way to Savh.
Took *Lizzie Baker* in afternoon.

19 Wednesday. We reached Savh. about 7 o'cl. this A.M. Capt.
Cobb left for Macon at 7 o'cl. P.M.

20 I got out my license as Capt. of our little Steamer to-day &
left for home on *Carrie* at 4 o'cl. P.M.

21 Reached Doboy about daylight this morning & got over
home in a rowboat during the forenoon.

22 I took command of our little Steamer to-day & made a trip
in her to Darien. Made $4.75 on the trip. The British ship
Great Britain Capt. Chilcott arrived last night.

23 Sunday. Little sick & did nothing.

24 Went with Bourke to carry beef to Doboy. Afterwards went aboard the *Great Britain.*

25 We to-day change the day of our beef delivery, so as to carry it over the same day as I go to town. Started to Darien but the injector on my boiler not working I did not go farther than Doboy.

26 Wednesday. Busy sawing wood & getting water aboard for tomorrow's trip.

27 My thirty-third birth-day. Tom was kind enough to run the boat to town, to let me spend the day at home. Capt. S. E. Clark the Tax Receiver spent the day at my house taking in tax returns.

28 Sawing wood & taking fresh water aboard for trip to Darien tomorrow.

29 I carried the boat to Darien to-day. Took Sallie up with me. Two cabin passengers.

30 Sunday. Spent the day at home doing nothing.

31 Sawing wood &c. for tomorrow's trip.

JUNE

1 Made a trip to Darien to-day, but the Steamboat foamed so badly that my passengers went up in a sail boat. I brought them down however. Reached home about 1 o'cl. to-night. Hired Joe Blue on the Steamer.

2 Wednesday. Nothing unusual occurring.

3 Hiltons & Foster's large saw mill on Pumpkin hammock took fire last [night] & burned down together with several hundred thousand feet of lumber & two schooners. Bourke & I took up a load of hands from Doboy to help save what they could.

4 Butchering day. Killed three beeves. Nothing else of interest occurring.

5 Went to Darien in Steamboat—got back by dark. Little Kate's (Taylor) eleventh birth-day.

6 Sunday. Lucy Cobb & her children left on the Str. *Carrie* this morning, on their way to Athens. Bourke accompanies

them as far as Savh. where he goes to get out license as engineer.

7 Usual routine of butchering & sawing wood.

8 Carried the beef over to Doboy early & then went on to Darien. She is travelling very well now—making about 8 miles an hour. Some rain to-day.

9 Wednesday. I intended to carry a load of cow hides up to-day but they got wet.

10 Made a pleasant trip up to Darien. Met Bourke just from Savannah with his engineer's license.

11 Carried 50 dry flint cow hides to Darien, 723 lbs. Sold them to J. A. Atwood & Bros. @ 12¢. Took Sallie up with me.

12 Went to Darien on my regular trip. Hired a cook named Hester this evening.

13 Sunday. To-day would have been Sister Kate's thirty eighth birth-day had she lived. Bourke & I carried the Steamboat up to Darien to move Dr. Kenan's family down in the morning.

14 Got loaded & with a flat in tow left town about 9 o'cl. this morning. Got nearly to his house when our boiler began to foam & we had to put them all in the flat to drift up to their landing.

15 In order to work on our boiler, we sent the beef in a canoe. Went hunting & I killed a buck in Gum Pond drive.

16 Wednesday. Butchered beef as usual to-day. Nothing of interest occurring.

17 I carried the beef over to Doboy in the Steamer & lay there all day having the boiler repaired.

18 Made an extra trip to Darien to accommodate some of the ship Capts., but only one went up with me.

19 Bourke & I towed the sail boat down to Wolf Is. to get her repaired, but did not succeed. We took the ladies along with us. The Steamer did very badly.

20 Sunday. Spent the day doing nothing.

21 Butchered as usual to-day.

22 My month for running the Steamer having expired last night, Tom takes command this morning. He took his wife to Darien to-day on her way to Athens—he accompanying her as far as Sterling on the Rail Road.

23 Wednesday. Tom not having returned with any order for beef, we did not butcher to-day.

24 Bourke & I got up at daylight & butchered a beef which he afterward took over. Tom returned this afternoon with the Steamer. Wm. Nightingale came with him.

25 We hunted this morning, but the weather being too hot & dry we killed nothing. Afterwards drove up cattle & butchered one.

26 Wm. Nightingale & Jno. M. McIntosh (who came down on the 18th inst.) left for Darien in the Steamer. By the latter I send $312.50 to Savannah to be expressed by him to F. L. Upson, Lexington, Ga., it being the interest due him to 1st July 1875.

27 Sunday. Nothing unusual occurring.

28 Butchered one beef for Doboy. This afternoon Capt. Chilcott of the ship *Great Britain*, came over on a visit.

29 The Steamboat, on account of the few ships in port & her own bad condition, has stopped her passenger trips to Darien.

30 Wednesday. Killed one beef this afternoon.

JULY

1 I went down the river fishing this morning for the first time this season. Caught, all of us, twenty nine scale fish.

2 Tom has gone with the Steamer to Darien to take a committee of County Commissioners to look up a quarantine ground.

3 Tom returned this morning, the boat having given out on the trip. This is little Willie Cobb's ninth birth-day.

4 Sunday. The weather has been dry for more than a month & the crops are burning up. Our cattle can barely find water to drink.

5 At 1 o'cl. this morning Bourke, Charlie & I started in the Steamer for Cambers Is. We carried 18 cowhides & sold them to Strain[5] at 11½¢. When we got to Cambers we took

5. Presumably a tanner living on Cambers Island.

Wm. Nightingale aboard & took in tow his flat with three horses—then went to Hammersmith landing & took in two more horses & Wm. Pritchard & a young man named Roland. Then steered for home down the channel back of Butlers Is. & through three mile cut. Reached home about 11 P.M.

6 Twenty eight years to-day since my Mother's death. Yesterday having been a hard day with us, we rested to-day. The cowhides sold yesterday make 187 we have sold so far this season. The weather is getting to be alarmingly dry. Cow holes all dried up & cattle suffering.

7 Wednesday. The whole party went hunting. Pritchard killed one buck at Hog hammock. We hung him up & hunted on & while we were hunting, the buzzards eat the deer. Had to have a cow hole dug to-day to get water for our cattle.

8 Most of the party went on the Steamer to Doboy to carry beef.

9 Twenty one years to-day since my Sister Caroline died. The party went hunting again. I killed a doe at the patch of pines in Bell & on the next stand Roland shot a buck which the dogs afterwards caught. He was the biggest deer I ever saw on Sapelo—his saddle weighing 42 lbs. We bloodied Roland well as it was his first deer.

10 Most of the party again went to Doboy with the beef. Weather still dry & crops are burning up. Corn crop ruined.

11 Sunday. What with hunting, driving cattle & butchering all week, I am pretty well broken down, & rested to-day.

12 Went hunting again to-day. I missed a deer in a bunch above Bell drive.

13 Our visitors left us for home this morning on the steamboat & I must say I am glad they are gone.

14 Wednesday. The steamboat returned this afternoon. Heavy blow from N.W., but only a sprinkle of rain here.

15 Went to Doboy on a collecting tour. Hottest day I ever saw on Sapelo. Thermometer 102°.

16 Drove up cattle & butchered one beef. A light shower last night & this morning.

17 Scraping & painting the steamboat's hull.

18 Sunday. Spent the entire day at home.

19   We killed one small beef this afternoon—only 137 lbs., but as there are only three vessels at Doboy, we will stop killing for the season, unless more vessels come in.

20   We sent the beef over by a small boat & afterwards worked on the steamboat.

21   Wednesday. The fourteenth anniversary of the 1st battle of Manassas. We started to carry Clara Barrow to Hammersmith landing, on her way home, but unfortunately we accidently got some bilge water in the boiler that [the steamboat] foamed so that after getting to the middle of the Sound, we had to turn back & come home.

22   Started out before daylight for Hammersmith—got there all right & put Clara Barrow out all safe. On our way back Wm. Wylly ran us aground & we had to stay there until nearly 10 o'cl. at night. Got to Darien about 11 o'cl. Eleventh anniversary of our battle near Atlanta in which Genls. Walker & McPherson were killed.

23   Reached home late this afternoon. A very good swell on the Sound.

24   Not being very well, staid at home most of the day. No rain yet & crops burning up.

25   Sunday. Spent the entire day at home. No rain yet.

26   Wooded & watered the steamboat. Mollie Livingston is very sick. No rain.

27   We started in the steamboat with the flat in tow for Doboy to get lumber, but owing to muddy water in the boiler she foamed so that we did not go more than half a mile. No rain yet.

28   Wednesday. After washing out the boiler yesterday & putting clear water in, we started for Darien, taking the flat as far as Doboy. Tom loaded it there with timber & the rest of us went on to Darien. John & Wm. Nightingale returned with us.

29   Did nothing to-day but unload the lumber flat. No rain yet.

30   Went hunting this morning but killed nothing. Afterwards wrote a deed for Tom to Jas. or rather Catherine Cromley, for the Light house island, or most of it.[6] No rain.

6. Members of the Cromley (sometimes spelled Crumbley) family were the longtime keepers (1873–1933) of the Sapelo lighthouse. The actual

31 Went hunting again this morning but again killed nothing—
the deer running the wrong way. The ground is so dry it is
with the greatest difficulty the dogs can even run a deer.

AUGUST

1 Sunday. Spent the day at home. No rain.
2 Went hunting again this morning and at the upper end of
Hog hammock—on the stand next the trunk, two bucks
sneaked out to me. With one barrel I wounded one badly
(which Tom afterwards killed) & I killed the second. Jno.
Nightingale killed a doe. A light sprinkle of rain.
3 Went hunting again to-day, but after a long run only got a
fawn—killed by Tom. Mr. Bass & Charlie are both sick with
fever. No rain.
4 Wednesday. We went to Cabaretta beach to catch shrimp,
but it was a failure.
5 Having no corn to feed our horses, we did not go hunting
to-day. This afternoon we had a tremendous rain—the first
good one since April. Mr. Bass & Charlie are both very sick.
6 We all went to Darien for the doctor for the sick. Jno.
Nightingale went home.
7 Having nothing to do & being fatigued from yesterday's
trip, I rested to-day.
8 Sunday. We carried Dr. Kenan back to Darien this morning
& afterwards we went on to Cambers Is. Wm. Nightingale
did not return with us. Nellie went up with us & went to
Church. Good shower.
9 Mr. Bass taken suddenly worse tonight & had to send up for
the doctor.
10 Bourke returned with Dr. Kenan about 8 o'clock this morning. Tom bought him a green parrot on yesterday.

---

lighthouse property (five acres) had belonged to the federal government
since 1820. This transaction sold the Cromleys about fifty acres, including
marsh, between the lighthouse and the south end of Sapelo. The Cromleys
were known as bootmakers and rattlesnake catchers. See July 30, 1875, and
February 28, 1877, and the Ella Barrow Spalding letter in this volume.

11 Wednesday. Had very heavy rains last night. I had to sit up last night, as did all the others with Mr. Bass who is very ill indeed. Rain.

12 Bourke & I carried the Dr. back to Darien on the Steamboat. Purchased groceries & got back about 10 o'cl. P.M. Good rain.

13 Nothing unusual occurring except nursing Mr. Bass who is still dangerously ill.

14 Still sitting up with Mr. B. at night & sleeping during the day.

15 Sunday. Nothing unusual going on. Still sitting up with Mr. Bass.

16 Rested after sitting up last night. Tom & Bourke gone to Doboy for lumber. We find to-day one of our finest cows killed by a blow from an axe in the hands of some negro.

17 Nothing unusual occurring to-day.

18 Wednesday. We started in the steamboat at 2 o'cl. A.M. & carried Nightingale's flat to Cambers Is. We afterwards brought the steamer back to Darien & put it in the hands of John & Wm. Parry for thorough repairs to the boiler & machinery for which we are to pay them $300. The job to be finished by the 1st day of October.

19 Bourke & I returned home in a row boat just at day break, leaving Tom in Darien to look after the steamboat.

20 Nothing unusual going on.

21 I have been hard at work moving my fence lumber from the landing to my yard. Tom returned.

22 Sunday. Tom left on Str. *Reliance* this morning for Savh. to meet his wife.

23 I went to Darien this morning in a row boat to see about our steamboat. I drew up & had signed by Parry, the machinist, a contractor. Afterwards I paid him $150 in advance. A tiresome day.

24 Left Darien at 3 o'cl. A.M. & got home to breakfast.

25 Wednesday. I had my two mares, Kate & Sallie, hitched to the buggy & took Sallie (my wife) & Katie Taylor to ride. Also carried Mr. Bass to Livingstons' on a visit.

26 Sallie [has] been very busy moving into another kitchen. The wind for the past three days has been from the N.E. Weather clear.

27 Tom & his wife arrived this morning on Str. *Reliance* &
came from Doboy in a row boat. A large negro excursion
came down on the Steamer *Clyde* & landed at Bourke's.
They soon went back, however, disgusted at the cool recep-
tion given by Sapelo negroes.

28 Nothing unusual occurring. The N.E. wind which has been
blowing, without a drop of rain, for nearly a week past, has
shifted.

29 Sunday. Mollie Livingston came down on a visit this afternoon—staying at my house.

30 A big negro fight between two Sapelo negroes. Anthony
Sams & Glascow Grovenor. Warrant &c.

31 A constable came for Anthony with a warrant charging him
with assault with intent to murder.

SEPTEMBER

1 Wednesday. Nothing of unusual interest occurring to-day.

2 My Mother's birth-day. This morning just after daylight I
was handed a telegram from my Father informing me of the
dangerous illness of my brother Andrews. I will go to Darien
tomorrow & if I hear no better news from him, will go to
Milledgeville.

3 Sister Sarah, my wife & myself went in Graybill's sail boat to
Darien. I telegraphed from there to Dr. White as to Arny's
condition—his answer was "condition critical—danger extreme." We took Str. *Lizzie Baker* at 9½ o'clock at night for
Savannah.

4 Reached Savannah at 11 o'cl. A.M. Left there on C. R.R. at
7.30 P.M.

5 Sunday. Reached Milledgeville this morning. When we
reached Father's found that poor Arny had been dead forty-
five minutes. He died of a 15 days' attack of bilious fever.

6 Sallie's 31st birth-day. We buried Arny this afternoon at
5 o'clock with military honors by his company (Baldwin
Blues), with the following pall bearers Lieut. W. A. Jarratt,
Sergt. O. T. Kenan, prvt. C. L. Case, prvt. P. A. West,
prvt. B. A. White, prvt. I. A. Quinn.

7 Taking care of Father & Mother. The latter takes Arny's
   death very much to heart.
8 Wednesday. Father having bought a large lot in the cemetary, I have been engaged to-day in removing Katie's
   remains to the new lot beside Arny.
9 Howell left for Athens this morning taking Mother with
   him. Willie is already there. Guy & I have been busy all day
   exhuming sister Caroline's remains at Beulah & removing
   them to the new lot in town. She now rests beside Sister
   Kate and brother Andrews. Thank God.
10 Having had a very prostrating day's work yesterday, owing
   to the extreme heat, Guy & I have been resting to-day. Sister Callie had been buried 21 years and although she was
   buried in a metallic case, yet the coffin was full of water. The
   cloth over the coffin (black broad cloth) was in almost perfect
   preservation.
11 Went with Father to the cemetary this afternoon—the first
   time he has been there since Arnie's funeral.
12 Sunday. None of us went to church. The wind having shifted
   to the N.E. it has been blowing hard & the weather is quite
   cold—rendering a fire necessary.
13 Mr. Goetchius[7] having been called to Columbus last Friday,
   returned this morning. Father very busy fixing up indian
   arrow heads for shipment to the Smithsonian Institute,
   Washington City.
14 Father still at work on his indian arrow heads. Nothing else
   unusual occurring.
15 Wednesday. Nothing unusual occurring.
16 Sallie spent the day with her cousin Clifford Williamson.
   Father got letters calling him to Athens.
17 Father left for Athens this morning to bring Willie home—
   as we suppose to die.
18 Father & Mother returned this afternoon with Willie. Poor
   fellow, I don't see how any man can be so emaciated & be

7. George T. Goetchius, of a prominent Columbus, Ga. family, was the
minister of the Milledgeville Presbyterian Church from 1872 to 1879,
succeeding Charles W. Lane. He married Julia McKinley, half sister of
McKinley.

alive. Howell Cobb who started with them had some thing like an apoplectic fit at Union Pt. & had to turn back.

19 Sunday. Nursing Willie.

20 Still nursing Willie. Poor fellow is most gone.

21 Nursing Willie night & day.

22 Willie better to-day—worse tonight.

23 Thursday. Willie a little better to-day, though he does not improve.

24 Sister Sarah, Kate Taylor & Tom Spalding arrived from Sapelo this morning. Willie as usual.

25 Willie a good deal worse to-day. He does not like for any but Tom & myself to nurse him. He rallied a little in the afternoon.

26 Sunday. Poor Willie almost went about noon but rallied & lived until twenty minutes after five o'clock (5.20) this afternoon, when he died suddenly. He told us in the morning that he would die some time during the evening.

27 Sister Mary, baby & Howell Cobb arrived this afternoon. Raining heavily.

28 We had intended to have Willie's funeral at 10 o'cl. this A.M. but it was raining so heavily that it was postponed till 3 o'clock P.M. He was buried beside Arnie, with military honors. The following were his pall bearers—Lieut. J. L. Hunter, Lieut. W. A. Jarratt, Sergt. T. L. McComb, Prvt. Chas. Case, Prvt. B. A. White, Prvt. Robt. Hunter.

29 Wednesday. Father & Mother seem to be utterly crushed by the loss of their two sons & beg me not to leave them yet.

30 Spent the day at home—a little sick. This day closes up a fatal month to us.

OCTOBER

1 Nothing unusual occurring.

2 Went into Milledgeville this morning.

3 Sunday. Guy & myself went with Sallie to the Episcopal Church—the first time that she & I have heard a sermon in over two years. Weather getting quite cool here.

4 Howell Cobb, who went to Macon with his brother John last Saturday, returned this morning.

5 It is just one month to-day since I arrived here—but what a month it has been. Within the month I have helped to bury two grown brothers & have reinterred two Sisters.

6 Wednesday. Tom Spalding & Sister Sarah left for home (Sapelo) this afternoon. Thus the family gathering begins to break up, and sad as was the cause of the gathering, I dislike very much to separate.

7 My Father left for Wilkinson Court this morning before day. I carried him over & a dark drive it was too. At 7.15 A.M. Howell Cobb, Sister Mary & baby left for home (Athens) taking my niece Kate Taylor with them. This is a bitter pill to Sister Sarah & myself as we have had her since her Mother's death (Feb. 4, 1873), but she must have schooling. Geo. Goetchius (Julia's husband) left for Washington Wilkes County to attend Presbytery. I have been abed all day with a terrible sick headache.

8 I am well to-day, but very sick from yesterday's head ache. Weather quite cool & fire very comfortable morning & evening.

9 Father returned late last night from Irwinton, where he had been to Court.

10 Sunday. Father, Sallie, Guy & I attended Presbyterian Church. Mr. Cunningham preached.

11 Poor Willie's birth-day. He would have been twenty-four years old to-day had he lived fifteen days longer. He is the first member of my family who I have seen die, except Sister Callie, & the memories of his death-bed haunt me in the dead of night nearly every night.

12 Nothing unusual occurring. The weather is getting on to the frost point.

13 Wednesday. Ben Barrow, Mr. Goetchius & Dr. Harris went partridge shooting & killed *two* birds.

14 Been busy packing mattresses for Mother to ship to Sapelo. Sallie took dinner yesterday at Bernard Herty's & spent last night at Cliff Williamson's—returning home this morning.

15 Father went to Sparta this morning to attend Hancock Court & returned this afternoon. I spent the morning in Milledgeville. Rain all afternoon.

16 I was to have started for home this afternoon, but owing to a change of schedule among the steamboats, I postpone it til Monday. Spent the entire day at Father's.

17 Sunday. The first frost of the season and a heavy, killing one at that. Attended the Presbyterian Church. [*Marginal note: Frost on Sapelo too.*]

18 Left Milledgeville for home. The schedule of the C. R.R. having been changed without our knowledge, Sallie & I took M. & A.[8] to Macon. It is the first day of the Fair & the latter place is crowded. Left Macon at 9.35 o'cl. P.M.

19 Arrived in Savannah at 7.15 o'clock this morning & spent the day with the family of Mrs. Sallie McIntosh.

20 Wednesday. Left Savh. at 10 o'cl. this A.M. on Str. *Lizzie Baker*. After a pleasant run outside reached Doboy about dark, where Charlie met us with a boat & hands. Reached home about 9 o'clock.

21 Did nothing all day at home.

22 Sick all day with diarrhoea. Mr. Rodriguez arrived from St. Catherine to buy seed cotton.

23 Mr. Rodriguez left this morning. I am still sick. Tom & Charlie are very busy painting our Steamboat—getting her ready for inspection.

24 Sunday. A quiet, warm, pretty day.

25 Tom went to Darien this forenoon to see about paying taxes. I have been quite sick.

26 One month this afternoon since my brother Willie died. Tom returned this afternoon.

27 Wednesday. All hands busy painting & repairing the wood work of the Steam boat. Weather very warm.

28 Still at work on the steam boat. Weather warm.

29 After finishing what repairs we could do on the boat, we commenced taking water aboard to go to Darien with. Sent there to-day for an engineer to take us up tomorrow.

30 When I woke up this morning I found a South rain falling. The engineer that we sent for failed to come to-day.

31 Sunday. Attended services at Tom's house.

8. The Macon and Augusta Railroad, completed 1872.

NOVEMBER

1 The engineer that we expected arrived this afternoon & we left our wharf, in our steamboat at 4.15 P.M. reaching Darien about 7.30 this evening.

2 Machinists putting the finishing touches on our boiler for inspection tomorrow.

3 Wednesday. Our boat (*The Sapelo*) was inspected to-night. She passed satisfactorily. The inspectors increased our passenger list from 13 to 25, but require us to carry a small boat and another steam gauge.

4 We came home this afternoon—reaching here sometime after dark.

5 Tom & I went grass hunting to-day, but although we rode several miles we did not succeed in finding a deer.

6 Not having killed a deer yesterday and all the houses being entirely out of meat, Tom & I killed a small beef this afternoon.

7 Sunday. Spent most of the day at home.

8 I got my single wagon back home to-day. Mr. Livingston broke it several months ago & would not bring it home. It has just been repaired. Weather cloudy with a cold N.W. wind blowing.

9 Nothing unusual occurring.

10 We expected Bourke & his wife back to-night, but they did not come. Very high West wind blowing.

11 Thursday. Weather moderating. Sent to Darien yesterday for the mail, but got no letters.

12 Weather still getting warmer.

13 To-night, just before going to bed Mr. Swoll of Savannah came up to my house. He got off his boat at Bourbon & it went on to Blackbeard Island.

14 Sunday. Spent the day going from house to house with Mr. Swoll. I forgot to say that Mr. Rodriguez arrived here yesterday with a sail boat on a cotton buying trip.

15 Tom & I went with Mr. Swoll to Blackbeard Is. where we met his friends Mr. Jno. Taylor & Capt. Westcott of Savh. Tom killed a doe & Billy Hillery a buck.

16 We all came over to Sapelo last night & hunted here to-
day. I killed a doe—a large one—in old marsh & so did
Mr. Taylor & Jack—Mr. T., a young buck.

17 Wednesday. Hunted Bell & other drives in that direction.
Mr. Swoll wounded a deer in Big Hammock & Mr. Livingston shot at one in Bell. Neither one got his deer.

18 Bourke & his wife returned from the up country last night
per Str. *Lizzie Baker*. Messrs. Taylor & Westcott left for
Savannah in their sail boat late yesterday evening. Bourke &
I went to Darien in our Steam boat. Mr. Swoll accompanied
us and remained in Darien with his German friends.

19 We returned early this morning. This is the ninth anniversary of my marriage day.

20 Busy covering our steamboat boiler with felt. Weather
very warm.

21 Sunday. Rode up to the Livingstons' & Mollie returned with
me. Very warm.

22 Working at the steam boat most of the day. A disagreeable,
damp, raw day. Ten years since I courted my wife.

23 Have been helping to build a trough from the pump to the
steamboat. Weather much warmer.

24 Wednesday. Went to Darien in the steamboat. Tom &
Bourke took their wives. Got no pay passengers going up,
but one coming back.

25 Found Mr. Rodriguez when we returned last, again here
trying to buy cotton. Killed one beef for home consumption.
To-day is Pres. Grant's thanksgiving day.

26 Did nothing particularly except to put water aboard the
Steamer.

27 Went to Darien on a passenger trip. Got from the Custom
House our Certificate of Inspection for the coming year.

28 Sunday. Eight years to-night since our baby son was born &
died.

29 Getting ready to serve as grand juror the balance of the
week.

30 Father's 66th birth-day. I went to Darien to attend Court.
Carried up on steam boat 10 full & 2 half passengers.

DECEMBER

1 Wednesday. I was elected yesterday foreman of the grand jury. Am staying at the Wyllys'. Weather cold & damp.

2 Tom & Bourke came up in the Steamer to-day. In two hours after they left for home the grand jury was discharged until the 5th January. Cold & damp.

3 Amused myself attending Court which adjourned this afternoon until next month. Weather still cold & lowering.

4 I at last got off from Darien late this afternoon. Brought down three passengers.

5 Sunday. Raining rather heavily this forenoon. H. C. Wylly is staying at Tom's.

6 Tom & Bourke gone to town on a special trip to take Mrs. Spalding & Mollie Livingston.

7 Three Capts. chartered us to carry them to Darien for $10.00.

8 Wednesday. Went to Darien on our regular passenger trip.

9 Nothing unusual occurring.

10 Went to Darien on our regular passenger trip.

11 Went to Doboy with Steamer to get lumber. Had a big talk about beef. We wish to sell to McKenzie & Jno. Ingraham & Steadwell are opposed to us.

12 Sunday. Nothing, except putting water aboard the Steamer, occurring.

13 Went to Darien on our regular passenger trip.

14 Chartered by a Capt. to-day to take him to Darien & back for $10.00.

15 Wednesday. Took over yesterday one beef—the first—of the season. Went to Darien on regular passenger trip. The Steamboat has been making about $25.00 a week.

16 Killed one beef yesterday & delivered it down Back river & to McKenzie this morning.

17 Made our usual passenger trip to Darien.

18 Delivered beef in Back river.[9] The coldest I ever felt on Sapelo. The thermometer stood 17° at 10 o'cl. A.M. in the

9. A tributary of Doboy Sound on the south side of Commodore Island, the mooring for vessels waiting to load at Doboy Island.

house & the ground remained frozen & ice continued to form all day.

19 Sunday. Weather still very cold, but two or three degrees warmer than yesterday.

20 Made our usual passenger trip to Darien. Weather moderating.

21 After delivering beef this morning, we went jump hunting. I got two shots—wounding one & getting none.

22 Wednesday. Made our usual trip to Darien.

23 After delivering our beef, Dick Clark chartered us to carry him to Darien.

24 Made usual passenger trip to Darien.

25 Christmas. After delivering beef, Capt. Chilcott gave us some brandy & wine & we came home & had a merry time.

26 Sunday. Weather warm as Summer.

27 Made the usual passenger trip.

28 Delivered beef in a dense fog.

29 Wednesday. Usual passenger trip.

30 Sister Mary Cobb's 31st birth-day.

31 Made our usual passenger trip—taking up 13 & bringing back 8 passengers. This day ends the year 1875—a year full of afflictions to my family. May the next be a brighter one is my prayer.

1876

JANUARY

1 New year's day. Twenty two ships in port to-day.
2 Sunday. A day of rest with me.
3 Ran a regular passenger trip to Darien.
4 After delivering beef the steamboat took Sallie & myself to Darien where I have to attend Court tomorrow as a grand juror.
5 Court met this morning, but there being no business for the grand jury, we were discharged until tomorrow morning.
6 Thursday. The grand jury was discharged this morning & I was immediately caught as a talis petit juror, but the judge let me off this afternoon & I left for home. Have been staying with the Wyllys.
7 Made our regular passenger trip to Darien.
8 Coming back from Doboy we got out of fresh water & tried to use salt water in our boiler, but it foamed awfully.
9 Sunday. A pleasant rest day with me.
10 Bourke, Charlie & I took the Steam boat to Pumpkin Hammock to work on the boiler. I had to walk into Darien to get the mechanic.
11 At work on the boat all day. Charlie went home to get us provisions to-night.
12 Wednesday. Charlie got back tonight & reports a very rough Sound. We finished work on the boiler at mid-night.
13 After getting water aboard, we left Pumpkin Hammock about midnight & steamed home handsomely.
14 Went to Darien with passengers.

15 After delivering beef, four ship Capts. came back with us & we had to carry them rabbit hunting. The whole party killed forty rabbits.

16 Sunday. Our visiting Capt. after spending the night, left for Doboy this morning.

17 Went to Darien with passengers.

18 After delivering beef we came home & have been busy expanding the tubes in our boiler.

19 Wednesday. We made a passenger trip to Darien—the tubes are at last tight.

20 Delivered five beeves to the shipping.

21 Made a passenger trip—the best we have ever made yet, I having booked about thirty-two dollars.

22 After delivering beef, three Capts. chartered the boat to carry them to Darien. The tubes commenced leaking worse than ever. Did not leave town till after dark—when nearing the Doboy wharf I fell overboard, but swam ashore all safely.

23 Sunday. Sick in bed to-day from having to keep on my wet clothes last night until I reached home.

24 Still confined to my room. Tom & Bourke killed 5 beeves.

25 Sent the beef over in a rowboat. We now deliver to McKenzie on the Doboy wharf at 8 cts. per lb. commencing to-day.

26 Wednesday. We have a man named Riley expanding the tubes with a Prossir expander & caulking & beading them down.

27 Tom carried the beef (3) to Doboy. The large fleet of vessels that have been in port is rapidly dwindling.

28 Finished repairs on the boiler about 10 o'clock to-night. Butchered three beeves for Doboy this evening.

29 This morning at day break we took the beef on for Doboy. After delivering it at Doboy, we went on to Darien, Sallie, Nellie & Mrs. Spalding going with us.

30 Sunday. It commenced to rain & blow last night & we have had a cold raw day of it to-day.

31 Butchered three beeves to deliver tomorrow. Had my cow Spot & young calf brought up this afternoon.

FEBRUARY

1   Have changed our running day, so that now we deliver on the Doboy wharf & then go on to town. Made the first trip to-day under the new schedule.

2   Wednesday. Killed three beeves to carry to Doboy tomorrow.

3   Delivered the beef & went on to Darien. Met Wm. Nightingale & Dr. Greene at Doboy on their way to Sapelo. They could get no boat to cross the Sound in & had to stay with us all day.

4   Went hunting with the visitors, but killed nothing. Weather very warm in the morning. About 1 o'clock, in one instant turned piercingly cold.

5   A young gale blowing & very cold, but Bourke & I made our usual passenger trip to Darien.

6   Sunday. Wm. Nightingale, who is staying at my house, has been very sick all day with chill &c.

7   Dr. Greene & Bourke have gone out jump hunting. I have been busy most of the morning writing to Father in the legislature in Atlanta.

8   Our visitors left this morning on Steamboat. Tom & his wife left for Brunswick—the former to attend State Agricultural Convention.

9   Wednesday. As Tom is in Brunswick, Charlie drove up the cattle yesterday. Butchered four.

10   Made the usual passenger trip to Darien, making $26 in cash.

11   We took the Steamboat to Doboy to meet Tom &c., just before we reached Doboy we met the Capt. of the Ship *Atlantic* of Nyborg with Tom & wife & Uncle David. We went aboard the *Atlantic* & spent a pleasant hour or so.

12   Made the usual passenger trip to Darien but only had 4 passengers up & 3 down.

13   Sunday. Just had settled myself for a good nap when Bourke & Nellie came for me to go with them and Uncle David to the beach. Owing to *peculiar* circumstances I had to go.

14   St. Valentine's day but "nary" a valentine hereabouts. Butchered four beeves. Heavy rain.

15 My brother Guy's 18th birth-day. Made our usual passenger trip.

16 Nothing unusual going on. Butchered a beef this afternoon.

17 Thursday. At the urgent request of some people we put off our morning trip to Darien & went this afternoon in order to take up all who wished to attend an Episcopal Church festival in Darien tonight, and thereby lost nearly all our passengers. Spent the night at the Wyllys.

18 Left Darien at 6.20 o'clock—no passengers. Butchered six beeves this afternoon. Tom left yesterday for Valdosta via Savannah, to buy beef cattle.

19 Sold two of beeves to Ingram & Steadwell. Usual passenger trip to Darien.

20 Sunday. Have enjoyed my rest to-day. Nellie is very sick, having had a miscarriage on the 17th inst.

21 Butchered three beeves.

22 On returning to Doboy from Darien at sunset, we met a row boat going for a doctor for Nellie. We went back immediately for Dr. Kenan—reaching home between midnight & 1 o'clock. Uncle David left for home this morning.

23 Bourke's 25th birth-day. He & I had to butcher alone.

24 Thursday. This afternoon W. H. Atwood, Jno. Dunham came down with us. They are road commissioners sent down to examine & report the utility of a public road from Raccoon Bluff.

25 After the arrival of Arthur Bailey—another commissioner—I drove them over to Raccoon Bluff to examine into things. They left in a row boat this afternoon. I think they will advise against another public road.

26 Made our usual passenger trip. Father sent me a copy of new game law.

27 Sunday. Did nothing but rest.

28 Weather warm & Springlike—grass growing very rapidly.

29 After taking the beef to Doboy we went on to Hammersmith landing to meet Tom with his cattle. We went first to Myhall Mill for a supply of wood—thence to Jno. Nightingale's place for a flat which we towed to Hammersmith via Champney Island.

MARCH

1 Wednesday. Busy all day building a cattle pen.

2 The cattle having arrived yesterday, we put them in the flat & started for home about 11 o'cl. Our steamboat tows finely. A N.W. gale blowing.

3 Killed beef for Doboy.

4 Took Nightingale's flat home by the same route we went for it. Afterwards went through Generals cut to Darien.

5 Sunday. Nothing unusual.

6 Butchered as usual for Doboy market.

7 Began our regular passenger trips to Darien again to-day.

8 Killing beef as usual. Our new stock is very poor.

9 Thursday. Usual passenger trip.

10 Nothing unusual occurring.

11 In getting to Doboy this morning we found the little steamer *Daisy* running as an opposition (to us) passenger boat between Doboy and Darien, but the salt water made her boiler foam so badly that she gave up the idea this afternoon.

12 Sunday. Rested to-day.

13 Butchered as usual.

14 Changed our time of leaving Doboy from 9 to 8 o'clock passenger days.

15 Wednesday. Nothing unusual going on.

16 Tom & his Mother started for Savannah on some law business, but meeting in Darien Col. Brown & Capt. Barnwell looking for a site for the penitentiary, he returned with them to Sapelo.

17 Tom & I took the visitors over his & the Kenan place. They desire to organize a joint stock company & buy a sea island on which to locate the Georgia Penitentiary on a twenty-year lease.

18 Made our usual passenger trip.

19 Every thing going on as usual. We hear yesterday of the loss of the British ship *Great Britain*, Capt. Chilcott. The Capt.'s two sons were lost & in [fact] most of the crew— the survivors living by eating the dead.[1]

1. The *New York Times*, March 17, 1876, verifies the details of this March 11 incident.

20 Monday. I drove up cattle for the first time this season. I was in a pouring & driving rain for 5½ hours & when I got home I was so cold & stiff that I could scarcely get off my horse. Killed three beeves.

21 My exposure yesterday brought on a chill, so that I did not go with the steamboat as usual. Bourke & Charlie carrying her. The wind is blowing a gale from the West. Very cold—thermometer 35°.

22 Wednesday. Killed three beeves for Doboy.

23 Tom returned from Savannah last night. On getting to Darien this morning Bourke received a telegram informing him that Ben Barrow had died on Tuesday of a hemorrhage (consumption). He was buried yesterday in Athens.

24 Killed three beeves for Doboy to-day.

25 Made our usual passenger trip to Darien. The number of our passengers is beginning to fall off. The weather is moderating, but still rather cold.

26 Sunday. The weather is beginning to get Spring like again, but is not as warm yet as it has been.

27 We carried Bourke's mare Bess over to Little Sapelo this morning in our steam boat. On the way we broke one of the eccentric rods, but managed to patch it up. Three beeves to-day.

28 Made our usual passenger trip. The number of our passengers though is on the decrease.

29 Wednesday. Butchered as usual.

30 Sallie went to Darien with me this morning. She found her Aunt, Mrs. Wylly, so ill that she did not come home.

31 Mrs. Wylly died last night.

APRIL

1 Sister Sarah's 29th birth-day. Mrs. W. was buried at the family cemetery this morning. My wife did not return.

2 Sunday. I slept at Bourke's last night. Tremendous rain nearly all night.

3 Slept at home last night. Heavy rain all night.

4   Sallie came home to-day & Sister Sarah took her place with Sallie Wylly.

5   Wednesday. Nothing unusual.

6   We went to Darien this morning expecting to go to Egg Island for a lot of cattle, but could not get a flat. Henry McKinley arrived on the *Daisy* & came down with us.

7   Butchered as usual.

8   Made our usual passenger trip, but got very little money from it. We discontinue our regular trips to Darien after to-day, until we can get more passengers.

9   Sunday. Nothing unusual going on except sleeping in the day time.

10 Only killed 153 lbs. beef to-day as there are only 8 square rigged vessels loading now.

11 After delivering our beef we came home & went deer hunting for the first time in a long while. Henry McK. let one run by him & I killed a young buck at the upper part of New Orleans drive.[2]

19 My Sister Julia (Mrs. George Goetchius) gave birth on the 8th inst. to a son & a telegram informs me that she died suddenly on the 15th inst. I leave Sapelo this morning for Milledgeville to see about Father's condition. Left Darien at 1 o'clock P.M.—left Sterling 4.45 P.M.

20 Arrived in Macon at 4.30 A.M. by Macon & B. R. Rd.[3] Arrived at Milledgeville about 7 o'clock A.M. No one expected me. I find Howell Cobb & Sister Mary at Father's. I find Father & Mother very much broken by Julia's death.

25 Left Milledgeville for Savh. to attend a democratic convention tomorrow to nominate delegates to St. Louis to nominate a democratic candidate for president.

26 Attended the convention this A.M. I telegraphed to Sallie to meet me here, as I want her at Milledgeville for company for Mother. I shall wait here till she arrives. Am stopping at Carr's hotel.

29 Sallie arrived about 1 o'clock P.M. & we left on the C. R. Rd. at 7.30 o'cl. this evening.

30 Sunday. Reached Milledgeville this morning at 10 o'clock.

2. Entries here become sporadic until January 1, 1877.

3. Macon & Brunswick Railroad, completed 1871.

JUNE

5 After staying more than a month with Father & Mother, we start home this afternoon.

6 Reached Savh. this morning & left there this afternoon.

21 Henry & Clara Barrow having been some time on Sapelo for the benefit of the health of the former, left for home this morning accompanied by Bourke. They go via Brunswick, but Henry poor fellow was too weak, he died at 9.30 o'clock tonight in Brunswick. They carried his remains to Athens.

SEPTEMBER

1 Yellow fever raging in Savh.[4]

5 James I. McKinley, my 1st cousin died of Yellow fever in Savh.

27 The McIntosh family fleeing from Yellow fever have settled on us temporarily. They arrive to-day.

28 Bourke & Willie Cobb, the latter of whom arrived on Aug. 28th, left for the up country to-day.

OCTOBER

3 Francis Cummins McKinley, another first cousin died of Yellow fever in Savh.—making four first cousins of mine gone this year—also a Sister & niece.

NOVEMBER

21 The McIntoshes left for the Ridge to-day.

4. In the summer and fall of 1876, yellow fever was epidemic in Savannah, Macon, and Brunswick.

1877

JANUARY

1   Monday. After having neglected my journal for several months, I now resume it & hope to be able to keep at it regularly. On the 18th of last month Charlie Bass & Mr. Livingston coming from Doboy in our sail boat capsized in the middle of the Sound in a high W. wind. After drifting for an hour-&-a-half they were picked up by a Doboy boat but we have not been able to use our boat since—the sail being destroyed. We killed our first beef for the Doboy market this morning.

2   Wind N.W. & so high that we would not carry the beef in the boat which we had—a canoe. Weather very cold—ice plentiful.

3   Wednesday. Very cold. Tom took the beef to Doboy & staid there to try to sell it. I went hunting & killed two partridges.

4   All hands are busy making a new sail for our boat. Bourke's wife is quite sick, having had a miscarriage to-day.

5   Still working hard at our sail.

6   Finished our sail at dark this evening. Tom returned from Doboy, having sold only two quarters of beef.

7   Sunday. Tom, Bourke, Charlie Bass & myself went to the Light House & saw the new iron beacon which has just been erected. Tom is clearing up at the South end preparatory to building there.

8   We carried another beef to Doboy. Charlie is staying there now to sell our beef.

9   Went to Darien with Bourke & Mr. Bass. Mrs. Livingston returned with us. Weather very cold.

10 Called with Bourke on Capt. R. K. Chilcott at the Livingstons'. He now [*page bottom eroded*].

11 Thursday. Killed a beef & Tom took it to Doboy tonight. Bourke left for Savannah on private business.

12 Doing nothing all day but reading. Tom & his wife very busy clearing at South End. Weather very warm. So far this has been the severest winter around here for a great many years.

13 To-day would have been Sister Caroline's thirty-seventh birth-day had she lived. Rode down to South End where Tom is clearing up, preparatory to building.

14 Sunday. Spent the day doing nothing. Weather still very warm.

15 Tom & I drove up & butchered one beef which Charlie carried to Doboy.

16 Tom went to Darien before daylight. Bourke returned from Savh. this morning, bringing with him a mule which he bought there for $135. After getting him to his wharf in a flat, he jumped overboard & swam across the creek, giving a great deal of trouble to get him back.

17 Wednesday. Killed a beef this morning which Bourke carried to Doboy in the sail boat. Heavy fog most of the day. Thermometer 68°—trees budding.

18 Had to get up at daylight & with Tom drive up & butcher a beef. Sent it to Doboy & got an order for another immediately which Tom drove up but not in time to butcher this evening. Bourke has taken him self off to Darien with all his servants, leaving Tom & me to do the work.

19 Got up at daylight & butchered a beef which Tom afterwards carried to Doboy. Bourke returned late this evening.

20 We killed two beeves late this afternoon to carry to Doboy Monday morning. Weather very warm & foggy.

21 Sunday. Just at dark a thunder storm came up & rained very heavily. While it was going on a flash of lightning struck a tree in less than 100 yards of my house—by the butcher pen, startling us very much.

22 Charlie Bass carried the beef over before daylight. Weather warm with some rain.

23 Tom left for Brunswick this morning to buy lumber for his house. Bourke & I drove up & butchered two beeves.

24 Wednesday. We carried the beef over in the sail boat & delivered it down Back river.

25 We killed two beeves this afternoon. Tom returned from Brunswick to-night. A new steamboat put on the line from Savh., called the *David Clark*.

26 We all carried the beef over this morning & delivered it to Charlie. Peter McKenzie is anxious to sell our beef for us.

27 In changing back to our old beef delivery days, to-day comes in as an idle day.

28 Sunday. My old mare Kate got down between the corn rows & would have died if we had not found & helped her.

29 Had great difficulty in finding the cattle this morning. Killed three of them.

30 Killed one beef to-day which Tom took to Doboy. The weather is getting very warm & Spring like.

31 Wednesday. Having left all the beeves which we drove up Monday, in the pen we did not have to look for them this time. We killed three of them. Bourke took them to Doboy & kept on to Darien.

FEBRUARY

1 Nothing special occurring to-day. Willie Wylly & Dr. Kenan came down this afternoon with Bourke.

2 I have been suffering for several days with a pain in my back—so much so that I could not help to drive up cattle to-day. Killed two beeves.

3 Tom went in the sail boat to Pumpkin hammock. Willie Wylly went home with him.

4 Sunday. News came last night that our steamboat had sunk at Cambers Island and Bourke went up this morning to see about it. A little rain.

5 I hired a cook named Di[*illegible*]mon this morning at $5.00 a month. Butchered three beeves & sent them to Doboy from the South End.

6 I received a letter from Father to-day, asking me to break up here & come & live with him. As our firm is about dissolving, I have determined to comply with his wishes & leave Sapelo finally. It feels to me like parting from an old & dear friend. Wm. Nightingale arrived to-day. He has bought Tom's [old] house & brought down a flat load of things. Bourke returned after getting the Steamboat all right again.

7 Wednesday. Killed three beeves. Wind high from N. raining & stormy.

8 Tom & I hunted for cattle this afternoon but could find none. Heard tonight that the steamboat was sunk again.

9 Got up beef this morning. Killed two & took them to Doboy & then all hands went on to Cambers Island to raise the Steamboat. Arrived there about 7 o'clock this morning.

10 Find the Steamer sunk half way her smoke stack at high water. I sold out my interest in her tonight to Bourke Spalding for 15 dry cows payable 1st 1879—7 per cent interest from date on $225—the agreed valuation of the cows.

11 Sunday. Finished with the steamboat at dark & started home. Got nearly to Darien & found a large number of rafts jammed across the river which we could not pass. Had to pass them in a pile of rice straw on Generals Island.

12 Reached home about 3 o'cl. P.M. & went for beef but could find none.

13 Killed two beeves. While butchering them the wind suddenly blew a gale from N.E. It blew so hard that we could not think of carrying the beef to Doboy.

14 Wind still blowing tremendously, but Bourke carried the beef on shortened sail. After getting to Doboy though it was blowing too hard for him to beat back. A tug towed him to the Lighthouse & he rowed up South end creek. Dr. N. Greene came over with him.

15 Thursday. My brother Guy's 19th birth-day. Wind gone N.W. but still very high. Rain most of yesterday. Weather very cold.

16 Killed two beeves this afternoon.

17 Went deer hunting. Three deer ran out to Dr. Greene at Cox drive. He killed one of them—a large doe. Caught a negro named Joe Jones setting fire to Cotton Savanna. Tom

says he is going to prosecute him, as it is an offence against State law.

18 Sunday. Nothing doing.

19 Had a long tedious ride for cattle—having had to ride about twenty five miles for them. Bourke in a rage all day because he had to drive cattle when he wanted to go to Darien.

20 Killed two beeves which Charlie carried over. This ends my connection with the butcher business. Bourke will continue that business—Tom & I retiring. I commenced now to make my preparations for a removal to Milledgeville. I sold all my horses (8 head old & young) to Tom for $500.00 half cash & half payable in one year.

21 Wednesday. Bourke got his first beef from Stebbins delivered at High Pt.

22 Went to Darien with Bourke. Carried 24 hides = 408 lbs. Sold them at 12¢. Paid my last years tax—$9.88 and the firm's tax—$15.55. Tom paid me Fifty dollars this morning. Dr. Greene left for Brunswick this afternoon.

23 Tom & Wm. Nightingale went to Union Island for lumber. Bourke went to High Pt. for beef.

24 An idle day with me.

25 Sunday. Pretty weather but a cold March wind blowing.

26 My servant boy Jerry whom I picked up a little boot black in Wilmington, N.C. in 1874, left me to-day to go to Tom. All however on account of my breaking up. Helped Bourke to butcher one beef & then went on to Darien with him where we met Wm. Wylly, Jno. Nightingale & Tom Gignilliat. No Yankee dared come near us all night.

27 Returning we reached home this afternoon.

28 Walked down to the South end with Sister Sarah to meet Tom with his raft of lumber, but he did not come. Got my boots half soled by Cromley.

MARCH

1 Thursday. Tom got in with his raft this morning. He is very tired. Jas. K. Clark & a friend came over this A.M. to hunt. We hunted toward the N. end & jumped seven deer, but killed none.

2 Clark & his friend left this morning. Rained all last night & to-day & blew very heavy from E. last night. We went out this afternoon & Bourke killed a doe in the lower Pine barren.

3 I started to Darien at 3½ o'cl. this A.M. on my way to attend the Agricultural convention on the 6th inst. at Milledgeville. Took cars at Sterling at 9 o'cl. P.M.

4 Sunday. Arrived in Macon at 7.30 A.M. & spent the day at the Brown House.

5 Arrived in Milledgeville at 7.20 o'cl. this A.M. & spent the day at Father's.

6 Convention met this morning. Father delivered the welcoming address on behalf of the citizens of Milledgeville. Willie Wylly arrived last night.

7 Wednesday. Attended the convention all day. Meet a large number of friends.

8 Went to the Asylum this morning with Wm. Wylly, Capt. Jno. Floyd & Guy. The convention adjourned this morning, after a very pleasant session. Milledgeville entertained the delegates very handsomely. Heavy rain & wind all evening.

9 The heaviest storm last night that I ever witnessed. I am anxious to hear from its effects at home. Sister Mary gave birth to-day to her 6th child & 4th son, whom she names Archibald Carlisle, for myself.

10 Spent the day with Guy on the plantation. Weather very cold.

11 Sunday. I did not go to Church this morning. In the afternoon I took a long walk with Father.

12 This morning Guy & I drove out to Francis Minor's, Bankrupt, in Hancock county. I set apart his homestead while there. Father left this afternoon for Savannah to attend the U. S. Court.

13 I left Milledgeville this A.M. on the fast line from New York to New Orleans. Left Milledgeville at 11.20 o'clock and reached Macon at 12.40 o'cl.—36 miles. Left Macon for Brunswick at 7.30 P.M. Rained all afternoon & night.

14 Wednesday. Reached Brunswick at 7 o'clock this morning & took Steamer *Reliance* at 7 this evening. She stuck near Broughton Is. river & staid there all night.

15 Got afloat about 7 o'cl. this A.M. Ran down to Buttermilk
Sound & took from a Schooner 100 sturgeon. Met Tom in
Darien & took my luggage off Steamer & came home with
him in sail boat. We landed at the South end & I reached
home on foot about six o'clock this evening.

16 I staid at home & did nothing to-day.

17 We all went from the South end to Doboy to have a settlement with Charlie Bass. We find that he has squandered our
money so that our beef did not bring us cost price. Rain all
afternoon.

18 Sunday. Spent the day visiting around.

19 To-day is the 12th anniversary of my last battle at Bentonville, N.C.

20 Beautiful Spring weather. Tom & Bourke both building &
Wm. Nightingale preparing to plant corn tomorrow.

21 Wednesday. After a very stiff S.E. wind nearly all day, we
wound up late this evening with a thunder squall from N.W.

22 Weather cold & disagreeable with a high N.W. wind blowing.

23 A beautiful Spring day. Thermometer at 64°. I shut the
hogs, which I have sold to Wm. Wylly for $15, up to-day.

24 Nothing unusual happening to-day.

25 Sunday. The day commenced with high S.E. wind which
later on brought very heavy showers.

26 As I am waiting on Tom to pay me for my horses & he is
waiting on Wm. Nightingale to pay him for his land, I am
having a very idle time of it.

27 A very high N.W. wind blowing.

28 I measured & staked Sallie's land to-day—it being her
twenty five acres around the house. Weather Spring like.

29 Thursday. For the first time in many years the month of
March has [freely] sustained her reputation for bluster.

30 I went to Doboy with Bourke early this morning where we
met Uncle David Barrow, his wife & Clara. Had all the wind
we wanted coming back, from N.E. & very flarry.[1] A dead
beat most of the way.

1. A gusty wind.

31 I went to Darien with Wm. Nightingale & Charlie Bass, after putting out two beeves for Bourke at Doboy. Willie Wylly paid me $15 for hogs. Wm. Nightingale paid me $75 on Tom's behalf. Willie Wylly returned with us to Sapelo. He rents the house I have been living in. Paid Jerry $34.31—in full to 1st inst. Paid my cook Di $5.

APRIL

1 Sunday. Sister Sarah's 30th birth-day. All hands rode down to the South end this afternoon to look at her new home in the Grove.

2 Commenced our packing to-day, preparatory to our move to Milledgeville next Saturday. Some negroes at the South End yesterday killed seven rattlesnakes (large ones) in a den in Barley field.

3 Still packing up. I have burnt I suppose several old letters. I had no idea that I had so many in the house.

4 Wednesday. Helped Bourke to butcher two beeves & afterwards, at Uncle David's request went with him & Bourke to Doboy. Still very busy packing up.

5 All hands busy packing up everything.

6 We went deer hunting this morning. Two ran out of Bell drive in sight of the upper stand where I was. I shot at them, but they were too far to be injured. I suppose this is my last deer hunt. Dr. Greene arrived this morning.

7 Sallie & I left Sapelo in our sail boat this morning on our way to Milledgeville, there to live.[2] Tom, Bourke & Charlie Bass went with us as far as Darien. We took Str. *Reliance* for Savannah at 7 o'cl. P.M. We carry Lizzie Barrow as far as Milledgeville on her way home in Athens.

8 Sunday. Reached Savannah at 10 o'clock this A.M. Amused myself the balance of the day carrying little Lizzie Barrow around town. Stopping at Pulaski House.

2. At his father's request, McKinley was moving back to Milledgeville to help his father with both farming and the law office. See McKinley's letter of December 27, 1876, in this volume. In 1880 the McKinleys returned to Sapelo to live out their lives.

9   After making some necessary purchases in Savh. We left
    there at 7.30 o'clock this evening on the Central R. Road.
10 After travelling all night, we arrived at Milledgeville at 10
    o'clock this morning. Father met us at the depot. Mrs. &
    Miss Goetchius of Columbus arrived this afternoon on a visit
    to George.
11 Wednesday. Father left for Savannah this afternoon to attend
    U.S. Court there. Pope Barrow arrived tonight to meet his
    daughter Lizzie & take her home.
12 Pope & Lizzie Barrow left for Athens early this morning.
    I then started to Irwinton to serve & file a "bill of excep-
    tions" for Father. Got back home about 8 o'clock at night.
    Commenced to rain just as I got home.
13 Rained all last night & all day to-day. Oconee rising rapidly.
    Travel stopped by it.
14 Spent the day at home, as I could not get to town on account
    of the river.
15 Sunday. Father returned from Savannah. River impassable
    & could not get to Church.
16 I set into work this morning by taking charge of the farm &
    hands, relieving Guy, who for the present is having a pleas-
    ant time with Miss Goetchius.
17 Father left for Clinton (Jones Court) this morning at 5 o'clock.
    Mrs. Dubignon & Miss Fleming Dubignon called on Sallie
    to-day.
18 Wednesday. I brought Clif. Williamson out to see Sallie
    this morning & carried her back around noon. Mrs. & Miss
    Goetchius not at all polite to Clif.
19 Busy all day bedding cotton land in the new ground next to
    Joneses'.
20 Walked into town this morning to see about some phos-
    phate, but did not get it.
21 The phosphate came this morning. Sallie spent the day with
    Cliff Williamson.
22 Sunday. Neither Sallie or I attended Church.
23 Planted our first cotton this morning, on the new ground
    acre—putting 75 lbs. of phosphate in. On the field behind
    the stable I put 100 lbs. Sallie went to see Mrs. DuBignon.
24 Mrs. & Miss Goetchius left for home (Columbus) this morn-
    ing.

25 Wednesday. Busy plowing cotton land.
26 This being "Decoration Day," all the stores in town closed & there was a general turn out of the people at the cemetery. Father had a chill to-day.
27 Mother's 62d birth-day. Father staying at home, very unwell.
28 Plows running in Johnsonville field.
29 Sunday. Guy & I attended the funeral of Green Medlin at Blackspring. He died last Friday, aged 63 yrs. We went from the funeral to Beulah & got some laurel.
30 Guy starts to school this morning to study up for college later in the year. Father went to his office for the first time since Thursday.

Later
Entries

[After April 30, 1877, McKinley ceased to keep a day-by-day account in his journal. Following are disjunct, sequential entries.]

APRIL 5, 1884

I see by the newspapers a notice of the death of my friend Charles W. Compton, familiarly known among his friends as "Pat" Compton. We have been thrown very much together since I was ten years old & his death affects me very much. He was a little younger than myself—40 or 41 years old. He died March 30, 1884. Both of us served in the Western Army 1861 to 65 and were both captured at Vicksburg, Miss. by the Yankees July 4, 1863.

AUGUST 31, 1886

Earthquake—August 31st 1886 [1]

Tonight at about twenty minutes after nine (9.20) o'clock I was in my bed, which stands with head to South East

---

1. This was the famous Charleston Earthquake of 1886. See note to May 6, 1871.

and foot to N.W., lying down, when suddenly the foot of the bed rose up—then sinking back, the head rose and sank the same way. It was an Earthquake and the heaviest I ever felt. I felt one shock on June 14th 1856, and one in 1866—both near Milledgeville, Georgia, but this to-night (on Sapelo Island the coast of Georgia) was by far the severest that I have ever felt. The feeling experienced during the first shock, while I was in bed, I can best liken to the feeling experienced by one in a small boat at sea, riding a long rolling swell. I immediately sprang out of bed, calling to my wife—"Earthquake—get out of the house." Her mother, Mrs. Spalding, had in the meantime joined us— much alarmed, as indeed we all were. We got out of the house hastily—(I, bear footed, the others not having gone to bed yet). In trying to reach the outer door, we staggered like drunken persons—the house swaying to and fro, and cracking and creaking like a ship in a storm at sea. This, the first shock, was by far the severest. They continued, at intervals of about fifteen minutes until we had experienced three distinct shocks—gradually decreasing in severity. All the others aver most positively that there were *four* distinct shocks, but I myself, can only swear to the genuineness of three—for I can feel them (in imagination now—sixteen hours since the first shock).

During the continuance of the shocks, it was almost a dead calm. Soon afterwards a light North East wind sprang up. The earthquake was greatest in intensity in the first shock—gradually decreasing in force with each successive shock.

Some negroes who were caught by it at Doboy, on a raft of lumber, assure me that the wharves there, several hundred feet in length swayed to and fro, as if they were reeds in a heavy wind. A negro meeting was in progress there at the time, but I hear that the Church was emptied as if by magic—several taking to the river.

Archibald C. McKinley

SEPTEMBER 1, [1886]

All the others in the house, viz. my wife, Mrs. Spalding
and Chas. L. Bass, aver *most positively*, that another earthquake shock occurred tonight between eleven and twelve
o'clock—strong enough to make the house creak. I was
asleep and did not therefore feel it. Evidently our part of the
country is being stirred to the depths.

2 Earthquake shocks still continue, though modified in
severity.

3 A very heavy shock tonight at ten o'clock and forty minutes—rolling me from side to side in my bed. It is hardly
necessary to say that I did not stay in that bed long. Every
night seems to begin with a shock, more or less severe. After
that they decrease in severity, but a tremor—a pulsation as
it were, with a few minutes intervening irregularly—is ever
with us, day and night, sometimes more, sometimes less.
As I write now it sways me gently—sometimes to and fro,
sometimes forwards and backwards—then again from side to
side, but an ever present tremor, when not a shock, all day,
all night. When will it cease?

4 Only one shock of any severity tonight—but the ever
present tremor still with us. Wind from N.E. & clouding.
Barometer, which has been slowly rising for a day or two,
stationary to-night. The tremor has a slightly nauseating
effect. I can best describe it by saying that it feels like a dish
of jelly looks when jarred.

5 The tremor or pulsation incessant in the early morning but
abating to a great extent as the day wears on, but at the
regular time tonight, we are run to the piazza by a heavy
shock—not so heavy however as that of the 31st of August.
The *tremor* still continues, but, I imagine, is on the de-
cline, as well as the shocks. I hope so at any rate, for six
successive days and nights of shock and tremble—causing
loss of sleep—is wearing us out. We are all worn out—
getting only what sleep we can snatch from our duties in
the day time while the earth only trembles, but does not
rock. Like pickets in an army, we snatch a few minutes sleep
between times.

6   The earthquake shocks still continue—though with much
    less violence. They are as regular as clockwork.
7   Earthquake about the same as yesterday. Continual quiver-
    ing.
8   Still the same tremor going on.
9   [Still the same tremor going on.]
10 [Still the same tremor going on.] Excessive rain to-night,
    with very heavy thunder & vivid lightning. This is the
    eleventh day of continued earthquake shocks.
11 Same state of affairs continues.

Letters

[McKinley to his father, William McKinley, December 27, 1876. This unsigned letter, from McKinley to his father, was found laid inside the journal. Whether this copy was a draft or a copy, or indeed whether the letter was ever sent, is not known. The following April, however, Archibald and Sallie McKinley did move to Milledgeville.]

Dec. 27th 1876

Dear Father.

Yours of 18th inst. recd. & studied attentively. It is a tempting offer. But like everything else of the sort it has its drawbacks, one of which is the heavy expense to you. I am afraid that I would not make a successful lawyer. I believe that I could make as good an office lawyer as the average man, but you know that I am no speaker & have not a good flow of language & you know also how far these two qualities go toward making a successful talking lawyer. Before deciding either way there is one point upon which I would like some more light. Through all the correspondence I have not heard a word as to how Mother is disposed toward my return to M. What does she think of your putting yourself to all this expense to get me back? She has been very kind to both my wife & myself & it would be exceedingly unpleasant to us to go back to M. with Mother unfriendly to the manner of our return. I and you know it would be too late to remedy the matter after we got there even though we lived in different houses.

Excuse my plain & direct questions, but a little plain talk now, by bringing about a perfect understanding, may save a great deal of unpleasantness here after. Another question I will ask—in two years from now Guy will be grown & as he expects to go into your office I would like to know how this plan corresponds with his wishes. Now on the other hand. As I wrote you last week, in 30 or 40 days our firm will dissolve which would leave to my share say 25 or 30 head of stock cattle. Now if I would be making my living at some thing else & I have got to find now shortly some business to go at, either here or elsewhere without touching them, they together with my stock of horses ought in a few years to accumulate into a very neat little property, if I don't have to kill them off, for you know they would be increasing at a compound rate of interest. In conclusion. Do you think that either you or I, or both together will be able to make a lawyer of me?

[McKinley to his nephew William McKinley Cobb, November 4, 1898. This letter was found in an Athens, Georgia, antique store in the 1980s and is reprinted courtesy of Jeff West of Athens.]

Inverness Ga.[1]
Nov. 4th 1898

Dear Willie

Your kind letter of Oct. 13th recd. & I would have replied sooner, but we have been exceedingly busy trying to patch up the damage done us by the terrible hurricane and tidal wave of Oct. 2d. For four weary hours we stood, (your Aunt & myself) waist deep in water. The waves coming across the island—direct from the ocean covered the tops of our windows.[2] In the house the water was nearly 3 feet deep—in the yard nearly 6 feet on a level. The waves in our yard were fully 12 feet high. Your Aunt S. was sick in bed with fever, but when her bed began to float, she had to get up & stand waist deep in water for hours. We lost most of our possessions either outright or from damage by salt water. All of our furniture is dropping to pieces, and my bibles—my own, my father's & my grandfather's with all the family records for three generations, were ruined, as the bibles were under water for hours. I hope however that I can copy the family records.

We are distressed over the sad news from your brother

Tom.[3] Your father writes very hopelessly about his condition. It is the saddest case I ever knew. Your Aunt Sallie thanks you for your kind & sympathetic message. We shall always be glad to hear from you. Are you still in the Interior Department? Let me know when you change your address.

    Your Aunt Sallie joins me in much love to you.

Yr. Aff. Uncle
A. C. McKinley

This envelope was under water. Since writing the foregoing, I see by the Charleston paper that poor Tom is dead. You all have our sincerest sympathy.

    1. Inverness was the Sapelo Island post office, where Sallie McKinley was postmistress and McKinley her assistant. Given the McKinleys' Scottish ties, one might suppose they selected the name Inverness.

    2. The McKinley house was on the landward side of the island. The area between there and the beach was cleared for agriculture, thus there was nothing to break the waves coming across.

    3. Thomas R. R. Cobb, McKinley's nephew, an Atlanta attorney.

[Sallie McKinley to Ella Barrow Spalding, November 9, 1898. The original of this letter is housed at the Georgia Historical Society, Spalding Family Papers, coll. 750, item 74.]

Sapelo. Nov 9th 1898

My dear Nellie

    I am going to try and write to you this morning, but how long I can hold out I dont know, for I am so weak and nervous, for I have gone through so much lately that I often wonder how I have lived through it. I want first to tell you and Randolph some little of the last hours of my most precious Mother. All Saturday she was very restless and walking from one door to the other and wanting to go out on the ground she said. I promised her I would send for Mammie to help me and we would take her out, which I did, for I found too, that I did not have the strength to keep her from falling and I had had light fever constantly and no sleep for weeks. Mammie came as soon as she got my message but it was after dark. We persuaded her to lie down on the couch and rest awhile, and she had walked so much all day that I thought the long heavy sleep she took was natural, but about

one oclock she woke up and I saw there was a great change in
some way, and when she stood on her feet they suddenly gave
way, and she sank to her knees, and it was all that Mammie and
I could do to lift her on to the couch and she lay from that time
until she died without moving. On Sunday morning early Archie
got Jack and we sent to Dr. Nydegger[1] in March Carters buggy,
and he came very kindly and promptly. I told him before he
saw her that I knew there was nothing that any one on earth
could do for her, but I wanted him to examine her and tell me
what was the matter with her, that the terrible swelling had increased so, and her feet up to her knees were so swollen, and
her face under her eyes, were painful to look at. He examined
her most carefully in every way and then told me that there was
not a sound organ in her body, that it was her age and natural
giving way of natural forces, he left [*illegible*] with me to help
her heart, as that organ he said had been very weak for a long
time. As Spalding[2] was sick I have sent for him often to see her
and he has examined her often, and when he left, he told me if
it would be of any comfort to me to send for him day or night
and he would come, but as night came on I saw that she would
not last very long, and oh' Nellie I had to sit all alone, but for
Archie and Charlie, who the doctor sent back in the buggy, and
see her die,[3] and then had to bathe and dress her for the last
time, only with Mammies help, and Jane Johnsons, who came
to help me as soon as she heard it. I have lived over it all again
and again and when I close my eyes, it comes back to me and I
can get no rest, I suppose it is going so long through so much
all alone. Charlie left at daylight to get the *Black Hawk* and to
get the casket, but when he got to Darien he found the *Hawk*
was not running and he did not know what to do for all the tugs
were at the North end and but for Dick Wylly[4] who we can
never feel grateful enough in this life, telephoned there for the
Dandy we would have been obliged to bury her here on Sapelo.
All this delay of course made it very late before we could get
up to Darien. Jennie & Rosa Powers with Mollie Livingston and
Cammie,[5] and some other gentlemen came down for us, and we
did not get to Darien until after night. They decided to take her
right to the Church and though Cammie asked me to go to his
house, I decided to go to Jennie's, as she and Mollie promised

to go with me so I could spend a part at least of her last night
on earth with her, but I only got in the house and Jennie made
me lie down and my fever rose and I had it all night long and at
six o'clock I tried to get up and went to the Church and stayed
until the people began to come, but I was sick, sick, in heart and
body. I suppose it must have been the ride to the Cemetery[6] but
when I got there and they were almost through I was taken with
another hard chill and Mollie and Jennie put me in the carriage
and drove me to the Livingstons, and tho they all protested,
I got up the next morning and got Charlie to bring me home.
I wanted the rest, and there were so many people coming all
the time to see me, I know they meant it kindly, but I thought
I should die if I could not get some rest. I took a big dose of
Calomel that night, and on Thursday I was so weak that Archie
wrote to Dr. Nydegger for advice and he said if we could send
for him he would rather see me so Archie sent [for him] and he
said he knew I would be sick, that he had seen it for a long time,
and the best thing Archie could do would be to take me to the
highest mountains he could find that it was prostration and low
fever, and now comes the most awful, awful, experience I ever
had in my life, this terrible Hurricane, that we had no thoughts
for hours that we would ever live through. I had had the fever
all night, and it was still on me. I was on the bed but had my
wrapper on, when Archie came in and told me the tide seemed
to be very high, this was early in the morning, but I got up and
looked out of the front winder saw it all over our yard and rising
very fast and Archie and I began putting two chairs together,
and putting our trunks up, on the beds, tables, and every thing
we could find to take them off the floor, and while we were busy
about that in one second it seemed, the water began rushing into
the house and was knee deep and in one minute time it was up
to our waist. And the waves from the grave yard[7] was beating
against the house almost mountain high and would dash to the
very tops of our windows, and Archie stood for a long time with
his shoulder against our back door to keep the waves from bursting the door open. I knew he could not stand it long, so began
trying to find him a bed slat and two nails that he could try and
strengthen it some and went to Mama's bed and found all the
beds floating, and every piece of furniture turning over and over

and floating from one room to the other. I at last found the slat
and some nails but nothing to drive them with, and all that time
poor Archie trying to hold that door, and with each wave the
house would shiver and we would feel the floor rise and I cant
see what kept them from going as the house would grind and
hoist, and we would feel each second would be our last. I felt all
about my feet for a hammer or something to drive the nails and
at last felt an old iron near the fireplace, and put my foot through
the handle and in that way got it, for the water was too deep to
reach anything with my hand, and he would try between the
waves to drive the slat on and in that way relieved himself, but
he was white in the face keeping that door from bursting in, for
we would certainly [have] been lost if those waves had forced the
door we would have been drowned in ten minutes. I was afraid
to go up on the ladder for the house would have parted between
the bedrooms and dining room and I sat on the ladder for a short
while but the feeling was so dreadful that I came down and I
wanted to be with Archie if we went. It was hours we stood in
that water expecting every breath to be our last. At last Archie
said he thought the water was falling, and it went down very
slowly, it seemed to us, and such a house, I know you never saw
in all your life, the dreadful marsh mud was over every thing,
the trunks which were unlocked were entirely empty of their
contents and soaked. Marsh mud which was ankle deep every
where as you have seen the floor of the bathing house and such
a smell, it was beyond every thing and for two days I could get
no one for love or money to help us clean it up, and I felt so sick
I could not hold up my head to do one thing, and what makes
me most miserable of it all I have lost every *single thing* that
belonged to my poor Mother not one thing left for Randolph and
I to keep to remember her by. We had to take hoes and drag
the things out in the yard, in piles of mud, and broken paper
boxes that came from her trunks and I have tried to search them
over today and find some little keepsake in vain. It made me
sick. I lost even her prayer book, and poor Archies family Bibles
are a terrible sight to look at. I hate to see them. We have lost
every thing on earth we had, and it is hard to start life at our
ages with nothing. Most of the furniture is all broken up, and the
books smell awful. I cant tell you what we have lost. I have been
trying for days to dry things and when we bring them in at night

we find that by next morning they feel as wet as ever, the salt never drys. I have hired two girls and they do their best, but it seems we can never get the house dry, and all my bed clothes being wet so long before I could get help have mildewed. Willie Wylly came the next day to see if we were alive and kindly and thoughtfully brought us some flour and lard, a ham and coffee. Which was a most merciful help at that time for we had not one mouthful in the house. We lost our back piazza and steps and the kitchen almost gone, our little out house entirely swept away with every thing in it, and so much for ourselves. Mr. Sawyer[8] said the water came up into his house about knee deep, but the house did not shake. When he saw it rising he tried to get to us, but met the water rising so fast he could not get here, so went back home, he was better off than we were, but it was bad being alone, old Mr. Bell said it was knee deep at the tabe,[9] but they suffered terribly at the Marsh Landing. Tell Uncle David that the wharf is *all* gone, every stick of it, and the negroes say the water was about neck high all over the yard, but it must have been far over that, for it came into the house, and the Russells say it was high in the house. They got alarmed when they saw the water rising so fast, so he took his wife and baby with a Miss Armstrong on a visit to them and started for the South end, and when they got to the grave yard[10] they met Mr Terrill and there the waves from the ocean came so fast that they went into the woods where a tree had been blown down and they got above the water in the branches and there had to stay in all that wind until the tide went down with that little baby, and they had all of Harry William's family with them,[11] they lost all their goods, a large store they had in one of the out houses. The Light house dwelling is gone, all washed away but the bricks. William Cromley found the house was going, took one of his children and swam with it, and put it in the Light house, went back and took the other, and last his wife, and in that way saved the three. Poor Galliard the negro who married your old servant Patience was drowned on Doboy with his wife and four children, she has not been found yet with two children, they found him and two children buried waist deep in the mill basin. I know you must be tired of reading such a long letter, if indeed you can read it atall, but it is hard for me to write. Give our best love to Uncle David and Aunt Pool, and tell Randolph he can never know how

I appreciate his letters to me they were a comfort to me. Thank you too for yours with all my heart. Archie joins in best love to all. I am always most affectionately

Sister Sallie

We cant find any paper to write on, this is some I found in an old blank book and dried but it writes dreadfully. Archie says I must tell Uncle David the water was six feet high by measurement on the side of our house. I lost the Parrot,[12] he was drowned in the gale, he ran away the night before and we could not find him.[13]

1. The director of the National Quarantine Station on Blackbeard Island.
2. Dr. Spalding Kenan.
3. Mary Dorothy Bass Spalding died on September 19, 1898.
4. A second cousin to Sallie McKinley, son of Thomas Spalding Wylly.
5. Alexander Campbell Wylly.
6. St. Andrews Cemetery, Darien.
7. Behavior.
8. Amos Sawyer, of Rhode Island, owned the Randolph Spalding estate of 7,000 acres on the north end of Sapelo from 1881 to 1908. He lived at Chocolate when in residence on Sapelo.
9. Refers to the tabby ruins of the Thomas Spalding house on the south end of Sapelo, today the restored and modified "Big House."
10. Again Behavior. This entry implies that to get to the south end from Marsh Landing during the storm, they had to go some distance north to get around Oakdale Creek. See Map.
11. A black family that lived at Shell Hammock.
12. See April 18, 1874.
13. The McKinleys lived in a house built before the Civil War for an overseer. It was, and is, located south of Long Tabby on Barn Creek.

[Ella Barrow Spalding to Charles Spalding Wylly, August 1914. This letter is apparently a typed copy of an original holographic letter sent to Charles Wylly to assist him in his Story of Sapelo, *commissioned by Howard Coffin. Wylly sent copies of the letter with copies of the "Sapelo" manuscript to family members. This letter is reprinted courtesy of Helen Treanor.]*

Savannah, Georgia
August 1914

Dear Sir:

Your letter asking me to write of Sapelo as I knew it, has been received. I wish my pen were adequate to the task. I wish

I could transcribe from mind to paper the story of the life which made the years years of interest as well as happiness. But as Locksley says, "Man can but do his best." So too with women.

My first acquaintance with the dear and beautiful place was in 1870, before the Spalding family returned to the island after the war.

In the spring of that year I went for a visit to my cousin, Mr. A. C. McKinley, who had married Miss Sarah Spalding. They were living then with her mother, Mrs. Randolph Spalding, widow of Colonel Randolph Spalding, C.S.A. who died during the war on the Ridge[1] near Darien.

During my visit we went on a maroon to Sapelo, a very delightful experience for a girl from the country, and a most delightful and attractive introduction to the Island.

Mr. Alex C. Wylly and Thomas Spalding were living at the Kenan place, and were our hosts. The Spaldings were ever charming to visit. Their guests were made welcome, and all things done for their comfort and pleasure, with generous hospitality as free then in days of restricted means, consequent upon the war, as in the old days of luxury and high living.

But to go back a little. You will remember that Sapelo was abandoned by the family at the beginning of the war, owing to the presence of Federal gun-boats in the sounds; that it was taken possession of by vagrant runaway negroes, and held by them during the war and for some time after; how the Spalding negroes flocked back as soon after emancipation as possible, Sapelo being the Mecca of their desires. They had been moved en masse to a rented plantation in Baldwin County, Georgia near Milledgeville, when they refugeed to that place.

Upon the return of the Spaldings to McIntosh County in 1865, they sent a representative to the Island to take possession for the owners. But, give it up? No indeed! When ordered to leave, the negroes declared the land was their's, and in turn ordered Mr. Bass[2] to leave, threatening to kill him if he did not go. And go he did, there being nothing else to do.

Georgia was still under martial law, so Mr. Charles Spalding, acting as guardian of his brother's children, made supplication to the General in command of the Department, for the recovery of the Island. General Tilton, who was stationed in

Savannah, sent a detachment of U.S. troops with Mr. Spalding to Sapelo, dispossessed the negroes, and turned the property over to the rightful owners. All negroes but the Spalding people were made to leave then and there.

Later on, the North End, Mr. Randolph Spalding's plantation, comprising all the land except Raccoon Bluff, from Sapelo High Point to the Kenan line, was sold to a Mr. Griswold of Rhode Island, who hoped to make untold dollars, raising sea-island cotton. But his hopes failed of realization, and he in turn sold to Mr. Cassin.[3]

Finally the place was bought by Mr. Amos Sawyer, who held it till purchased by Mr. Coffin. So time ran on.

The Spaldings decided to return to the Island to live. Their home had been destroyed, but Mr. Griswold, during his tenure, had built a very comfortable cottage at High Point, which Mr. Cassin, the then owner,[4] let to them until a house of their own could be built or repaired.

By January 1871 Thomas Spalding was married to Miss McKinley, sister of Mr. A. C. McKinley, and all the family moved to the Cassin house, and lived there until the winter of 1871–72. In the meantime making the Long Tabby[5] into a most comfortable dwelling. There they lived after leaving the Cassin house. Later Mr. and Mrs. McKinley moved a quarter of a mile beyond into a house built long years before the war. It is still standing. It's framing timbers of live-oak are so hard it is next to impossible to drive a nail into them.

I visited my cousin Mrs. Thomas Spalding in 1873, and became quite acquainted with Island life, and found it greatly to my liking. In November 1874 I was married to Thomas Bourke Spalding, Colonel Randolph Spalding's youngest son. We lived about as far on the west side of the Long Tabby as the McKinleys lived on the east.

My mother-in-law lived with us, and added very much to the happiness of my life. She was an exceedingly pretty woman, very capable, and a most interesting companion. At that time, and for some years to come, the three families lived almost in sight of each other on the shores of Barn Creek, a beautiful salt stream, tributary to Duplin River. It is very crooked, it's bends and turns making little promontories upon which to build. Our home was on the prettiest point, having also the best landing. The house was built before my marriage upon a small tract of land my husband bought from his brother. Nothing remains now but the land but it is the dearest spot of all to me. One could sit on the piazza, and there in front ran the creek, beyond for miles the ever beautiful marsh. Over there lay Little Sapelo. Beyond the marsh was Doboy Sound, ever changing, ever beautiful. Across it one could see Doboy Island, Cain Creek, and then "Afar the dim coast line. A long low reach of palm and pine."[6]

It was very lovely, most times calm and peaceful, and oh, how dear!

How one's heart turns with love and longing to the past days! They seem so sweet and fair. There were dark days, sad days, which must come to everyone, but looking back, down the vista of time, sadness and darkness shrink out of sight, one scarcely perceives their shadow, leaving only the sweetness and the fairness. And it is good that it is so. Will any people ever live there on that Island who will love as did those three families, who had homes and happiness on Barn Creek's shore? I trow not.

But our story lingers. At that time Doboy was a great shipping port for yellow pine. I have seen ships lying in Doboy Sound four deep at the wharves. At Doboy, at Cane Creek, and in Back River they were moored as many as half an hundred at one time. Not coast-wise schooners, but big square riggers of every nationality, from across the seas. The industry was a great feeder to Darien. The timber, virgin pine of the highest grade, was cut in the interior and rafted down the Altamaha to Darien. There it was measured and sold. Thence to Doboy and loaded on ships for export.

There was a big saw-mill on Doboy, and one on Cain Creek, where the logs were "squared" before loading.[7] Thousands upon thousands, yes, millions of feet of lumber were burned to get rid of it, the smoke and flame of the burning rising night and day. The big thick slabs were carried by an endless chain to the pit, pitched off and burned. If the lumber companies had it now they would be rich indeed.

My husband, seeing the opportunity, bought cattle to raise beef for the shipping. At first he was alone in the enterprise, but later his brother and brother-in-law desired to join him, forming a company. They bought a little steamboat for delivering the beef and such truck as was raised, and to carry the Captains to Darien for business or pleasure. But the forests were cut away, the bar filled up, and the end had come for Doboy.

When I was first married a great many of the old negroes were still living. It is hard to believe those now on the Island are their descendants, the old people were so far superior. They were a kindly, gentle people, industrious and honest—yea, verily, honest—many of them respectable and trustworthy. They had been trained in these good ways, had been kindly treated, loved their owners, and were kindly thought of by them. For some the family had a feeling of attachment, hard to realize now.

Let me give an instance to prove my point.

Mr. Randolph Spalding's old "Yebo" nurse, Maam Hannah, lived with her husband, old Carolina, in a little house quite near the Long Tabby, free of rent of course, and doubtless fed and cared for by the family, who felt a real affection for the old people. One day their house caught fire, and the old couple, too terrified, too infirm to escape, were in great danger of burning. When the white family heard of it, those who were at home, rushed to the burning house. My husband (this was before our marriage) ran into the burning building, and bore away both to safety in his arms, making both trips at great peril to himself. Maam Hannah took him to be his father, and called him by his father's name several times. The old people died of their burns shortly after.

Of course the natural instinct of brave men is to save life, but he was actuated also by affection for these faithful servitors of his family.

They had curious superstitions, these negroes, among others, this: that one must be baptized on the "first ebb," else the flood tide coming in would meet the sins just washed away on their way to sea, and bring them back to the poor sinner left shivering on the bank.

The church then stood in the Kenan field on the banks of Hanging Bull Creek, which emptied into Barn Creek just west of our house, so they would need to be dipped at tip-top high water, for it is many a mile to sea at that point. Ghosts played a large part with them. I had a little serving boy, who, before sweeping anything out of a door *at night,* would pause on the threshold, and say "Move Friend!" addressing any ghost which might be standing there. It was bad luck to sweep them out.

And again, another little boy I had, who ran about and waited on me, went with us to a picnic to High Point. He was sitting at the back, with his feet hanging over, very happy and singing merrily in a sweet little voice all the way along. We liked to hear him, so let him sing away. In the afternoon on the return trip, Robert was silent. Not a note did he sound. We needed cheering after the long day's outing, so I said, "Robert why do you not sing?" "I can't." "But yes you can. You sang all the way up this morning." "Yes'm, but de Ghos steal all me voice." Poor little chap, he was tired, and laid it all on the ghost. They all believed, big and little, that ghosts roamed the place day and night. I do not think that they thought them harmful, if certain rules were observed, due deference given. Quite a few of the older negroes were in the U.S. Navy during the war. I asked one of them, Jimmie Lemon, "Daddy Jimmie, what made you fight with the Yankees against your own people? That was wrong." To which he replied, "They steal we Missus. We bin biling salt on Sapelo River, an de ship boats slip up behin, and tak us prisoners to de ship." That is how it came about according to Daddy Jimmie. I reckon he told the truth. Who's to say he did not? Jimmie Walker, who was a preacher, a great strong man, able to work all day in the hold of a ship, applied for a pension, and my son asked him on what possible grounds. He said he tripped on a grape vine, and fell during the war, and when preaching he "squalled" and it made his head hurt. He got his pension.

Time ran on, and our Barn Creek Colony was broken up. Thomas Spalding moved to the South End. The McKinleys returned to Milledgeville, to be with their father, and we built at Marsh Landing, and moved there to live in 1882. My son Randolph was born at Riverside, our Barn Creek home, in 1879, his sister[8] in 1881, the only children of the family name. The Long Tabby changed hands several times. Mr. William Nightingale bought the place, and lived there for a year or two, but gave it up, and afterwards Mr. William Wylly rented it, and made it his home. His sister lived with him, and, finally Mrs. Treanor,[9] a niece of Mrs. Thomas Spalding's and Mr. McKinley, who had lived much on the Island, bought and made the Long Tabby her home for several years.

My husband was born at "Chocolate" on the North End place. The only one of his generation born on Sapelo. The house at Chocolate was a two-story frame building on a tabby basement. It was built in the early 30s by Dr. Rogers, a Northern man, who also built the big barn. The servants' quarters were tabby cottages in rows at the back of the dwelling, with the avenue of fig and pomegranate trees between. In front, from door-step to the river's edge, was a grove of oranges, and I have heard my mother-in-law say she could stand on the piazza and gather the luscious fruit from the trees.

Instead of fences, the yard, stable, and barn were enclosed by sour orange hedges, portions of which were still standing when I first knew the Island. It is said the piece of marble over the barn door near the eaves, giving date of building, was a piece of the slab from the tomb of the Marquis de Montalet.[10] The rest Dr. Rogers used for sun-dials. I do not know where the sun-dials have gone, but the piece in the barn is still there, to be verified, should one wish. But this I do know. There has been nothing to mark the lonely grave at High Point as De Montalet's *save tradition*. Since I have known the Island—now nearing 45 years—the tabby tomb and tabby wall about it was there till the storm and tidal wave of 1898, when the sea encroached, tore open the grave, and scattered the bones upon the shore.

Poor man! Verily he spent his years as a "tale that is told." No one truly knows whence he came. That he lived and his being, is almost a tradition, kept alive mainly by the family of the one man, it would seem, who called him friend. His name comes down with them in kindly fashion. My sister Mrs. McKinley writes me "I have often heard my Aunt Mrs. Brailsford say 'The old Marquis was a dear good old gentleman.'"

Let that be his epitaph.

There never were any French on the South end of the Island, and they were all gone from the North end when Mr. Spalding bought from Dr. Rogers, at the time of his son Randolph's marriage in 1843. There was one other owner on the North End at that time, Mr. Thomas King, of the Liberty County family of that name. He lived in Bourbon Field, owning a place of 500 acres, which Mr. Spalding bought after his marriage.

But to return to the 70s. Mr. Spalding Kenan followed the others to Sapelo, and lived for a while on his mother's place. After he went to Darien to resume the practice of his profession. His father-in-law, Mr. Livingston and family, lived at the Kenan place for several years. Later on they moved to Darien. After his mother's death, Dr. Kenan purchased the interest of the other heirs, and gave the property to his wife. His son, Dr. Randolph Kenan, followed his example, and at the time of his death, was sole owner. He left it to his younger brother, Spalding. Mr. Sawyer's family spent each winter at Chocolate after he bought, so we had quite a colony.

The McKinleys had returned by this time, and completed our number as a family. In the course of time the National quarantine station[11] was established on Blackbeard, and the doctors with their families were pleasant neighbors, and a visit to them made a very nice break in our lives. They seemed as glad to have us as we to go. A desirable neighbor being an acquisition, and we were very desirable. I have often been asked by poor city-bred people, if Sapelo was not "dreadfully lonely." One lady said "One would as well be a convict as live there." How could it be lonely? We had our household duties, the affairs outside which belong to a housekeeper in the country, we had many pleasant diversions. We read, we rode, we sailed, we took long lovely walks, we fished, we crabbed, we swam the waters—in the bath-house for still-water bathing—and when inclination led, all would meet on the beach for a glorious surf bath. When all else failed, one could fold one's hands, look abroad, and rest one's soul.

All our friends loved Sapelo. Not many months passed but some one of us had visitors, old and young. The most exciting adventure upon which we sallied forth was to watch "Crumbleys" catch rattle snakes. This horribly fascinating pursuit was followed only in winter, when the snakes were torpid and lay in their dens. They come out on bright sunny days and bask. Whoever saw one, sent forthwith to let the Crumbleys, who lived at the light-house, know [and] who came with a good stout string tied in a slip noose in the end, and, of all things in which to put a dead beast, a peaceful fishing basket strapped on the back. When the den was reached, Mr. Snake was gently prodded with the staff until roused enough to grow angry, and ventured out to see who dared. When he put his head out, he put it through the slip-noose lying ready. A quick turn of the wrist, a jerk, and there he was captured. My, how angry he would be! That eye, how it glared! Move where you would, it followed, full of evil, full of hate. After capture they were drawn up by the noose to a convenient height on some neighboring tree, and executed by having the head cut off just back of the murderous jaws, *after* being carefully skinned. They were careful the snake should not bite himself, for they extracted and sold the oil from the bodies as a liniment for rheumatism, getting a good price per ounce. They also cured the skins, mounting some, selling others for belts. Horrid to read of, isn't it? But most exciting to witness, furnishing many thrills to the minute, and gratifying to know there was one snake the less.[12]

But to pleasanter themes. Our dear delight was "jump hunting" for deer. Those hunts were always on horseback, hence a large part of the delight. The early start in the freshness of the morning, the riding through highways and byways, and across savannahs, until we happened upon [one] sleeping in his bed, was a delight. The noise of our coming would rouse the innocent sleeping creature, and off it would fly like the wind. The deer was always given a chance. To shoot one in his bed, was a disgrace too great for words. A sharp lookout had to be kept, or the deer would make his escape. Once Mr. Spalding and I were out hunting, he riding in front, and I close behind in the narrow path. A deer jumped out after we had passed. He heard and looked back. He saw the deer but I was directly in his way. He quietly waited for me to ride forward a bit, then turned in his saddle, shot over his shoulder, and the deer was our's. We got another that same day. Mr. Spalding was a splendid shot, as was his brother. Few equaled them in any of the sports incident to island life. None surpassed them in the noble qualities which go to make the highest type of men.

I recall his killing an eagle once with his rifle. Another long shot, and a good one. Having loaned his shot-gun to a visiting friend, he had used his rifle on the hunt, from which they were returning. The bird was flying directly over his head, way up. He stopped his horse, fired, and the bird of liberty came tumbling down. Six feet he was from tip to tip of wing.

Sometimes, as an especial favor, we might be permitted to help drive cattle. That was great fun, even though we did not participate fully. We generally kept to the road or path, keeping them in hearing if not in sight, with their guns across our laps, if the drive chanced to come after a jump hunt; while they rode in the woods, gathered up the cattle, and drove them along, sometimes at a wild rate if it was a wild bunch. We, my sister-in-law Mrs. Spalding, and myself, had all we could do to keep in sight or sound if they got running. It was equal to any fox hunt, but we followed fast, and followed far. We "stopped not for brake." We paused not for briar. We were young. We liked to be in the open, with a good horse under us, and could easily find our way home without the gentlemen, if need be. Permit me to say we did not ride "cross saddle."

We had rides too for the ride's sake. Driven to and fro to visit each other, or to see what was going on abroad in the Island. We went seining on the beach quite often. It was entertaining to watch them stretch out a line in the surf, straight out, with the net then curving, and bring the long net in, sometimes a water haul. Then again the silver fish would jump and flounder in the meshes, with crabs stacked about. Occasionally we went clamming. That pursuit—one can hardly call it a pleasure—needs to be seen to be appreciated. We did not take part except as on-lookers, though sometimes our girl visitors did for the fun of it.

We grew older presently, and gave up our rides and hunts, taking to more sedate pursuits, but found life none the less happy. But the end of our happiness there was drawing to a close. Mrs. Thomas Spalding and I left the Island. My son and I in the fall of 1884, Mrs. Spalding in the spring of 1885.[13]

None of us were left on the Island but my mother-in-law and the McKinleys, till 1891. That year my father and mother went with my son and myself to live at Marsh Landing. Mrs. Thomas Spalding, now Mrs. William Wylly, returned to the South End shortly after we left the Island in 1897, not to return except for brief visits.

My place was sold to C. O. Fulton of Darien, and after Mrs. Wylly's death, the South End passed into the hands of parties in Macon.

Here the story ends.

Much more I could write, but at the risk of wearying those who read, as perhaps I have already done. I trust that what I have written may add as much to Mr. Coffin's pleasure to read, as it has been mine, to write it.

Very sincerely

Ellen Barrow Spalding[14]

1. Spalding is evidently in error here. Colonel Spalding died of fever while on duty with the Confederate army in Savannah, March 17, 1862.

2. Allen G. Bass.

3. James Cassin, of New York, owned the Randolph Spalding estate on the north end from 1873 to 1879.

4. Spalding is in error here. The estate and house were owned by J. N. A. Griswold until October 1873. As the *Journal* indicates, Griswold rented to McKinley. Also see McIntosh County Deed Book A, 196.

5. The Long Tabby was built as the sugar processing building next to the Round Tabby on Barn Creek.

6. The quote should properly read: "Far off I see the dim coast wall, / A long, low reach of palm and pine," from "Sapelo," Carlyle McKinley, *Poems* (1904).

7. Most of the timber shipped internationally through the Darien-Doboy port was shipped as squared logs, not sawn lumber.

8. Clara Lucy, born May 27, 1881, died September 3, 1881.

9. Mrs. Edward D. Treanor, Kate McKinley Taylor, daughter of McKinley's sister Catherine and the mother of Helen Treanor.

10. Jean Berard Mocquet de Montalet fled the slave uprisings in Santo Domingo and came to Savannah about 1797, where he purchased the Hermitage plantation on the Savannah River. He married Angelique Servanne Charlotte de Picot Boisfeuillet, the eldest daughter of one of the five French who purchased Sapelo Island in 1789. After his wife's death in 1805, he inherited her share of her father's estate on Sapelo. Exactly when he came to live at High Point on Sapelo is questionable, but it was after 1803. He died there in 1814. Montalet's homesite and other actions have been highly altered by Charles Spalding Wylly as well as subsequent authors.

11. Opened on Blackbeard Island in 1880, the National Quarantine Station was initially the quarantine station for Georgia, Florida, and South Carolina. These stations were established primarily for the control of yellow fever.

12. See *Atlanta Journal*, January 17, 1891.

13. Her husband, Bourke, had died in 1884 and Thomas Spalding in 1885.

14. Her proper name was Ella.

Epilogue

Sapelo Island from the period of the journal to the present has undergone many changes. Tom Spalding in the 1880s laid out two "subdivisions" at Shell Hammock and Hog Hammock and sold these parcels to the former slaves. The "Street" lands at Raccoon Bluff were purchased in the 1870s by a consortium of freedpeople known as the William Hillery Company and divided among them. Amos Sawyer, owner of the Randolph Spalding estate, sold several parcels to freedpeople. Various parcels at Riverside were divided and sold. Mrs. Bourke Spalding sold her holdings. The lands of Tom Spalding, mortgaged by his widow, were lost to foreclosure by William Wylly, her second husband, and became the property of a Macon hunting club.

In 1912 Howard E. Coffin, an automobile industry magnate from Detroit, began to acquire the island. From subsequent owners he bought the various Spalding properties as well as the Kenan and Sawyer holdings. He purchased the several small tracts at Riverside from the McKinleys, Treanors, and others, giving Archibald and Sallie a life estate on their place. By 1925 Coffin owned most of the island as well as Little Sapelo Island and the hammocks west of the Duplin River. Pressures of both the Depression and the costs of his development of the Sea Island resort to the south forced Coffin to find a buyer for Sapelo, and in 1933 Richard J. Reynolds, Jr., became the owner. By purchase and land swaps Reynolds acquired the lands at Shell Hammock and Raccoon Bluff and consolidated the resident black population at Hog Hammock.

In 1953 Reynolds established the University of Georgia Marine Institute at the south end of Sapelo, underwritten by his Sapelo Island Research Foundation. Much important basic research in estuarine and marsh ecology has since come from the Institute. After Reynolds's death in 1964, the northern portion of the island was purchased by the state of Georgia and became the R. J. Reynolds, Jr., Wildlife Refuge. In 1976 the state purchased South End, and, with portions of the refuge, established the Duplin River National Estuarine Sanctuary. Thus Sapelo is today owned by the state of Georgia with the exception of about 450 acres held by the descendants of Spalding slaves in Hog Hammock.

Directly across Doboy Sound from Sapelo mute evidence exists today of the former shipping traffic in Doboy Roads. Nine small islands adjoining Commodore Island are composed entirely of ballast. The timber vessels arrived in ballast and cast out the material at moorings before loading timber. Remaining ballast indicates material available at the ship's last port of call. Often used were stream cobbles and gravel, represented in several of the islands. One island is composed almost entirely of broken terracotta, another of cast-iron fragments, and yet another of flint that has been identified by fossils as being from the Dover Cliffs of England.

On Doboy Island itself, which once had, in addition to the sawmill, two hundred residents, a church, a restaurant, and stores, almost nothing remains from the period of the journal: only fragmentary ruins of the steam boiler, foundations, and a large masonry wall constructed of ballast stone. (This wall was where the slabs were dumped over to burn.)

During the period McKinley kept his journal, Sapelo Island had been largely cleared for agricultural purposes, as it had been since the late 1700s. Today, except for Hog Hammock and the various facilities of the state and the university on South End, it has reverted to pine–live oak forest, much as it must have been before English settlement.

Index

Wilson, Anthony, xlii
Winans, D. C., 66
Wolf Island, 137
Wright, Chauncey M., 144
Wyat, Bayley, xxvii
Wylly, Alexander C., 16, 35
Wylly, Alexander W., 108
Wylly, Charles S., 16, 111, 248
  (n. 10)
Wylly, James Hamilton Couper,
  29, 35
Wylly, Mrs. Alexander W.

(Elizabeth S. Spalding), ix;
  death of, 214
Wylly, Mrs. William C. (Sarah
  McKinley), 247
Wylly, Richard, 234
Wylly, Sarah Leake, 19
Wylly, Thomas S., 118
Wylly, William C., 1, 28, 35, 237;
  rents McKinley's Sapelo
  house, 224

Yankees, 5, 25, 28, 149, 221